Stigma

Concepts in Social Policy

General editors:

Vic George, Professor of Social Policy and Administration and Social Work, University of Kent

Paul Wilding, Professor of Social Administration, University of Manchester

Initiated to open up and broaden discussion of theory within the study of social policy, this new series presents texts covering concepts which have particular relevance to this field. Each text will analyse a concept or related concepts from theoretical and multi-disciplinary standpoints, and will discuss their usefulness to the development and practice of social policy.

The concepts to be covered will include:

† PARTICIPATION
* RATIONING
* POWER
* PREVENTION

† already published
* forthcoming

Concepts in Social Policy Two

Stigma

Robert M. Page

Routledge & Kegan Paul
London, Boston, Melbourne and Henley

302.5 PAG

First published in 1984
by Routledge & Kegan Paul plc

39 Store Street, London WC1E 7DD, England

9 Park Street, Boston, Mass. 02108, USA

464 St Kilda Road, Melbourne,
Victoria 3004, Australia and

Broadway House, Newtown Road,
Henley-on-Thames, Oxon RG9 1EN, England

Set in 10/12pt Times
by Columns of Reading
and printed in Great Britain
by T.J. Press (Padstow) Ltd, Padstow, Cornwall

Library of Congress Cataloging in Publication Data

Page, Robert M.

Stigma.
(Concepts in social policy; 2)
Bibliography: p.
Includes index.
1. Stigma (Social psychology) 2. Social service –
Great Britain. 3. Great Britain – Social policy.
I. Title. II. Series.
HM291.P25   1984   302'.12   83-24638

British Library CIP data also available

ISBN 0-7100-9786-7

For my parents, Monica and John, who have shown such remarkable resilience in the face of adversity

Contents

Tables and Figures

Tables

Figures

Acknowledgments

The completion of this book owes much to the help and advice I have received from various sources. I have benefited greatly from the comments and criticisms I have received from members of the Board of Studies in Social Policy and Administration and Social Work at the University of Kent. In addition, other members of the Faculty of Social Science at Kent have provided valuable assistance with particular sections of this book, though needless to say I alone am responsible for all errors and omissions.

I also owe a debt of gratitude to my series editors, Vic George and Paul Wilding, who have commented perceptively on successive drafts of this book. In particular, I would like to thank Vic George for his constructive advice and help during my years as an undergraduate and postgraduate student at the University of Kent.

I would also like to thank the SSRC for their financial assistance during my period of postgraduate research.

Finally, I would like to thank: my parents for the encouragement they have given me over the years; Fulham football club and Worcestershire County cricket club for keeping me entertained; all my friends and colleagues (especially Graham Stevens, Chris Gerrard, Mick Griffiths, Linda Keen, Rob Young, Steve Burt, Libby Graham, Chris Morgan, Tim Marks, Phil Bell and Mike Harmer) whose success in making me laugh is much appreciated; Joanna Treacy for her Mansfield accent and her affection.

The author and publishers are grateful to the following for their kind permission to reproduce the tables and figures used in this book: Her Majesty's Stationery Office, for tables 2.1, 2.2, 2.3, 2.7, 2.12, 3.1, 3.2 and 3.3, which are Crown copyright;

Cambridge University Press, for tables 2.4, 2.5, and 2.6; Heinemann Educational Books, for tables 2.8, 2.9 and 2.10; Penguin Books Ltd and University of California Press, for table 2.11; Robert Pinker, for tables 2.13 and 2.19; Policy and Politics, for tables 2.14, 2.15, 2.17 and 2.18; the Commission of the European Communities, for table 2.16; and the University of Surrey, for figure 3.1.

1   The anatomy of stigma[1]

References to stigma are now commonplace in the media and in general discourse. The term is readily applied to any 'disreputable' person, group, activity, occupation[2] or location. However, stigma remains a relatively imprecise concept. As Titmuss reminds us, 'the concept itself is as elusive and complex as other key concepts like class, alienation, participation, democracy, poverty and so forth.'[3] The relevance of this statement can clearly be seen if one considers just a few of the ways in which the term stigma has been defined in the social science literature.

Whether it is a visible mark or an invisible stain, stigma acquires its meaning through the emotion it generates within the person bearing it and the feeling and behavior toward him of those affirming it. These two aspects of stigma are indivisible since they each act as a cause or effect of the other. (J. and E. Cumming)[4]

In the final analysis, stigma might best be considered to be the negative perceptions and behaviors of so-called normal people to all individuals who are different from themselves. (English)[5]

In its most general sociological sense, the term stigma can be used to refer to any attribute that is deeply discrediting and incongruous with our stereotype of what a given type of individual should be. (Kando)[6]

Given the differences in these definitions (at least in emphasis), it is not surprising that the notion of stigma has acquired something of an elusive reputation. To counter this shortcoming it is necessary to distinguish clearly between the various aspects of this concept.

Stigmas

In its most literal usage the term stigma refers to some form of mark or stain. As Osborne points out:

> 'Stigma' dates back to the Greek word for 'tattoo-mark,' a brand made with a hot iron and impressed on people to show that they were devoted to the services of the temple or, on the opposite spectrum of behavior, that they were criminals or runaway slaves.[7]

More recently, however, the term stigma has tended to be associated almost exclusively with 'inferior' forms of physical appearance, conduct or ethnicity.[8]

Any discussion of socially inferior attributes (stigmas) necessarily requires some consideration of the question of social normality. A number of commentators have given attention to this subject.[9] For example, Merton and Nisbet[10] have outlined six distinctive dimensions of social norms:

  (i) Norms may prescribe or proscribe conduct or merely indicate the type of behaviour which is preferred or permitted.
 (ii) The extent of agreement concerning such norms will vary within society.
(iii) There are likely to be varying degrees of commitment amongst those who accept a particular norm.
 (iv) Informal or formal sanctions may be applied to those who fail to conform to a particular social norm.
  (v) Norms differ in the type of adherence required (i.e. norms may require implicit or explicit support).
 (vi) The 'elasticity' of norms will vary. With some norms adherence to a restricted range of conduct may be required whereas greater flexibility may be permitted with others.

Although this classification is useful, it does not provide any means for precisely identifying prevailing social norms. Indeed, any classification is likely to be deficient in this respect given the diversity of opinion over the question of what actually constitutes a social norm. Nevertheless, there is likely to be some agreement concerning what can loosely be regarded as the 'major' social norms in society (many of which will be embodied in legal codes). As Plummer contends:

> Groups may reject societal definitions, but they cannot wish them away or remain unaware of them. You cannot steal, murder, rape, be blind, deaf or mentally ill without being aware that you are violating some publicly held norms.[11]

However, in a discussion of societal and situational deviance, Plummer clearly acknowledges that the relative dimension of social norms cannot be ignored.

> A simple distinction must be made between 'societal deviance' and 'situational deviance'. The former is that conduct des-cribed as deviant in the public, abstract and reified values systems which all societies must have – even though individual actors may dissent from them, and even though such systems need not be clear, non-contradictory, or without competition. The latter is that conduct which emerges as deviant in interpersonal encounters. The former – while relative cross culturally – is perceived as absolute by most members of a society and possesses moral authority; while the latter is capable of considerable relativity. The former thereby sets constraints on what can be called deviant in any given society though these constraints are far from being rigid and fixed.[12]

It would appear, then, that reactions to norms infractions are likely to vary to some degree. As Cohen points out, the public may respond to deviance in a number of ways.

> It can be *indifferent* – the problem doesn't concern us, 'let him do his thing'; it can *welcome* the deviance, heralding it, for example, as pointing the way for society to advance; it can be *punitive*, advocating deterrent and retributive measures, rang-

ing from £5 fines to the death penalty; or, finally, it can be *progressive*, advocating various treatment and therapeutic measures ostensibly designed for the deviant's 'own good'.[13]

It seems, therefore, that stigma will not necessarily attach to all types of norm infractions. For example, adults who indulge in activities associated with childhood such as 'train-spotting' may well be regarded as odd or eccentric but it is unlikely that they will be stigmatized unless their conduct is perceived as evidence of an established stigma attribute such as mental illness.

In general, stigma has tended to be associated with those inferior attributes which are commonly regarded as major norm infractions. Certain attributes, such as physical handicap, have had stigmatic connotations for many centuries[14] whilst others have only been negatively regarded for much shorter periods of time.[15] (It should also be noted that the stigma which attaches to a particular attribute in one historical period may decline in another e.g. divorce.[16]) In addition, the rationale for a particular stigma may change over time. For example, the unmarried mother was stigmatized in earlier centuries because her conduct directly contravened the teaching of the Christian church. However, since the mid-sixteenth century the dependency of unmarried mothers on public aid has been the main reason for such stigma (see chapter 3).

Goffman has identified 'three grossly different' types of stigma which exist in contemporary society.

> First there are the abominations of the body – the various physical deformities. Next there are the blemishes of individual character perceived as weak will, domineering or unnatural passions, treacherous and rigid beliefs, and dishonesty, these being inferred from a known record of, for example, mental disorder, imprisonment, addiction, alcoholism, homosexuality, unemployment, suicidal attempts, and radical political behaviour. Finally there are the tribal stigma that can be transmitted through lineages and equally contaminate all members of a family.[17]

According to Goffman:

In all these various instances of stigma . . . the same sociological features are found: an individual who might have been
received easily in ordinary social intercourse possesses a trait
that can obtrude itself upon attention and turn those of us
whom he meets away from him, breaking the claim that his
other attributes have on us.[18]

Goffman also outlines two ways in which each type of stigma
can be 'carried'[19] (discredited and discreditable). Goffman uses
the term discredited to describe those who presume that their
stigma is known about already or is immediately obvious to
others (usually because it is visual in nature). In contrast, the
term discreditable is used by Goffman to describe those who
believe that their stigma 'is neither known about by those present
nor immediately perceivable by them.'[20] (See Table 1.1.)

Table 1.1 Stigmas and the ways in which they may be carried

Types of stigma	Ways in which stigmas may be carried	
	Discredited	*Discreditable*
1 PHYSICAL	Paraplegic in a wheelchair	Woman who has undergone a mastectomy
2 CONDUCT	Well-known criminal e.g. Myra Hindley, Ronald Biggs	'Secret' homosexual
3 TRIBAL	Negro	Jew

In general, those with physical or tribal stigmas will tend to be
discredited rather than discreditable. For example, the blind or
the physically handicapped will find it difficult to 'conceal'
information about their stigmas from others. There will be
exceptions. A paraplegic sitting at an office desk which effectively
conceals any hint of disability may be thought of as physically
able by others who do not know of her disability.

Individuals with conduct stigmas are more likely to be
discreditable than discredited. In many cases, such individuals are
able to limit public information about their discrediting attributes. For example, a lesbian may decide to 'pass' as hetero-

sexual with colleagues at work and with casual acquaintances. For others, such passing may not be possible. For instance, 'Great Train Robber' Ronald Biggs has become so well known that his name has even been used by a British car manufacturer in an advertising campaign (The Mini: Nips in and out Quicker than Ronald Biggs).

It must also be noted that varying degrees of blame attach to the types of stigma outlined by Goffman. In general, those with physical or tribal stigmas are granted a measure of social acceptance because they are not considered to be personally responsible for their 'failing'. As such, they may tend to elicit favourable rather than unfavourable reactions from others. As F. Davis states in a discussion of the physically handicapped: '. . . in our society the visibly handicapped are customarily accorded, save by children, the surface acceptance that democratic manners guarantee nearly all.'[21]

There are exceptions to this generalisation. For example, Cahnman argues that the obese are perceived as blameworthy.

> . . . contrary to those that are blind, one-legged, paraplegic, or dark-pigmented, the obese are presumed to hold their fate in their own hands; if they were only a little less greedy or lazy or yielding to impulse or oblivious of advice, they would restrict excessive food intake, resort to strenuous exercise, and as a consequence of such deliberate action, they would reduce. Actually, the moral factor which is thus introduced aggravates the case. While blindness is considered a misfortune, obesity is branded a defect.[22]

Those with conduct stigmas are generally considered to be personally responsible for their failings. It is commonly believed that such individuals have deliberately chosen to behave in socially unacceptable ways. As such, they are liable to be treated unfavourably by others. Again, there are exceptions. For example, a woman who gives birth to an illegitimate child as a result of being raped may be seen as blameless rather than blameworthy.

Pardo has paid particular attention to this blameless-blameworthy dimension of stigma in his research in Canada.[23] Using a non-stigmatized 'normal' as a baseline for comparison,

Pardo attempted to discover how a group of undergraduates would respond to various stigmatized individuals: a blind man – physical stigma; an ex-convict – moral stigma; a blind ex-convict – multiple stigma. Pardo tested three hypotheses.

1 People will tend to evaluate a blind man more favourably than an ex-convict. (Pardo termed this a justice effect.)[24]
2 People will tend to compensate a blind victim of an accident more generously than an ex-convict who has experienced an identical mishap. (Social responsibility effect.)[25] (In order to test this particular hypothesis, Pardo asked his respondents to award damages (of between 1,000 and 3,000 dollars) to individuals (with the various stigmas mentioned above) who had suffered identical injuries (a hip fracture and bruising) as a result of being hit by a driverless bus which had faulty brakes.
3 An individual with both a physical and moral (conduct) stigma will tend not only to be evaluated in an unfavourable way by the public but will also tend to be denied material support because of the overtrumping effect of moral turpitude. (Overtrumping effect.)[26]

Pardo found that his subjects responded in the manner predicted with regard to both his first (the blind man was evaluated far more favourably than the ex-convict) and second (larger amounts of compensation were awarded to the blind plaintiff than to the ex-convict) hypotheses. In terms of the third hypothesis the results were less conclusive. Although the respondents formed a negative impression of the blind ex-convict (as predicted) they nevertheless decided to award this person the highest amount of compensation.[27]

Despite the numerous methodological objections that can be raised about research of this kind (e.g. a highly selective group of respondents; the use of hypothetical case-studies) it can be confidently asserted that Pardo has provided valuable evidence to support the contention that the blameless-blameworthy dimension is of importance for the study of the concept of stigma.

The idea that the notion of stigma should be associated exclusively with major, negative, norm infractions has been rejected by a number of writers. Goffman, for example, has expressed certain reservations about this approach. Although he acknowledges that 'there are important attributes that almost everywhere in our society are discrediting',[28] Goffman still maintains 'that a language of relationships, not attributes, is really needed. An attribute that stigmatizes one type of possessor can confirm the usualness of another, and therefore is neither creditable nor discreditable as a thing in itself.'[29] This argument has found favour with others. For instance, Reisman argues that stigma attaches to General Practitioners because they are 'less technically expert than the specialist, the scientist or the consultant in a big hospital.'[30] Similarly, Tony Benn has stated that stigma tends to attach to Labour party politicians with intellectual reputations.[31] Posner, who has paid particular attention to this idea (in an article entitled 'The stigma of excellence: on being just right'[32]), contends that in addition to those who fail to live up to a particular norm *'those who personify it or go beyond it* may at times feel uncomfortable, guilty and stigmatized.'[33] In support of this assertion Posner cites the case of the male 'non-drinker'. She argues

> that the basis of the non-drinker's stigma is his flaunting of ideal behaviour. We all know drinking is bad for us, but we all do it, and if there's one thing that really irritates us it is a superior moral person who has himself totally under control and who therefore reminds us of our own failings![34]

From this basis it would appear that stigma can just as easily attach to the Queen, doctors, clergymen, mothers, children, manual and non-manual workers as it can to groups such as the disabled, homosexuals or ex-prisoners. However, such a contention squeezes the useful life out of the concept of stigma. Accordingly, it is maintained here that the term should be used exclusively in connection with inferior as opposed to normal or superior attributes. As Dinitz et al. assert:

> there are certain persons at the extreme who are defined as unfortunate – the severely retarded, the midget . . . etc. Others, who are also at the extremes, such as the genius, the seven-foot-tall basketball player . . . and the overendowed female, may be positively valued. . . . Both ends may be

equidistant from the average or norm. This underscores the point that it is not the extreme, the variation, or the freakishness in itself that defines social deviation; the extreme has to be evaluated by the society in a negative fashion.[35]

Even if one accepts that the term stigma should only be applied to negative attributes, there is still likely to be considerable disagreement over questions such as the extent of stigma in society. For example, Goffman is of the opinion that:

it is not very useful to tabulate the numbers of persons who suffer [stigma] . . . the number would be as high as one wanted to make it; and when those with a courtesy stigma are added [friends, family and associates of the stigmatized], and those who once experienced the situation or are destined, if for no other reason than oncoming agedness, to do so, the issue becomes not whether a person has experience with a stigma of his own, because he has, but rather how many varieties he has had his own experience with.[36]

Stigma recognition

There are two main ways in which individuals tend to come to recognize that they possess a stigma. This process may, firstly, take the form of self-recognition. As a result of socialization most members of society will gain some understanding of the various types of prevailing stigma. They will thus be in a position to compare their own conduct or appearance with existing stigma types. If they find that their appearance or conduct mirrors a particular stigma type it is possible that they may come to the conclusion that they possess a stigma. As Plummer, in a discussion of homosexuality, argues:

a person who experiences a homosexual feeling does not have to be hounded out of town, sent to prison, or treated by a psychiatrist to come to see himself as a homosexual – he may quite simply 'indicate' to himself, through the 'interpretation' of the given feeling and the accompanying awareness of the societal hostility, that he is a homosexual.[37]

For those with inborn physical or tribal stigmas such self-recognition is likely to take a different form. As Goffman points out, such individuals 'become socialized into their disadvantageous situation even while they are learning and incorporating the standards against which they fall short.'[38]

The second main way in which individuals come to recognize that they possess a stigma is through the reactions of others. Such reactions may be of a direct kind. One homosexual recalls such an incident: '. . . when I was about sixteen and had a romp with a boy friend in the street, another boy suddenly called me "queer".'[39] Alternatively, such reactions may be of a more indirect type. For example, a woman (upon hearing her friends discussing the behaviour of agoraphobics) may come to the conclusion that her own behaviour could be perceived as evidence of mental illness.

Finally, it is important to note that many individuals may come to recognize that they have a stigma by a combination of self-recognition and audience reaction.

Stigmatization

An individual may be stigmatized by the intentional or 'unintentional' actions or comments of officials (e.g. magistrates, police officers, social workers), employers, fellow employees, other family members, friends, neighbours or strangers.

Intentional stigmatization may take a variety of forms ranging from snubs or adverse comments to legal sanctions. In all such cases, attention is focussed on a particular inferior attribute of the individual concerned. As Suchar states:

> The individual . . . is assigned a 'master status trait': homo-
> sexual, drug addict, prostitute, juvenile delinquent, or
> others . . . this label will dominate all other 'characteristics' of
> the individual; 'good athlete,' 'good conversationalist,' 'good
> dancer,' and the like are subordinated to or negated by this
> trait, which is immediately felt to be more central to the
> 'actual' identity of the individual.[40]

The class, status and power of the stigmatizer can be of

importance in terms of the impact of stigmatization. For example, someone classified as mentally ill by members of the medical profession may find it difficult to refute such typing or convince others that such labelling is inappropriate.[41]

Although the precise effects of official labelling are far from clear cut,[42] it can be argued that such labelling tends to create more problems for an individual than 'lay' labelling. For example, a young offender describing his relationship with the police states:

> You can just be walking down-town with millions of shoppers and they'll stop *you*. If they know your face you're fucked. If you've done a bit of robbing and they don't like your face, that's it.[43]

It must be noted, though, that those who have not been stigmatized by officials may still experience difficulties in their day-to-day lives because of the possibility of such labelling[44] or because of the hostility of other members of the community.

Intentional and explicit forms of stigmatization tend to be directed towards those with conduct or tribal stigmas. In contrast, those with physical stigmas rarely experience overt hostility from others. The stigmatization of this group takes a different form ('unintentional' stigmatization). Evidence from a number of studies[45] indicates that 'normals' tend to be over-sympathetic or inhibited during contact with the physically stigmatized. For example, in a study in the 1960s, Kleck[46] found that his subjects were more inhibited when they were in the presence of an assistant who had assumed the role of a left leg amputee than they were during interaction with a physically normal assistant. Subjects interacting with the 'disabled' assistant were found to have:

(i) Displayed greater relative motoric inhibition (i.e. they didn't move about as much as they did with the normal assistant).

(ii) Formed a more positive impression of this particular assistant.

(iii) Distorted their opinions in the direction of making them more consistent with those assumed to be held by disabled persons.

Although it can be argued that this form of stigmatization is preferable to overt hostility, it must be remembered that such 'stereotyped' responses can have important implications for the life chances of the physically stigmatized. For example, such individuals have frequently been 'cared' for in separate communities, ostensibly for their own good. However, the physically stigmatized may find such segregation extremely distasteful.[47] For instance, a girl recalling her first impressions of a home for the blind states:

> I was to spend the rest of my life making mops with other blind people, eating with other blind people, dancing with other blind people. I became nauseated with fear, as the picture grew in my mind. Never had I come across such destructive segregation.[48]

The relationship between stigmatization and stigma types can depend upon what Goffman has termed the known-about-ness of a particular attribute, its obtrusiveness and its perceived focus.[49] In the case of those with physical stigmas, explicit forms of stigmatization may be avoided provided that they observe certain forms of social etiquette and accept that interaction with normals will tend to be superficial. Indeed, F. Davis has compared the position of the visibly handicapped in 'mixed' social situations with the 'poor relation at the wedding party . . . sufficient that he is here, he should not expect to dance with the bride.'[50] However, if those with physical stigmas become too obtrusive, they may suffer explicit stigmatization. Berk, in a study of patrons at a dance hall in the United States, gives an example of such a situation.

> A number of paraplegics in wheel chairs arrived at a dance, and their presence in one of the halls where the dances were held resulted in an exodus of over two hundred and fifty of the approximately seven hundred patrons in the room within a half hour. Patrons fled the immediate vicinity so as to avoid contact with 'those misfits' as they were described by several patrons who felt that the handicapped should have had the good sense not to come to such places and embarrass everybody.[51]

The stigmatization of those with conduct stigmas may also vary in relation to known-about-ness, obtrusiveness and perceived focus.[52] Members of a local community may, for instance, refrain from stigmatizing an elderly, acknowledged, homosexual who lives in the vicinity on the grounds that his conduct poses no form of threat. In contrast, a local school teacher with a recent conviction for gross indecency may experience intense hostility from members of the same community.

Felt stigma

All individuals who carry stigmas are likely to experience feelings of stigma to some degree. For those with conduct or tribal stigmas such feelings may be induced by the adverse comments or actions of others. For example, a former mental patient (recalling a discussion with a colleague after being discharged from hospital) comments: 'I said: "That argument doesn't make sense: you're mad," and he replied: "At least I've never been a patient in a mental hospital." I was desperately hurt. . . .'[53] Such feelings may also result from 'official' stigmatization. A prostitute recalling her experiences of court appearances states:

You go in through that door and everyone's waiting for you and looking at you. I keep my head down and never look on either side. Then they say those awful words: 'Being a common prostitute . . .' and you feel awful, all the time not knowing who's watching you at the back of the court.[54]

For the physically stigmatized, feelings of stigma are more likely to be experienced as a result of the inhibited or over-sympathetic reactions of normals (see p. 11). For instance, a physically handicapped person confined to a wheelchair states:

I get suspicious when somebody says, 'Let's go for a . . . push with me down the hall,' or something like that. This to me is suspicious because it means that they're aware, really aware, that there's a wheelchair here. . . . A lot of people in trying to show you that they don't care that you're in a chair will do crazy things. Oh, there's one person I know who constantly

kicks my chair as if to say 'I don't care that you're in a
wheelchair. I don't even know that it's there.' But that is just
an indication that he *really* knows it's there.[55]

A one-legged girl, recalling her experiences with school sports,
provides a good illustration of how over-helpful reactions can
also result in feelings of stigma:

> Whenever I fell, out swarmed the women in droves, clucking
> and fretting like a bunch of bereft mother hens. It was kind of
> them, and in retrospect I appreciate their solicitude, but at the
> time I resented and was greatly embarrassed by their
> interference. For they assumed that no routine hazard to
> skating – no stick or stone – upset my flying wheels. It was a
> foregone conclusion that I fell because I was a poor, helpless
> cripple.[56]

For those with blameless stigmas any reorientation by normals
may result in feelings of stigma, even if such changes result in a
more favourable attitude being adopted. For example, former
England cricket captain Tony Grieg was perturbed by the
thought that the Australian cricket public might respond to him
more favourably after it was revealed that he suffered from
epilepsy.[57]

The frequency of felt stigma experiences is likely to vary from
individual to individual. For those who interpret all their life
experiences within a stigma framework (i.e. those who believe
that their stigma obtrudes in all forms of social intercourse) such
feelings may be relatively common. For instance, a criminal
states: '. . . I always feel this with straight people – that
whenever they're being nice to me, pleasant to me, all the time
really, underneath they're only assessing me as a criminal and
nothing else.'[58]

For others such feelings may be quite rare. As an unmarried
mother told me, 'I've very rarely felt stigmatized. It's just the odd
reaction from people . . . but then I sit and reason it out within
myself and think sod 'em.' Obviously, it seems likely that those
individuals who continually feel stigmatized will find life
extremely difficult to cope with (even if they are living within a

tolerant and understanding community). In contrast, those individuals who rarely feel stigmatized (especially those who make a determined effort to minimize such feelings) are likely to find life relatively unproblematic (even if they should be unfortunate enough to be treated unfavourably by members of their local community).

Earlier (p. 9) it was suggested that individuals may come to recognize that they possess a stigma by means of self-recognition. Similarly, it is possible to feel stigmatized without experiencing explicit stigmatization. As Weinberg and Williams point out in a discussion of homosexuality:

> Even if the homosexual himself has not actually been sanctioned because of his sexual orientation, the way he feels about himself can be damaged by his *imputing* negative reactions to the heterosexuals he knows and to people in general.[59]

Although feelings of stigma are more likely to be experienced by those who possess stigmas it is important to note that others may report similar feelings even though they do not possess a seriously discrediting attribute.[60] A comment from a nail-biter provides a perfect illustration in this regard:

> Going to a party and having to hold a glass is agony to me because my hands, and bitten nails, are so obvious, writing a cheque in a shop with the assistant gazing at my hand as I write is dreadful. I am aware of her scrutiny and my hand shakes. . . . The solitary pain of the true nail-biter, his sense of inadequacy and self-disgust and the condemnatory indifference to his plight which ordinary society bestows on him are not generally recognised.[61]

In addition, individuals may feel stigmatized merely by being present in a stigmatic situation. For example, a female researcher, recounting her feelings whilst visiting an area associated with prostitution states:

> The deserted appearance of the footpaths and the apparent purposefulness of any woman who did walk along them . . .

forced upon me the realisation that this area was reserved for prostitutes – it was a place set aside for them and would lend its colouring to anyone who chose to enter it. . . .[62]

It should also be noted that individuals with courtesy stigmas[63] (see p. 9) may experience feelings of stigma. For example, in a letter submitted to an advice columnist, a young girl writes:

Dear Ann Landers:
   I'm a girl 12 years old who is left out of all social activities because my father is an ex-convict. I try to be nice and friendly to everyone but it's no use. The girls at school have told me that their mothers don't want them to associate with me because it will be bad for their reputations. My father had some bad publicity in the papers and even though he has served his time nobody will forget it.
   Is there anything I can do? I am very lonesome because it's no fun to be alone all the time. My mother tries to take me places with her but I want to be with people my own age. Please give me some advice – AN OUTCAST.[64]

Interestingly, it also seems possible that the associates of individuals with 'stigmas of excellence' (see pp. 7-9) may experience feelings of stigma. For instance, the family of an Oxbridge student state:

After working extremely hard and giving up pastimes and pleasures, our son achieved his ambition and won a place at Cambridge. We are an ordinary family and were so proud of his success. However, we have been disillusioned by the resentment we receive from friends, workmates, even family, if we mention his locality. Whereas parents with children at other universities can discuss their offsprings' progress, and express natural pride in achievements, we are barred by looks, innuendo and rejected from participation.[65]

It is difficult to define precisely what constitutes a feeling of stigma. In order to cast some light on this matter it is useful to consider two other closely related unpleasant sensations – namely, embarrassment and shame.

According to Modigliani:

> Embarrassment is a common experience. It may be elicited by
> a surprising range of apparently dissimilar situations: being
> introduced to an unfamiliar audience, arriving at a social
> occasion under-dressed, talking to a person who stutters badly,
> mistaking a stranger for an acquaintance, and so on. Subjec-
> tively it entails a sense of exposure, of inadequacy, of awkward
> self-consciousness. It is sometimes accompanied by such
> distressing symptoms as blushing, sweating, tremor, fumbling
> and stuttering.[66]

As Modigliani points out, embarrassment appears to be a very
mild form of unpleasant sensation which we are all likely to
experience. Embarrassment generally occurs at a specific moment
in a social situation; is often instantaneous in effect; and rarely
has any permanent effect on the future actions or self-esteem of
the individuals experiencing it. However, in some cases an
individual may have felt so embarrassed in a particular situation
that future plans are geared towards ensuring that such
embarrassment is avoided in the future. For example, a woman,
embarrassed by her lack of proficiency at badminton, may decide
to avoid attending the club of which she is a member.

Shame[67] appears to be a more intense form of unpleasant
sensation. As with embarrassment, shame may be experienced in
a number of situations and may affect us all at some time in our
lives. We may experience shame as a result of a particular action,
such as deliberately travelling on a train without a ticket, or due
to some form of inaction, such as neglecting an aged relative.
Unlike embarrassment, a feeling of shame is likely to have a
more marked effect on the actions of individuals. Such a
sensation may result in determined efforts to improve one's
performance in a particular social role e.g. father, employee,
lover, gardener. By experiencing shame, individuals generally
acknowledge that their conduct in one or more social roles has
fallen below an accepted standard (such acknowledgment may be
self-initiated or result from the reactions of others).

A feeling of stigma appears, at least in theory, to be the most
severe form of unpleasant sensation. Those experiencing stigma
may feel that their whole identity is tarnished because of a

particular attribute. Such feelings may be intense; experienced in many situations; and persist for long periods of time. For example, a man convicted of shoplifting states:

> Though the whole business fell into some sort of manageable perspective, as time passed I still felt tainted by it all. . . . Every time I passed the store concerned, I would relive the experience. . . . I was never able to make myself go into the shop either. The fear of people finding out always worried me, and the chance that I might meet one of the solicitors from the court socially and they would recognise me was another constant, if highly improbable, worry.[68]

Many individuals who experience feelings of stigma may, like those who feel ashamed, accept that their physical appearance, conduct or ethnicity is evidence of inferiority. However, others who experience such feelings may hold the belief that it is the reactions of stigmatizers which is reprehensible rather than their own discrediting attribute (i.e. they question the assumption that they are inferior members of society. Note that further attention will be given to this subject in the next section).

Finally, it is important to note that the distinctions I have made between embarrassment, shame and stigma are highly speculative. In general and academic discourse these terms are frequently used as if they were synonymous.[69]

Responses to stigma acknowledgment

Individuals are likely to respond to stigma acknowledgment in one of two ways. They may either accept or reject the assumption that a particular attribute is evidence of inferiority.

For acceptors, 'the denial of respectability by their audience represents an accepted-as-accurate response to their genuine lack of respectability. This obtains in situations where there is consensus between the viewer and the viewed concerning a true lack of moral worth.'[70] Acceptance can lead some individuals to seriously consider changing their job, address, or even their name.[71] In contrast, others may view acceptance as being an important first step on the road back to normality. For example, a homosexual may seek medical help in an effort to remedy his sexual 'affliction'.[72] Similarly, a member of Alcoholics Anonymous may accept 'assignment to the role of alcoholic as a step towards overcoming his alcoholic behavior'.[73] However, as Goffman points out: 'Where such repair is possible, what often results is not the acquisition of fully normal status, but a transformation of self from someone with a record of having corrected a particular blemish.'[74] In some cases acceptance may have an instrumental purpose. For example, in order to obtain accommodation in a hostel run by the Salvation Army, an alcoholic may readily agree with the staff that heavy drinking is a social evil.

'Rejection' may also take a variety of forms. For some, a passive form of rejection may be adopted. Such individuals, though rejecting any notion of inferiority, are unwilling to commit themselves to more active forms of protest for fear of hostile reactions from others.[75] In contrast, other individuals may decide to draw attention to their stigmas in an effort to demonstrate the inappropriateness of associating a particular attribute with inferiority. For example, a prostitute may readily refer to her professional status during casual conversations with others. Similarly, a Jew may prominently display a Star of David necklace.[76] Such individuals may adopt this method of 'confronting' stigma in their public, as well as private, lives. For instance, a clergyman may decide to disclose the fact that he is a homosexual to his congregation.

Rejection may take a collective form.[77] Groups or movements, of varying degrees of political militancy, may be established to provide mutual support in countering existing, negative, public stereotypes. This process can be difficult. As Goffman argues:

> When the ultimate political objective is to remove stigma from the differentness, the individual may find that his very efforts can politicize his own life, rendering it even more different from the normal life initially denied him – even though the next generation of his fellows may greatly profit from his efforts by being more accepted. Further, in drawing attention to the situation of his own kind he is in some respects consolidating a public image and of his fellow-stigmatized as constituting a real group.[78]

Collective action may be undertaken for very different purposes. Certain groups, such as the disabled, may act collectively in order to achieve a greater degree of social acceptance within the existing framework of society. In contrast, other groups, such as militant homosexual organizations, may use collective action to challenge the existing social system. In addition, it should be noted that some groups (e.g. hippies) may demonstrate their rejection of prevailing social norms by establishing peripheral, 'alternative' communities.[79]

Stigma disavowal

Some individuals, upon experiencing stigmatizing reactions from others, may respond by attempting to neutralize such labelling.[80] This group, whilst accepting that certain attributes are evidence of inferiority, contest the applicability of such labelling in their particular case. Such neutralization may be of a formal or informal kind. Formal attempts at neutralization may involve an appeal to an official body (e.g. a mental patient who feels that she has been unjustly detained may appeal to a Mental Health Review Tribunal) or to members of the general public (e.g a criminal campaigning for a re-trial). At an informal level, individuals' ability to contest or neutralize adverse labelling will frequently depend on their class, status and power. This is especially the case with regard to infringements of the law.[81]

Stigma management

There are two main ways in which individuals can manage their spoilt identities – namely, passing or covering.[82]

(i) Passing

Individuals with information to manage (the discreditable: see pp. 5-6) may attempt to pass as normal during various forms of social interaction. Some individuals may pass frequently whilst others may employ this technique more sparingly.

Opportunities to pass will depend on the type of stigma an individual possesses. Those with physical or tribal stigmas will have fewer chances to pass because of the visibility of their stigmas. Nevertheless, such individuals may pass successfully in certain situations. For instance, a near-blind man recalls how he succeeded in passing as sighted with a girlfriend:

> I managed to keep Mary from knowing my eyes were bad through two dozen sodas and three movies. I used every trick I had ever learned. I paid special attention to the color of her dress each morning, and then I would keep my eyes and ears and my sixth sense alert for anyone that might be Mary. I didn't take any chances. If I wasn't sure, I would greet whoever it was with familiarity. They probably thought I was nuts, but I didn't care. I always held her hand on the way to and from the movies at night, and she led me, without knowing it, so I didn't have to feel for curbs and steps.[83]

Individuals with discreditable conduct stigmas will be able to pass more frequently because they will be in a position to control information about their discrediting attribute. Some individuals may decide to restrict information about their stigma to a small group such as their immediate family or closest friends, whilst others may be prepared to inform a much wider social audience.[84] The stigmatizing attribute possessed by an individual may be of importance in terms of the type of passing undertaken. For example, a prostitute may wish to pass as 'respectable' with both her family and the police whilst simultaneously remaining 'well known' to her potential clientele.

Even after the stigmatized have selected their confidantes they may still find that passing is fraught with difficulties. For example, an ex-criminal (who has passed in a new neighbourhood) may find his recently acquired respectability threatened by the appearance of a former prisonmate in the locality.

For some, passing may present numerous practical difficulties. For example, a stutterer recalls:

> having a very bad time with initial 'm's . . . and, very foolishly under the circumstances, travelling to Marble Arch. I could see the conductor coming down the corridor towards me and I

knew I would have to say, 'M-M-M-', and, finally, as often
happens with stammerers, a fantastic act of creation took
place. I said 'One to the arch that is made of marble, please.'[85]

Passing may be a painful experience for those, such as passive
rejectors (see p. 19) who feel that their discrediting attribute
should not be negatively regarded by others. As a homosexual
states:

> When jokes were made about 'queers' I had to laugh with the
> rest, and when talk was about women I had to invent conquests
> of my own. I hated myself at such moments, but there seemed
> to be nothing else that I could do. My whole life became a
> lie.[86]

The extent to which individuals engage in passing is likely to
depend upon whether they accept or reject (see pp. 18-20) that a
particular attribute is evidence of inferiority. It seems probable
that those who accept such an association will pass more
frequently than rejectors.

There may be occasions, though, when rejectors omit to refer
to their stigma during social interaction, not because of any fear
of hostile reactions but, rather, because disclosure is perceived as
inappropriate or unnecessary in the particular situation. For
example, an ex-prisoner engaged in casual conversation may
make no reference to his stigma because he believes that such
information is not relevant to the subject under discussion. Even
if a suitable opportunity for disclosure presents itself he may still
refrain from referring to his stigma on the grounds that personal
information should not be disclosed during casual meetings.
Although it could be argued that this man has engaged in
passing, it should be remembered that we are all likely to limit
the amount of information we disclose about our private lives
during brief discussions with comparative strangers. Indeed, we
would be surprised if brief acquaintances violated the rules of
social etiquette by divulging intimate details of their private
lives.[87] As such, it seems inappropriate to infer that individuals
have engaged in passing merely because they have omitted to
refer to their stigma during a particular social encounter. In
addition, individuals may engage in deliberate episodes of passing

for reasons other than a desire to minimize the possibility of receiving unfavourable reactions from others. For example, an epileptic may decide to avoid referring to her stigma when meeting people casually because she has found that disclosure results in inhibited forms of interaction (i.e. others feel obliged to express sympathy or restrict their conversation to the subject of epilepsy).

(ii) Covering

The discredited (see pp. 5-6) may attempt to manage their stigmas by means of covering. By engaging in covering an individual hopes to reduce tension during social interaction.[88] Although such individuals recognize that passing is inappropriate due to the visibility or fame of their stigma, they may nevertheless attempt to ensure that their stigma is as unobtrusive as possible during social interaction. For instance, a near-blind person who knows that others in his company are aware of his differentness may 'hesitate to read, because to do this he would have to bring the book up to a few inches of his eyes, and this he may feel expresses too glaringly the qualities of blindness.'[89] Similarly, a man with a previous conviction for theft may decide to withdraw his application for the post of treasurer at his local social club after acknowledging the possible tension that could be created.

As with passing, it seems likely that those who accept, rather than reject, the assumption that a particular personal attribute is evidence of inferiority will cover more frequently. For example, blind acceptors may try to ensure that they behave in ways regarded as normal by the sighted. This may involve such actions as 'looking' directly at other people when engaged in conversation.[90] In contrast, blind rejectors are likely to pay little heed to the norms of the sighted. Instead, they are likely to behave in ways which they consider to be expedient. For example, such individuals may use their hands rather than cutlery when eating in 'mixed' company.

Three final points need to be made in relation to stigma management. Firstly, intentional passing or covering by the stigmatized precludes any effective challenge to existing social values and, as such, is likely to reinforce contemporary patterns of stigmatization.[91] Secondly, passing and covering may also be undertaken by those with courtesy stigmas.[92] For instance, a prisoner's wife may inform neighbours that her husband's absence from home is due to temporary overseas employment. Thirdly, it should be remembered that we are all likely to pass in certain situations in an effort to maintain 'face'.[93]

In this chapter attention has been focused exclusively on sociological and social psychological approaches to the notion of stigma. In the next chapter consideration will be given to the rather distinctive way in which this concept has been used in the social administration literature.

2 Stigma: the social administration approach

Although the adoption of the notion of stigma by social administrators owes much to the work of sociologists and social psychologists it would be misleading to give undue emphasis to these particular influences. The importance contemporary social administrators attach to the concept of stigma owes far more to the deep-rooted historical association between this notion and certain developments in social policy. In particular, the concept of stigma has been inextricably linked with the treatment of the able-bodied poor over the centuries. For example, a series of repressive measures were introduced by Tudor governments during the sixteenth century in an attempt to curb the incidence of vagrancy.[1] The punishments meted out to those deemed to be members of the undeserving poor were intended not only to be physically unpleasant but also highly 'stigmatizing' (e.g. whipping, stocking, branding and ear-boring).[2]

In later periods the poor were often subjected to sanctions of a more 'exclusively' stigmatizing kind. For example, in the late seventeenth century a number of parishes introduced a regulation which required recipients of poor relief to wear a distinctive mark or badge on their clothing.[3] It was hoped that this stipulation would deter all but the most needy from applying for poor relief.

The deterrent value of stigmatization was also clearly recognized by the Poor Law Commissioners in their report on the operation of the poor laws (1834). Believing that parish allowance schemes were demoralizing the poor, the Commissioners recommended the introduction of a number of reforms based on the principle of less eligibility.[4] The Commissioners were of the firm opinion that a minimal form of poor relief (which ensured that the living standards of recipients were less favourable than those of the poorest independent labourers) would stem the demand for poor relief provided that such provision was linked to a workhouse test (i.e. applicants applying for relief should be required to: accept institutional care (a sanction which also applied to other dependent family members); forfeit their voting rights (where applicable); wear distinctive clothing; undertake monotonous and degrading forms of work). As Pinker points out:

> The concept of 'less eligibility' was a psychological device which, in the non-market context of a workhouse, reminded individuals in a forceful way of what they did *not* want. Since the economic market, in most instances, had never offered these paupers much more than marginally superior material rewards, the sanction of less eligibility took a necessarily psychological form. It imposed the pain of humiliation and stigma.[5]

The introduction of the new poor law was instrumental in ensuring that the subject of stigmatization was kept in the forefront of subsequent discussions about poor relief during this period. For example, local opposition to the workhouse system (with all its stigmatic associations) proved highly successful in forcing the Poor Law Commission to agree to the re-introduction of outdoor relief in 1842.[6] The resultant growth in outdoor relief found little favour, however, with the Local Government Board (which was established in 1871 to replace the Poor Law Board). Concerned about the growing cost of this form of provision the new board encouraged local unions to introduce an even more stigmatizing form of institutional relief. The first of these 'test' workhouses was established by the Poplar guardians in 1871. Inmates within this repressive institution were compelled to perform degrading and painful tasks such as stone breaking or oakum picking (separating the fibres of tarred rope). If they failed to meet the specified daily production targets (women, for example, were expected to pick 6lb of beaten, or 3lb of unbeaten, oakum each day) inmates were liable to be brought before a magistrate or placed in solitary confinement in the workhouse refractory ward on a bread and water diet.[7]

The overt stigmatization enshrined in this scheme was

markedly absent from other social policy measures of the period.[8] Indeed, efforts were made to reduce the stigma attaching to other institutionalized pauper groups (e.g. children, the sick and the elderly[9]). For instance, in the case of children the principle of less eligibility was gradually diluted by the introduction of educational provision and by the acceptance of the advantages of community care (e.g. scattered homes and boarding out).[10]

The question of stigma was also given consideration in the poor law reports of 1909. In their report, the majority (represented by, amongst others, the permanent heads of the Local Government Boards and members of the Charity Organisation Society such as Loch and Bosanquet)[11] argued that a distinction should continue to be maintained between the type of relief afforded to the deserving as opposed to the undeserving poor. Accordingly, they recommended that the former should be provided with relief (on more favourable terms) by Voluntary Aid Committees whilst the latter should be forced to seek sustenance from Public Assistance Committees. The majority acknowledged, however, that the public poor relief scheme needed to be modified in certain respects if it was to shed its stigmatic image. They therefore recommended that:

(i) Outdoor relief should be known in future as home assistance.
(ii) Applicants for relief should be classified as necessitous rather than destitute.
(iii) Disenfranchisement should be abolished for short-term claimants (i.e. under three months).[12]

Given their commitment to the introduction of specialised, non-stigmatized, public welfare services, the minority (B. Webb, Chandler, Lansbury and Wakefield) not unsurprisingly saw no need (unlike the majority) for the continued operation of a distinctive destitution authority.[13] Nevertheless, they did accept that stigmatizing measures were necessary, for the purpose of deterrence, in cases of idleness and malingering (reformatory detention colonies).[14]

Although both these reports had little immediate impact on government policy,[15] they were nonetheless highly significant in terms of ensuring that consideration continued to be given to the notion of stigma in subsequent income-maintenance programmes. Awareness of the stigmatizing propensities of poor law provision, and the consequent threat to public order posed by those members of the unemployed dependent upon such aid,[16] prompted governments of all parties to devise various unemployment income maintenance schemes during the early decades of this century.[17] A major aim of these schemes – to provide unemployment relief on more socially acceptable terms – was never fully realized because of continuous concern about cost and abuse. As a result these schemes became, to greater or lesser extents, tainted by less eligible procedures such as seeking work or means tests.[18]

Subsequent attempts to reduce the stigma attaching to non-contributory unemployment assistance (e.g. the abolition of the household means test in 1941[19]; the establishment of the National Assistance board in 1948)[20] have proved largely unsuccessful. A major reason for this failure centres around the belief that a distinction should continue to be maintained between contributory and non-contributory forms of income support. The means test remains the most significant administrative device for distinguishing between these two types of benefit. As Beveridge argued in his report on social insurance (1942):

> National Assistance must be felt to be something less desirable than insurance benefit; otherwise the insured persons get nothing for their contributions. Assistance therefore will be given always subject to proof of needs and examination of means; it will be subject also to any conditions as to behaviour which may seem likely to hasten restoration of earning capacity.[21]

The divisive nature of means-testing was a source of particular concern for a number of post-war academics in the developing discipline of social policy and administration. Fully aware of the stigmatizing propensities of residual forms of welfare, these commentators attempted to inform both the public and policy makers alike of what they considered to be the overwhelming social and economic advantages of 'institutional' welfare provision. It is to this collectivist tradition that attention will now be given in order to demonstrate how the concept of stigma has been used in the contemporary study of social policy.

This collectivist tradition, which can usefully be termed the Fabian socialist[22] or social democratic[23] approach to welfare is characterized by: (i) adherence to social values such as equality, freedom and fellowship; (ii) acceptance of the belief that capitalist society can be transformed by positive forms of government intervention; and (iii) whole-hearted support for benevolent public welfare services.[24] No one within this tradition has expressed greater faith in the part that social policy can play in creating a more socially just society than Richard Titmuss. Titmuss believed that social policy could, by providing opportunities for the expression of altruism, effectively counter the divisive and alienating aspects of economic life.[25] For Titmuss the decision to expand welfare services after the Second World War was an indication of the increasing influence of social as opposed to market ethics:

> the fundamental and dominating historical processes which led to these major changes in social policy were connected with the demand for one society; for non-discriminatory services for all without distinction of class, income or race; for services and relations which would deepen and enlarge self-respect; for services which would manifestly encourage social integration.[26]

According to Titmuss the blood donation system in Britain provides one of the best examples of the positive effects of social policy.[27]

> Unlike gift-exchange in traditional societies, there is in the free gift of blood to unnamed strangers no contract of custom, no legal bond, no functional determinism, no situations of discriminatory power, domination, constraint or compulsion, no sense of shame or guilt, no gratitude imperative and no need for the penitence of a Chrysostom.[28]

Titmuss was greatly encouraged by the fact that the majority of blood donors did not demand or expect any tangible form of reward for their services.[29] Instead, they tended to observe what Gouldner has termed the norm of beneficence.[30]

This norm requires men to give to others such help as they need. Rather than making help contingent upon past benefits received or future benefits expected, the norm of beneficence calls upon men to aid others without thought of what they have done or can do for them, and solely in terms of a need imputed to the potential recipient.[31]

The concept of need formed a central part of Titmuss's analysis of social policy. He argued that public welfare services should be provided on the basis of this principle rather than on criteria such as ability to pay, desert, or some inflexible notion of legal entitlement. In order to support his assertion that need-based, universal public social services could play a vital role in creating a more integrated and just society, Titmuss frequently referred to what he considered to be the deficiencies of private, and selectivist public, welfare provision.[32] In this examination of the relative merits and demerits of institutional and residual forms of welfare Titmuss utilized, and developed, the notion of stigma.

Titmuss drew attention to two main ways in which the private welfare sector could stigmatize the poorer members of the community. Firstly, he argued that the very existence of private welfare services within a market-dominated society was likely to have a detrimental effect on public welfare services. For example, with regard to education, he stated that:

Until we, as a society, can rid ourselves of the dominating influence of the private sector of education we shall not have the will to embark on an immensely higher standard of provision for all those children whose education now finishes when it has hardly begun.[33]

Secondly, and more specifically, he pointed out that the selection procedures most commonly used in the private welfare sector were inherently stigmatizing for particular groups in society:

Private enterprise social service institutions have to operate on the principle of excluding the 'bad risks' and the social casualties of change. Thus, private occupational schemes exclude the chronically sick, the disabled, the elderly, the mentally handicapped, new entrants, most categories of women – especially unmarried mothers – and so on. Private medical institutions similarly exclude 'the bad risks', the over-80s, the indigent and so-called charitable cases.[34]

Although Titmuss discounted any suggestion of deliberate stigmatization on the part of the private welfare sector,[35] he was none the less concerned about their marked lack of interest in the social effects of their services:[36]

[if applicants] are excluded because they cannot pay or are likely to have above-average needs . . . who can blame them if they come to think that they have been discriminated against on grounds of colour and other criteria of rejection?[37]

Titmuss also contended that selectivist public welfare services had stigmatizing propensities:

In the past, poor quality selective services for poor people were the product of a society which saw 'welfare' as a residual; as a public burden. The primary purpose of the system and the method of discrimination was, therefore, deterrence (it was also an effective rationing device). To this end, the most effective instrument was to induce among recipients (children as well as adults) a sense of personal fault, of personal failure, even if the benefit was wholly or partially a compensation for disservices inflicted by society.[38]

Titmuss argued that the residual nature of selectivist public welfare services was likely to create staff recruitment difficulties which would only serve to increase the possibility of stigmatization.

Insofar as they are able to recruit at all for education, medical care and other services, they tend to recruit the worst rather than the best teachers, doctors, nurses, administrators and other categories of staff upon whom the quality of service so much depends. And if the quality of personal service is low, there will be less freedom of choice and more felt discrimination.[39]

Titmuss was also deeply opposed to the major administrative procedure of selectivist welfare provision – namely the means test:

> If all services are provided – irrespective of whether they represent benefits, amenity, social protection or compensation – on a discriminatory, means-test basis, do we not foster both the sense of personal failure and the stigma of public burden? The fundamental objective of all such tests of eligibility is to keep people out; not to let them in. They must, therefore, be treated as applicants or supplicants; not beneficiaries or consumers.[40]

Titmuss contrasted the stigmatizing propensities of private, and selectivist public, forms of welfare with (what he perceived as) the status-enhancing qualities of universal public social services.

> One fundamental historical reason for the adoption of this principle was the aim of making services available and accessible to the whole population in such ways as would not involve users in any humiliating loss of status, dignity or self-respect. There could be no sense of inferiority, pauperism, shame or stigma in the use of a publicly provided service; no attribution that one was being or becoming a 'public burden'. Hence the emphasis on the social rights of all citizens to use or not to use as responsible people the services made available by the community in respect of certain needs which the private market and the family were unable or unwilling to provide universally.[41]

Titmuss welcomed the move towards universalism which occurred in areas such as education, housing and health care after the Second World War.[42] Titmuss was particularly proud of the developments in health care. He believed that the National Health Service provided the finest example of a non-discriminatory, non-judgmental, social service.[43] In *The Gift Relationship* he stated:

> Attitudes to and relationships with the National Blood Transfusion Service among the general public since 1948 can

only be understood within the context of the Health Service. The most unsordid act of British social policy in the twentieth century has allowed and encouraged sentiments of altruism, reciprocity and social duty to express themselves; to be made explicit and identifiable in measurable patterns of behaviour by all social groups and classes. In part, this is attributable to the fact that, structurally and functionally, the Health Service is not socially divisive; its universal and free access basis has contributed much, we believe, to the social liberties of the subject in allowing people the choice to give or not to give blood for unseen strangers.[44]

Though committed to the principle of universality, Titmuss was fully aware of the limitations of this approach.

Universalism in social welfare, though a needed prerequisite towards reducing and removing formal barriers of social and economic discrimination, does not by itself solve the problems of how to reach the more-difficult-to-reach [who are in need]. . . .[45]

For example, Titmuss recognized that higher-income groups were tending to make more extensive use of the National Health Service.

They tend to receive more specialist attention; occupy more of the beds in better equipped and staffed hospitals; receive more elective surgery; have better maternity care, and are more likely to get psychiatric help and psychotherapy than low income groups – particularly the unskilled.[46]

Titmuss accepted that certain selectivist measures were needed in order to overcome the deficiencies of universalism. However, the type of selectivity that Titmuss had in mind was qualitatively different from the negative form of selectivity associated with residual forms of welfare. Unlike negative selectivity (which merely attempted to identify those members of a particular population group who were eligible, by reason of extreme poverty, for some form of benefit),[47] the positive selectivity (discrimination) advocated by Titmuss was intended to provide additional help for those groups whose needs were not being fully met by existing universal services. As he states:

> The challenge that faces us is not the choice between universalist and selective social services. The real challenge resides in the question: what particular infrastructure of universalist services is needed in order to provide a framework of values and opportunity bases within and around which can be developed socially acceptable selective services aiming to discriminate positively, with the minimum risk of stigma, in favour of those whose needs are greatest.[48]

Titmuss's success in establishing stigma as a concept of central importance for the study of social policy cannot be overstated. The fact that academics, politicians, and others have continued to take both a theoretical and practical (e.g. the effect of stigma on the take-up rate for social security benefits) interest in the concept is due in no small measure to his pioneering contribution.

Further theoretical developments

Titmuss's ideas concerning the relationship between stigma and social policy have been critically examined by a number of other commentators.

Some writers[49] have expressed doubts, for instance, about the link between means-testing and stigma. For example, Klein asserts that:

> Stigma is the phlogiston of social theory: a label attached to an imperfectly understood phenomenon – when low take-up of means-tested benefits can be explained just as well, perhaps better, by the information costs involved, by the fact that expense in time, trouble and travel may outweigh the value of small benefits and by the ability of some people to manage on a given amount of money better than others (all of which indicate providing more free information and streamlining administrative procedures rather than condemning the means tests and discretionary benefits as instruments of policy.[50]

Although contemporary universalists have acknowledged that factors other than stigma might affect the take-up rate for means-tested benefits, they have none the less continued to reaffirm their belief that such procedures are inherently stigmatizing. This is clearly illustrated if one considers their response to the suggestion made by Rose[51] and others that it is possible to find examples of non-stigmatized forms of means-testing (e.g. income tax returns, student grant applications). For example, Room argues that the means tests commonly applied to the poor differ from the former in two important respects.

> First, secrecy and procedural complexities are often allowed to compound the general ill-informedness of claimants, so that the opportunity cost to the latter in terms of time and energy is high. Second the manner in which officials deal with claimants in their face-to-face contacts typically reinforces the sense of stigmatisation that claimants may expect of their neighbours and fellow citizens.[52]

As Reddin concludes: 'The middle class versions of the means test, such as that for university grants, tend to be more civilised and socially acceptable devices than anything to be found amongst the lower income groups.'[53]

Questions have also been raised about the status enhancing qualities of universal social services. As Pinker points out, client and official perceptions of the social services may differ quite significantly:

> Each user of a social service brings the subjective facts of his personal biography to the experience. These facts will be more authentic to him than the officially defined aims or traditions of the service.[54]

As he continues:

> The relationship between social services and citizenship is thus largely determined by subjective evaluations of the purpose of the service. For some citizenship is enhanced while for others it is debased by reliance upon social services. Perceptions of status vary according to service and category of need, and it is

no more true to say that all universalist services always endow
status than it is to claim that selectivist services always
stigmatize.[55]

Certainly, it seems likely that some recipients of universal social
services will experience feelings of stigma (particularly as such
feelings are highly subjective – see pp. 13-18). For example,
streaming or assessment procedures within the educational
system may induce feelings of stigma amongst pupils. Similarly,
patients with chronic complaints may experience a sense of
inferiority because of the priority which tends to be given to
acute conditions within the National Health Service[56] (the
creation of the NHS has done little, for instance, to improve the
quality of care afforded to groups such as the mentally
handicapped).[57] Even positive discrimination programmes may
have stigmatizing propensities. As Reisman states:

> Positive discrimination implies direction of resources without
> stigma towards a particular group. Here, of course, the
> question is not (as it is with a means test) whom to exclude but
> whom to include more intensively. Whether or not this can be
> done without stigma is another matter. Some groups may feel
> stigmatized by being selected (and therefore branded as
> deficient); and there is no *a priori* reason to think that the
> people in Plowden's Educational Priority Areas do not
> experience a collective sense of shame.[58]

Pinker has drawn attention to some of the underlying reasons
for the failure of contemporary welfare services to eradicate the
problem of stigma. He points out that dependency on public
welfare services is always likely to be potentially stigmatizing for
any citizen who has been socialized in a community where market
rather than welfare values predominate. 'In a society where self-
help and independence are powerfully sanctioned values, the
subjective facts of social consciousness . . . impose inferior status
on the dependent.'[59]

In addition, he argues that the stigma attaching to a particular
form of dependency (and the extent to which stigma is
experienced as a result of dependency) will vary according to the
dimensions of depth, distance and time.

'The first variable of depth refers to the extent to which the recipient is made aware of his dependence and sense of inferiority and accepts the definition of his status as legitimate.'[60] For example, individuals who are receiving benefits in recognition of past (e.g. industrial disablement claimants) or future (e.g. higher education students) service are unlikely to be made continually aware of their dependent status or to feel stigmatized by the receipt of such aid. The opposite is more likely to be the case with groups who contravene the norm of reciprocity[61] (e.g. the mentally handicapped) or who are deemed to be responsible for their public dependency (e.g. voluntary unemployed). Pinker contends, however, that certain groups may question the appropriateness of associating stigma with their particular dependency (see on this point pp. 18-20). 'Groups exposed to short-run risks of dependency, such as redundant able-bodied workers and minority groups with a high proportion of young members, are more likely to reject or be indifferent to prevailing forms of stigma.'[62]

Pinker also stresses the importance of the social or spatial distance between recipients of welfare services and their 'donors'. He argues that groups with tenuous grips on citizenship such as ethnic minorities and the institutionalized elderly or handicapped are much more likely to be made aware of their dependent status.[63] Finally, Pinker asserts that individuals who are dependent on welfare provision for long periods of time are most likely to experience intense or persistent feelings of stigma.[64]

In his discussion of the relationship between stigma and public dependency, Pinker also draws attention to the stigmatizing effects of personalized forms of welfare.

The aim of personalizing a welfare-exchange relationship is supposedly to identify more accurately the needs of the applicant, but by so heightening the sensibilities of 'giver' and 'receiver' we also risk making one party more acutely aware of his dependency.[65]

To counter this possibility, which may be compounded by the superior knowledge and expertise of welfare professionals,[66] Pinker suggests that greater use should be made of impersonal, non-stigmatized forms of welfare such as subsidised transport.

'Any user of a free service of this kind would enjoy an increase in disposable income without any risk of stigma and without any danger that ignorance or apathy might exclude them from maximum benefit.'[67] More generally, Pinker argues that the stigma attaching to dependency can be reduced if a variety of donors are involved in the process of providing aid for recipients.

> Dependencies of a stigmatizing or humiliating nature are most likely to be avoided when the individual receives aid of a partial nature from a number of providers. Since individuals require aid from both familial and organizational sources in order to enhance their life-chances, recipients are most likely to prosper when there is an element of competition between donors.[68]

Like Titmuss,[69] Pinker has also highlighted the fact that social policy has controlling as well as caring functions.

> Social services are used to transmit skills and a variety of goods and services designed to enhance the freedom and independence of individuals. They are also used to impose sanctions, and therefore stigma, upon individuals.[70]

These conflicting aims of social policy can clearly be seen to operate, for example, in the sphere of income support for the unemployed. The welfare objective – providing aid for the unemployed and their families (care) – is not permitted to overshadow economic considerations such as the need to reinforce the work ethic. Accordingly, sanctions (control) are applied to those individuals who have left their previous employment without good reason or who have failed to make satisfactory efforts to find a new job.[71]

Control of the poor inevitably increases the possibility of intentional or unintentional forms of stigmatization. Welfare personnel, by virtue of their relatively powerful position vis-à-vis welfare recipients, will often be the perpetrators of such stigmatization. In many cases welfare recipients will be unable to challenge the exercise of this authority because of the very nature of their dependency (i.e. a request for social service aid is often made as a last resort; as such, 'custom' cannot easily be withdrawn, especially if material aid is required). There is considerable evidence that the controlling activities of welfare officials creates feelings of stigma amongst recipients of social services. For example, groups such as one-parent families[72] and the unemployed[73] have frequently referred to their humiliating experiences with National Assistance and Supplementary Benefits officers. In addition, Jordan has expressed concern about the increased risk of stigmatization within the personal social services which (he argues) resulted from the implementation of the 1963 Children and Young Persons Act (section 1 of this act empowered social workers to provide material aid in cases where there was a risk of family break-up).

The obligation to provide poor relief has not only altered the whole structure and ethos of local authority departments; it has created a new kind of relationship between social workers and their clients, based not on principles of casework, but on principles of public assistance. Services which were once provided as best they could be, within the limited resources of local authorities as personal services, are now rationed according to the means-tested ideology of the supplementary benefits system, with all the humiliation of the recipient that this entails.[74]

The assumption that administrative procedures are uniquely responsible for the stigma that attaches to certain social services has also been challenged by Pinker and others:

In our present state of knowledge it is very difficult to understand the cultural processes by which social services and their users become stigmatized. It may be that some groups of users are held in such low public esteem that any service and personnel concerned mainly with their needs become stigmatized merely by association.[75]

Donnison, the former chairman of the Supplementary Benefits Commission, contends that any service dealing with 'vulnerable people who attract least public sympathy'[76] such as deserted wives, ex-prisoners and mental patients is always likely to become stigmatized by association. In the case of supplementary benefits, he argues that the service has only been able to retain some semblance of respectability because of the presence of a large number of deserving claimants (pensioners).[77]

Although there may be some disagreement as to which social service attracts the greatest degree of stigma[78] there seems to be little doubt that services which attract the least amount of public approbation tend to be those which are used predominantly by the lower social classes (e.g. supplementary benefits, social work services and public housing). In contrast, those social services which are patronized by clients from both lower and higher income groups tend to be regarded more positively (e.g. education and health services). Far from being subjected to disapproval or stigmatization, the users of these services are likely to be commended 'for their social competence'.[79]

The media, particularly the press, have played a significant part in creating and reinforcing negative public attitudes towards social services such as supplementary benefits and public housing. In the case of the former, attention has frequently been given either to the disreputable nature of claimants or to the supposedly widespread incidence of fraud and abuse.[80] Despite the lack of evidence to substantiate these allegations of abuse,[81] parts of the press have continued to mount campaigns against scroungers. Indeed, as Golding and Middleton point out: 'the very lack of evidence . . . is taken as proof that there must indeed be a hidden depth of social security abuse.'[82] Interestingly, after castigating the *News Of The World* for unfairly stigmatizing the supplementary benefits service and its clientele, the then chairman of the commission was himself subjected to 'stigmatization' by the same paper.

> Where has he been all his life? A different world to that most of us live in. His father helped run the Burma branch of the British Empire. The Prof went from Marlborough (Captain Mark Phillips's old school: fees £2,000 a year) to Magdalen (King Edward VIII's old college). It is a mystery why a gent with such a background should be regarded as an expert on poverty.[83]

Finally, it is important to note that criticism has been directed at the collectivist aim of reducing the incidence of stigma within the field of social policy. For example, Reisman argues that the movement towards a system of welfare rights has increased the likelihood of irresponsible and unacceptable patterns of behaviour within the community (e.g. voluntary unemployment, child neglect, excessive gambling or drinking). To counter this trend, Reisman advocates that the feckless poor should be subjected to potentially stigmatizing forms of control.[84] In similar vein, both Page and Boyson have stressed the need for explicitly stigmatizing procedures within income support schemes for the unemployed. Page suggests that it would be sensible:

> to arrange for daily signing on by all those who are
> unemployed for longer than three months, or, better still, to
> allow the officers concerned to use their discretion so that
> those who are making a genuine effort to find work need sign
> on only once each week, while those obviously 'swinging the
> lead' could be instructed to sign on more frequently and at
> specific times. For each day when such a person failed to sign
> on his money would be stopped.[85]

Boyson, meanwhile, believes that: 'A basic work test on roads, municipal parks, clearing waste land could be offered to the workshy at the place of their application.'[86]

Social administration and the concept of stigma: the complement provided by research

The development of social policy and administration as an accredited academic subject has led to a rapid growth in the number of research studies undertaken in this field since 1945. A number of these studies have been concerned with the relationship between stigma and welfare provision. In these investigations consideration has generally been given to one or more of the following themes:

(1) The effect of stigma upon the take-up rate for means-tested benefits.
(2) Experiences of stigma resulting from social service use.
(3) Public attitudes towards the social services.

(4) Public attitudes towards the poor and welfare recipients.

Each of these themes will be considered in turn.

(1) The effect of stigma upon the take-up rate for means-tested benefits

Given the collectivist and problem-solving tradition of social policy studies it is not altogether surprising that a good deal of research has been devoted towards the question of how the take-up rate for various means-tested benefits might be adversely affected by considerations of stigma. It is useful to examine this research according to the type of benefit under investigation.

(a) Social Security benefits
The fact that it is now commonly acknowledged that considerations of stigma may deter poor people from claiming means-tested benefits to which they are entitled is due in no small part to the efforts of a number of researchers who investigated the circumstances of the elderly during the 1950s and 1960s. For example (following Townsend's initial work on the elderly, which had drawn attention to the link between stigma and unclaimed benefit),[87] Cole and Utting collected data (during 1959 and 1960) on the economic circumstances prevailing in 400 'elderly income units' (one unit consisted either of a man or woman over retirement age *or* a married couple where the husband was over retirement age).[88] The authors found that 12 per cent of these units were not receiving benefits to which they were entitled. Stigma was identified as one of the reasons for non-claiming amongst this group.[89]

Further evidence of the detrimental effect of stigma upon the take-up rate for National Assistance amongst pensioners was provided in a government survey published in 1966 – *Financial and Other Circumstances of Retirement Pensioners*.[90] As Table 2.1 shows, pride, dislike of charity or reluctance to visit the National Assistance office were cited as reasons for non-claiming by a substantial proportion of pensioners. This direct indicator of the adverse effect of stigma upon the take-up rate for National Assistance amongst the elderly should not, however, be dis-

Table 2.1 Reasons for not applying for National Assistance –
June 1965

*Proportion giving the following reasons:**	*n=*	*Married couples (121,500)* %	*Single men (63,000)* %	*Single women (427,200)* %
Lack of knowledge or misconception		37.4	33.5	34.8
'Managing all right'		19.7	30.0	37.7
Pride, dislike of charity, dislike visiting National Assistance Board		33.4	26.5	22.9

Source: Ministry of Pensions and National Insurance, Table III.21, p.42.
Note: *Some pensioners gave more than one reason and are counted more than once in this table.

sociated from the other reasons given by pensioners for non-claiming. For example, a reason for non-claiming such as lack of knowledge can justifiably be linked to the notion of stigma. As George explains:

> a service which for one reason or another is considered by the
> public to be 'stigmatized' is likely to be both misunderstood
> and not adequately understood for the perceived 'stigma' tends
> to distort any information about the service that reaches the
> public.[91]

This particular study also highlighted the potentially intractable difficulty of eradicating the stigma associated with the claiming of means-tested social security benefits. As Table 2.2 shows, considerations of stigma were found to deter younger as well as older pensioners (who, one could justifiably assume, would be more likely to experience feelings of stigma because of their familiarity with previous forms of poor relief) from claiming benefits to which they were entitled. As Atkinson points out: 'On the basis of this evidence there are no strong grounds for expecting that the problem [of stigma] will disappear with time.'[92]
These studies of the elderly poor certainly had an impact on

government policy. In response to this and other evidence[93] the Labour government decided to establish a new semi-autonomous board – the Supplementary Benefits Commission – to carry out those duties previously performed by the NAB.[94] It was optimistically hoped that the abolition of the term National Assistance coupled with the proposed merger of local contributory and non-contributory benefit offices would improve the image of the means-tested sector. As Kincaid states: 'It was hoped that some of the respectability of national insurance would rub off on the supplementary sector.'[95]

Table 2.2 Retirement pensioners not claiming National Assistance to which they are entitled and reasons for not doing so by age – June 1965

	Percentage of those eligible not claiming			Percentage of those not claiming attributing it to pride, or to dislike of charity or National Assistance Board		
	Married couples	*Single men*	*Single women*	*Married couples*	*Single men*	*Single women*
Age:						
60-64	–	–	38	–	–	20
65-69	45	35	40	31	14	25
70-74	33	36	36	32	36	24
75-79	40	40	37	45	35	22
80-84	36	39	35	30	21	23
Over 85	37	42	39			
All ages	39	38	39	33	27	23

Source: Atkinson, A.B., Table 3.8, p. 59.

A number of specific administrative changes were made in order to encourage the elderly poor (who were to remain firmly within the means-tested sector) to claim their supplementary benefit entitlements.[96] First, elderly claimants were to be provided with a combined pension and supplementary pension order book rather than two order books (thus ensuring that they could not be easily identified as claimants during visits to the post office). Second, the circumstances of supplementary pensioners were to be reappraised after a year instead of six months. Third, this group were to be given the option of visiting their local supplementary benefit office if they did not wish to be visited at home. In addition, it was also hoped that the elderly poor (along with other claimants) would benefit from more general changes in the means-tested system such as: improved forms of publicity for the new scheme; the decision to pay long-term additions without regard to family circumstances; the rationalization and improvement of the 'disregard' regulations; the acceptance that claimants had a 'right' to benefit.

The fact that the elderly demonstrated a greater willingness to claim their entitlement to benefit after the introduction of the new scheme should not, however, be taken to indicate that the image of the means-tested sector had been dramatically improved as a result of the cosmetic changes outlined above. It seems more likely that this increase in the take-up rate was caused by improvements in the level of allowances and by the more generous system of 'disregards'.[97]

Evidence linking stigma with the non-take-up of means-tested social security benefits has continued to be found in more recent surveys.[98] For example, in a study of funeral expenses, Hennessey found that a number of people living on low incomes were unwilling to ask the Supplementary Benefits Commission for addtional help with funeral costs because of the stigma involved in claiming.[99] As Table 2.3 shows, thirteen respondents referred directly to the stigma associated with claiming when they were asked to explain why they had not requested assistance from the SBC. It should also be noted, though, that some of the other reasons given by respondents for not approaching the SBC can be linked to the notion of stigma. For example, those respondents who were critical of the social security system or who had used their own savings may have been indirectly referring to the effect of stigma.

(b) Rate/rent rebates/allowances

As part of a research project in the early 1970s, Meacher attempted to find out what effect stigma had upon potential rate rebate claimants in Islington.[100] To carry out this task, Meacher renewed contact (September 1971) with a group of eligible, non-claiming occupiers who had previously indicated (May 1971) that they would apply for a rate rebate. Having eliminated the factor

Table 2.3 Reasons why people with difficulties did not ask about extra help from the SBC

	Number of people giving this reason (weighted)
Didn't know about it/ never thought about it	25
Claiming benefits is degrading/ respondent too proud to go to DHSS or ask anyone for money/ only idlers ask for social security	13
Respondent knew that insurance/ estate would pay out eventually	10
Didn't think there was anything besides Death Grant/ didn't think they were entitled to or qualified for anything else	9
Respondent was working full time and knew SBC could not help	8
Social security are unhelpful/ don't care/ respondent had had claims for benefit(s) turned down in the past	7
Respondent used own savings/ cut down instead	6
Weighted total number of people asked this question	66

(More than one reason possible)
Source: Hennessey, P.J., Table 6.5, p. 86.

of ignorance (all members of the survey group had been clearly informed of their eligibility for this benefit), Meacher found that the worthlessness of claiming (low level of rebate not deemed to be a sufficient reward for the effort involved in claiming) and stigma were the two most important reasons for non-take-up. In terms of the latter Meacher found that:

(i) The elderly were more likely to be influenced by considerations of stigma than other eligible families.
(ii) Private tenants tended to refer to stigma as a reason for not claiming rebate more frequently than their council counterparts.

Given the deep-rooted historical association between stigma and means-tested benefits, Meacher was not surprised that the elderly tended to be deterred from claiming rebates to which they were entitled (because of stigma) more than other groups. As she points out:

Since we did our utmost for more than a century until the 1940s to inculcate feelings of guilt, shame and stigma, their presence among older people is evidence of the *success* of earlier publicity carried out over a very long period.[101]

In terms of her second finding, Meacher was prompted to hypothesize that:

acceptance of a Council house may itself be seen as a certain loss of independence, so that further claims are less inhibited. Several respondents in private accommodation made comments such as 'you're not your own once you claim these things' or 'they know all about you once you fill in those forms'. Council tenants may well feel that they have already revealed some personal information to the council so that to do so again is less a deterrent.[102]

Table 2.4 Principal reasons for not claiming given by non-claimers

Ignorance and misconception	23
Stigma, pride, dislike of charity	8
Don't know	5
Total	36

Source: Taylor-Gooby, P.F., 'Rent benefits', Table 5, p. 44.

In a survey conducted by the Batley community development project a link was also found between stigma and the non-take-up of rent rebates and allowances.[103] In a qualitative follow-up survey conducted in 1973, 36 tenants were asked to account for their failure to claim either rent allowances (12) or rebates (24).[104] As Table 2.4 shows, only a small number of respondents cited stigma as a reason for their reluctance to claim. However, greater significance was accorded to the factor of stigma when this group of non-claimers and a group of claimers were asked to speculate as to why eligible tenants were not claiming these benefits (see Table 2.5).

Table 2.5 Principal reasons why other entitled tenants do not claim

	Claimers	Non-claimers	Total
Ignorance	7	9	16
Stigma and pride	7	12	19
Scared of rebuff	9	4	13
Don't know	9	10	19
Other	3	1	4
Total	35	36	71

Source: Taylor-Gooby, P.F., 'Rent benefits', Table 6, p. 45.

According to Taylor-Gooby, the apparent discrepancy between these results may indicate, on the one hand, that respondents believe that stigma is an important influence upon others but not upon themselves or, alternatively, that there is some general reluctance to admit to personal feelings of stigma.[105] This latter explanation is certainly worthy of serious consideration given the fact that many of us would no doubt find it difficult, or even belittling, to admit to feelings of stigma.

(c) Free prescriptions and 'passport' benefits

In a study conducted in a Scottish city in 1972, Blaxter collected data on 237 former hospital patients of working age.[106] She found that the take-up rate for free prescriptions amongst those members of her sample who were entitled to this benefit was relatively low. As Table 2.6 shows, most of the non-claimers were entitled to this benefit on grounds of low income.

In attempting to account for this reluctance to claim, Blaxter found that her respondents distinguished between those benefits which were provided on the basis of a particular medical condition, insurance record or 'stage-of-life' criteria (e.g. children, pensioners) and those forms of assistance which were provided on a discretionary basis for those in financial need (i.e. ' "need" of itself: not entitlement because of belonging to a special group, or "need" because of special circumstances').[107] As Blaxter points out:

> To accept any benefit supplied by 'the welfare' was seen as passing a watershed. Many people refused to apply for free prescriptions even though they admitted money problems, because they thought that 'it means inspectors prying'; I'm not telling them how much money I've got . . . 'everyone says they make you feel degraded if you ask for anything free'; 'I'm not applying for charity'.[108]

Although Blaxter's non-claimers did not appear to feel stigmatized about being poor,[109] they did appear to be deterred (by considerations of stigma) from applying for those benefits which they did not believe they had a 'legitimate' right to receive.

Table 2.6 Grounds of entitlement to free prescriptions

	Receiving	Not receiving	Total
Low income	18	36	54
'Prescribed' diseases	9	2	11
Both income and disease	8*	2	10
Both income and service pension	1+	2	3
Both disease and service pension	1+	–	1
Pregnancy	1	–	1
Total	38	42	80

Source: M. Blaxter, Table 1, p. 43.
Notes: *Five of these respondents had received 'income' certificates and three 'disease' certificates.
+Both of these respondents were in receipt of service pension certificates.

In a survey of fatherless families receiving Family Income Supplement, Nixon also found that there was a link between stigma and the non-take-up of 'passport' benefits.[110] Although stigma was not found to be the main reason for non-take-up, it was found to deter a number of mothers from claiming a variety of benefits to which they were entitled (see Table 2.7). Interestingly, Nixon found that considerations of stigma affected mothers' decisions concerning claiming in both a direct and indirect way. For example, in terms of the latter Nixon discovered that 40 mothers had refused to claim free school meals because they felt that this would cause embarrassment for their children.

Table 2.7 Reasons for non-take-up of 'passport' benefits

	Type of 'passport' benefit not taken up				
	School meals	Prescrip- tion charges	Hospital fares	Dental/ optical charges	Legal advice
Base of percentages	400	314	823	518	700
	%	%	%	%	%
Did not know it was included with FIS	4	16	7	11	5
Did not think I was entitled	5	18	10	12	6
Embarrassing for children	10	1	0	1	0
Pride	4	5	1	3	1
Too much bother/ not worth it	1	6	3	3	1
Too much form filling	0	0	0	1	0
Total eligible	24	46	21	31	13

Source: J. Nixon, Table 3.5, p. 34.

(d) Free school meals
Evidence indicating that stigma contributes towards the non-take-up of free school meals has been found in a number of studies.[111] For example, in a 'snapshot' survey in 1974, Field found that the humiliating treatment meted out to 'free meal' pupils in certain schools (different payment schemes, separate entrances/tables, different/smaller meals) had deterred some poor parents from claiming this benefit on behalf of their children.[112] Davies also found evidence of an association between stigma and non-take-up in his meticulous study of free school meals, which was conducted

Table 2.8 Proportions of families with no experience of free meals and who had not considered applying for free meals giving various reasons for not considering applying (%)

| | Non-takers' sample* | | Payers' sample* | |
	U	O	U	O
Income too high	26	36	50	41
Ineligible because working	7	3	5	7
Ignorance about free meals scheme	19	5	3	2
Unwillingness to reveal personal information	2	0	2	2
Pride as parents	4	8	7	12
Embarrassment to child	2	3	2	7
Disagreement with free meals in principle	0	3	2	4
Thought ineligible	17	10	17	18
Parental preference	19	10	2	0
No answer	6	26	15	16
Families who had no experience of free meals and did not consider applying	100	100	100	100

Source: Davies, B. in association with Reddin, M., Table 3.2, p. 68.
Note: *U denotes 'under-achieving area': O denotes 'over-achieving' area. For details of this classification see Davies, B., pp. 19-20.

in the late 1960s.[113] In order to gauge the effect of stigma upon take-up, Davies asked a group of mothers to explain why they had not applied for free school meals. As Table 2.8 shows, only a relatively small proportion of respondents referred to stigma factors (e.g. unwillingness to reveal personal information; pride as parents; embarrassment to child. It should also be noted that the category parental preference may also include references to stigma).[114] However, when Davies asked his respondents to account for non-take-up amongst other eligible families he found that far greater weight was given to stigma factors (see Tables 2.9 and 2.10). Davies believes that there may have been three possible reasons for the discrepancy between these two results:[115]

(i) Respondents were unwilling to be completely honest with interviewers and thus avoided referring to stigma when talking about themselves.

Table 2.9 Proportion of respondents giving various explanations of why eligible families did not apply for free school meals

		Non-takers' families		Payers' families		Free meals receivers' families	
		U %	O %	U %	O %	U %	O %
(a)	Stigma (including parents' pride or shame, or the dislike of the invasion of privacy involved)	39	43	48	55	40	39
(b)	Ignorance (including not realizing that they are eligible, not knowing about free meals, not understanding the system	35	24	40	22	18	20
(c)	Dislike of food	12	18	5	7	19	17
(d)	Parents can afford to pay	6	0	2	7	2	1
(e)	Parents apathetic	0	4	7	6	12	10
(f)	Prefer to eat at home	4	11	0	3	5	10
(g)	Others	6	2	2	0	4	1
Total number of persons giving codable explanation	%	100	100	100	100	100	100
	No.	66	56	61	71	67	69

Source: Davies, B. in association with Reddin, M., Table 3.7, p. 82.

(ii) Respondents may have been unwilling to admit to feeling stigmatized about receiving a financially advantageous family benefit.

(iii) Respondents' ideas about what influences other people's behaviour may have reflected political mythology and stereotypes rather than their own knowledge, experience or feelings.

After examining each of these possible reasons, Davies concludes that 'the last is the most probable explanation; the second is less probable; and the first is much less probable.'[116] Davies's conclusion on this point is clearly open to question. It could be argued, for example, that he has not given sufficient consideration to the possibility that respondents may find it difficult to admit to personal feelings of stigma (see p. 48). This particular issue will be discussed in greater detail later in the chapter.

Table 2.10 Proportions of respondents agreeing with propositions as important explanations of why eligible children did not receive free school meals

	Non-takers' families		Payers' families		Free meals receivers' families	
	%	N*	%	N*	%	N*
'Under-achieving' authority						
(a) Do not need them	32	76	27	79	53	68
(b) Other children stigmatize receivers	58	77	61	79	56	68
(c) Teachers pick on receivers	30	77	15	79	10	68
(d) Thought to be charity	70	76	70	79	78	68
(e) Application too complicated	51	76	56	79	34	68
(f) Don't like stating incomes	44	77	70	79	76	68
(g) Don't like employer to know that applying	57	77	54	79	50	68
(h) Don't know about the service	74	77	70	79	60	68
'Over-achieving' authority						
(a) Do not need them	40	67	27	78	19	81
(b) Other children stigmatize receivers	68	68	65	79	62	81
(c) Teachers pick on receivers	12	68	15	79	12	81
(d) Thought to be charity	82	68	75	79	78	81
(e) Application too complicated	43	68	52	79	25	81
(f) Don't like stating incomes	65	68	63	79	74	81
(g) Don't like employer to know that applying	57	68	52	79	63	81
(h) Don't know about the service	63	68	47	79	46	81

Source: Davies, B. in association with Reddin, M., Table 3.8, p. 84.
*Number of persons giving an answer to the proposition. The percentages are proportions of this number.

(2) Experiences of stigma resulting from social service use

Much of the evidence linking social service use and stigmatizing experiences has come from surveys of claimants receiving means-tested social security benefits. In numerous instances researchers have found that the mere process of applying for, or receiving, such benefits can induce feelings of stigma. For example, 75 per cent of the female single parents interviewed by Marsden in the mid-1960s reported that they had felt very embarrassed when applying for national assistance.[117] In a survey of supplementary benefit recipients in the late 1960s, Townsend also found that a third of his respondents felt embarrassed to some degree about receiving this form of aid (see Table 2.11).[118] In another study, conducted in the early 1970s, Marshall interviewed a group of mothers who were dependent upon supplementary benefit.[119] She found that a substantial proportion of her respondents (particularly divorced women, separated wives and wives with sick husbands) felt stigmatized about receiving supplementary benefit (see Table 2.12). In terms of this particular study it is important to note that the extent of felt stigma amongst respondents should not be gauged solely from the category 'feelings of stigma or dislikes feeling of dependency'. Clearly, mothers who reported, for example, that they disliked: (i) visiting the local SB office; (ii) the questions posed by, or attitude adopted by, SB officials; (iii) 'just . . . being on it', may equally well have been referring to feelings of stigma.

Table 2.11 Percentages of elderly and younger recipients, according to their attitudes to receiving supplementary benefit

Whether embarrassed or uncomfortable at receiving supplementary benefit or accepting it like a pension or other income	Recipients aged 60 and over	Recipients under 60	Recipients		
			Male	Female	All
Very embarrassed or uncomfortable	5.3	19.2	8.0	9.7	9.1
A little embarrassed	20.7	19.2	18.4	21.2	20.0
Not embarrassed	74.1	61.6	73.6	69.1	70.9
Total	100.0	100.0	100.0	100.0	100.0
Number	189	73	87	175	265

Source: P. Townsend, *Poverty in the United Kingdom*, Table 24.11, p. 846.

Table 2.12 Dislikes about being on supplementary benefit

	Unem-ployed men (wives)	Sick men (wives)	Unmarried mothers	Separated wives	Divorced wives	Widows
	%	%	%	%	%	%
Dislikes going to local office, because of waiting times, lack of privacy, or unspecified reasons	24	28	29	36	36	30
Dislikes questioning by staff; type of question or attitude of staff	47	26	20	30	31	36
Feels that exceptional needs grants are not given to them when they should be	11	–	4	6	3	6
Feeling of stigma or dislikes feeling of dependency	24	37	29	37	41	26
Dislikes being short of money, income inadequate	22	11	20	16	18	9
'Just don't like being on it'	7	7	6	5	5	8
Nothing disliked, or favourable comments only	24	32	27	19	16	42

Source: R. Marshall, Table 59, p. 53.
Note: Percentages add up to more than 100 because several mothers gave more than one answer.

Various studies have also shown that the conduct of national assistance and supplementary benefits officers can induce feelings of stigma amongst claimants.[120] Claimants' complaints about the unfavourable attitude of officials have often been linked to particular administrative procedures. For example, in a study of the unemployed in North Tyneside, it was found that many of the respondents who had been refused exceptional needs payments were highly critical of the behaviour of the supplementary benefits officers concerned.[121] Two 'typical' comments can be cited in this regard.[122]

> He was snotty. He didn't ask to see the clothing .. . . a bugger,
> I was gonna sock him one.

> I'd asked for a grant for wallpaper and paint – the children's
> room is damp all winter and their blankets are no good – I just
> got cheek. I threw him out.

Lister[123] found that the majority of the eighteen wage-stopped claimants she interviewed in the early 1970s also felt aggrieved because of the treatment they had received from SB officers.

> They treat you like dirt. One woman was so rude you'd think
> she was talking to a tramp. Department of Public Humiliation I
> call it.

> The Social Security make you feel they're doing you a favour,
> that you should be grateful for everything you get. A frightfully
> demoralising experience the whole thing.[124]

Research has also shown that female claimants are particularly likely to be treated in a stigmatizing way by social security officials. Women suspected of cohabitation have frequently drawn attention to the totally unacceptable comments made by national assistance and supplementary benefits officers.[125] A comment from one of Marsden's respondents provides a good example of how feelings of stigma can result from a remark made by an official in these circumstances.

> They were really horrible. First one man came round, then
> another, saying, 'Do you sleep with Mr Barnes? Are you
> committing adultery with him?' And I told him it's my own
> private business, but the man says, 'You can't tell me that a
> man and a woman living in the same house don't go to bed
> together,' and I told him that's dirty talk and I don't like it at
> all.[126]

Comments made by officials during questioning about future employment plans[127] or the identity of a putative father[128] have also been shown to induce feelings of stigma amongst female claimants.

It should also be noted that feelings of stigma have been reported by other social service users such as council house tenants[129] and social work clients.[130] For example, in terms of the latter, Rees found that 35 (59 per cent) of his respondents had felt ashamed (to some degree) about being referred to a social worker.[131]

In addition, it is important to remember that evidence relating to felt stigma has not always been found in welfare consumer research. For instance, in a recent study of supplementary benefit claimants, Briggs and Rees[132] found little evidence to support the assertion that contact with SB officials is liable to induce feelings of stigma amongst the poor. As they point out:

> Some experiences regarded by claimants as humiliating were recounted to us, but they were not very common. Spontaneous favourable comments about the last interview and the manners and helpfulness of officers greatly outnumbered unfavourable ones. Among pensioners in particular, there appeared to be the raw materials for the emergence of a Supplementary Benefit Fan Club.[133]

A number of researchers in the United States have attempted to pinpoint the precise reasons for the link between felt stigma and the receipt of welfare benefits. In a survey of fifty, predominantly black, female recipients of AFDC (Aid to Families with Dependent Children) who were living in a southern state of America, Horan and Austin found that educated or longer-term beneficiaries were more likely to report feelings of stigma than other respondents.[134] In addition, it was found that (other things being equal) mothers who knew about the existence of local welfare rights organisations were less likely to feel 'stigmatized'.[135]

Horan and Austin's results contrast markedly with those obtained in a survey conducted by Handler and Hollingsworth.[136] After interviewing over 700 AFDC recipients, who were living in one of six Wisconsin states, these authors came to the conclusion that:

> although feelings of stigma do exist among AFDC recipients, our indicators of stigma are only very weakly related or not

related at all to the more obvious background characteristics of welfare recipients such as race, employment experience, education, type of community, length of residence, or friendships.[137]

Kerbo (in a study of 103 mothers who were receiving AFDC in a midwestern urban area)[138] also found little or no evidence to link felt stigma with race, employment experience, education, length of residence or age (over forties only). However, he did find that respondents who believed in individualistic explanations of poverty were more likely to feel stigmatized than those who favoured structural explanations.[139]

Kerbo's findings conflicted, however, with Handler and Hollingsworth's results concerning the effect of felt stigma upon recipients' attitudes towards the welfare system. Contrary to the evidence of the latter,[140] Kerbo found that respondents who had experienced intense feelings of stigma tended to adopt 'a passive uncritical orientation toward the welfare system'.[141]

(3) Public attitudes towards the social services

Evidence from a number of sources indicates that welfare services have stigmatic connotations for some members of the general public. For example, as part of an exploratory examination of the relationship between the individual and the welfare state, Pinker[142] asked three groups of male respondents (1 The chronically sick – bronchitics; 2 The acutely sick – coronaries; 3 A control group – 'fit' men) about their attitudes towards welfare services. He found that just over one third of his respondents believed that welfare dependencies were bad for self-respect (see Table 2.13). More specifically, Pinker found that respondents held the social security service in particularly low esteem. Some 80 per cent of his respondents contended that people took unfair advantage of this service, though only 30 per cent believed that there was large-scale abuse.[143]

Similar results to those obtained by Pinker were found in a recent survey (1977) conducted by Golding and Middleton in two English cities (Leicester and Sunderland).[144] For example, these authors found that nearly a quarter of their 650 respondents

Table 2.13 Attitudes towards seeking help from the welfare state

	Bad for self-respect	Not bad for self-respect
Bronchitics	11	19
Coronaries	10	24
Controls	5	11
Total (N=80)	26	54

Source: Pinker, R.A., *Dependency*, Table 4, p. 59.

believed that people who claimed social security benefits should feel guilty about living off taxpayers' charity.[145] In addition, some 97 per cent of Golding and Middleton's respondents believed that scrounging was prevalent within the social security system. Indeed, a third of this latter group were of the opinion that more than 25 per cent of all claimants were scroungers.[146]

Social security is not the only welfare service that has stigmatic connotations for the general public. For example, in a study of community perceptions of social work, Glastonbury et al. found that 30 per cent of their respondents held the view that social work clients were feckless and lazy.[147]

Evidence that the public tends to associate stigma with particular welfare programmes has been found in two other studies. Clifford[148] asked a cross-section of people living in three different parts of a large, southern Irish town to speculate about public attitudes towards three particular income support services (St Vincent de Paul – a voluntary Catholic organization which provides cash and other material aid for the poor; Home Assistance – a discretionary, family means-tested, income-support scheme for those unable to obtain other state benefits; Unemployment Assistance – claimants eligible for this benefit must:– (i) be aged betwen 18 and 69; (ii) have resided in the state for at least six months prior to their application; (iii) be not only capable and available for, but also genuinely seeking, work; (iv) be willing to submit to a means test). As Table 2.14 shows, most respondents believed that the general public would be reluctant, to some degree, about approaching either the St Vincent de Paul society or the Home Assistance service. In contrast, few respondents believed that the general public would be reluctant in any way about approaching the Unemployment Assistance service.

Table 2.14 Reluctance of people in general towards approaching services

Attitudes towards approaching services	Service (%)		
	Home Assistance	St Vincent de Paul	Unemployment Assistance
Very reluctant	30.0	31.4	4.6
Quite reluctant	22.6	26.6	5.6
A bit reluctant	27.2	27.9	11.8
Not reluctant	20.2	14.1	80.0
Total	100.0	100.0	100.0
Number	287	290	285

Source: D. Clifford, Table 4, p. 39

Table 2.15 Reasons for reluctance

Factors	Home Assistance	St Vincent de Paul	Unemployment Assistance
Pride and independence	45.5	29.6	41.7
Shame and embarrassment	16.1	28.2	27.1
Dissatisfaction with the service	2.3	1.7	2.1
Fear of being refused	10.6	6.4	4.2
Service seen as charity	10.1	12.8	4.2
Dislike of officials	7.8	3.8	2.1
Fear of being 'classed' as poor	5.0	11.5	8.3
Service too public	1.8	6.0	6.3
Felt obligation to pay back benefit	1.8	1.7	4.2
Total	100.0	100.0	100.0
Number of respondents to question	218	234	48

Source: D. Clifford, Table 5, p. 39.

Most respondents referred to stigma factors when they were asked to account for the public's reluctance to approach these various services (see Table 2.15).

Clifford suggests four possible reasons for the relatively superior public image of the Unemployment Assistance scheme (which was, incidentally, not only means-tested but also widely assumed to be open to abuse):[149]

1 Fixed rates of benefit.
2 The absence of discretion.
3 Benefits were paid at the same office as insurance benefits.
4 The high status of many of the claimants (low-paid smallholders were entitled to claim this benefit).[150]

In a study in the United States, Williamson asked 230 white women living in Boston (1972) to estimate the degree of stigma associated with various types of welfare programmes.[151] In terms of job training schemes, Williamson found that his respondents tended to give higher stigma ratings to those schemes in which eligibility was restricted to welfare recipients.[152] Similarly, two 'welfare' income support programmes – General Relief (a scheme in which cash payments are provided for low-income families who are unable to obtain any other means of support) and AFDC (an income maintenance scheme for low-income families in which dependent children are deprived of the support of one parent) were also given high stigma ratings.[153]

When asked to give reasons for their negative attitude towards AFDC, respondents referred to a number of factors: administrative procedures; the incidence of abuse amongst claimants; the characteristics of recipients (prostitutes, alcoholics, unfit mothers) and the inferior treatment accorded to claimants and their children by others.[154]

In addition to finding that the more highly stigmatized programmes tended to be those which were restricted to welfare claimants, Williamson also found some evidence which suggested that respondents with liberal views or from higher socio-economic backgrounds tended to give higher stigma ratings to the various programmes than their conservative or lower socio-economic counterparts.[155]

(4) Public attitudes towards the poor and welfare recipients

Much of the rather limited evidence concerning public attitudes towards the poor has come from research conducted in the United States. In general it has been found that the public hold rather unfavourable opinions of the poor. For example, in a nationwide survey of 1,017 Americans, Feagin found that 84 per cent of his respondents believed that many of those receiving welfare payments should have been working; 71 per cent thought that claimants made dishonest assessments of their own needs; whilst 61 per cent contended that female welfare recipients were deliberately having illegitimate children in order to increase their incomes.[156] Unfavourable public attitudes towards the poor were also found in a Gallop survey conducted in 1964. A third of the 3,055 white Americans inteviewed in this survey were of the opinion that poverty resulted from a lack of effort on the part of the poor themselves.[157] Three groups of respondents particularly favoured this explanation: (i) the young; (ii) the better educated; (iii) low-status white-collar workers and farmers.[158] Interestingly, Golding and Middleton (in their recent study of public perceptions of poverty in England) also found that their respondents tended to favour this 'victim-blaming' explanation of poverty.[159] In looking in more detail at the characteristics of those respondents who had linked poverty with prodigality (wasteful spending patterns, financial ineptitude, imprudent breeding habits and sheer fecklessness or lack of motivation of the poor), Golding and Middleton found that women, pensioners and people living in middle-class neighbourhoods were more likely to favour this particular explanation of poverty.[160] It should be noted with regard to the latter that unfavourable middle-class attitudes towards the poor have also been found, to varying degrees, in a number of American studies (e.g. Lauer,[161] Goodwin,[162] and Williamson[163]).

Golding and Middleton's evidence concerning 'victim-blaming' tends to confirm one of the findings of an earlier EEC study on public perceptions of poverty.[164] In this survey it was found that British citizens were more likely to accept individualistic explanations of poverty than their European counterparts (see Table 2.16).

In this study it was also found that lower income groups and

Table 2.16 Public opinion on the causes of poverty (EEC)

Causes	United Kingdom %	Whole community %
Laziness	45	28
Drink	40	28
Too many children	31	27
Lack of foresight	21	18
Chronic unemployment	42	27
Ill health	36	37
Old age and loneliness	30	34
Lack of education	29	39
Deprived childhood	16	46

Source: Commission of the European Communities, Tables 27 and 28, pp. 69-70.
Note: Totals higher than 100 per cent because of multiple replies.

the less well educated (throughout the community) were more likely to associate poverty with individual failings whilst higher income groups and the better educated tended to link poverty with social injustice.[165] In contrast, Golding and Middleton's evidence (relating only to England) suggests that it is claimants, manual workers and inner-city residents who are more likely to associate poverty with structural injustice.[166]

Three surveys in the British Isles have shown, in addition, that when the general public are asked to make assessments of the welfare entitlements of particular groups in society they attach great importance to the characteristics and circumstances of potential recipients.

Glastonbury et al. asked their respondents whether social work services (including material aid) should be provided, at public expense, for various groups in society (six of these groups were portrayed as having blameless or accidental dependencies whilst negative characteristics were ascribed to the remaining eight groups i.e. blameworthy or non-accidental dependencies).[167] (See Table 2.17.) The former (blameless) were seen to be the most deserving of support – 68 per cent of respondents said that they

Table 2.17 Respondents' attitude to giving help in specific family circumstances

Specified groups		Respondents' replies (%)			
	Yes	*Sometimes*	*No*	*Don't Know*	*Total*
1 Mothers and children where father is dead or deserted	90	2	3	5	100
2 Families who are homeless or in very poor housing	85	8	3	4	100
3 Poor families	74	19	3	4	100
4 Families where the father is out of work	54	37	5	4	100
5 People, like students, who do not pay taxes	52	20	22	6	100
6 Coloured families	51	25	20	4	100
7 Families in which father is in prison	82	6	7	5	100
8 Unmarried mothers and children	74	14	8	4	100
9 Families with delinquent children	68	11	20	1	100
10 Families with a lot of children	52	24	19	5	100
11 Families who have only recently moved to the area	33	29	33	5	100
12 Families in debt	25	44	26	5	100
13 Families with parents who drink, smoke or gamble	18	20	55	7	100
14 Families in which the father is unwilling to work	15	28	53	4	100

Source: B. Glastonbury, Table 3, p. 196.

would offer unconditional help; 19 per cent – conditional help; 9 per cent – no help at all. In contrast, the latter (blameworthy) were perceived as being relatively undeserving – 46 per cent of those interviewed stated that they would grant unconditional aid; 22 per cent conditional aid; 28 per cent – no aid at all.[168]

Not unexpectedly, a large percentage of respondents were willing to grant unconditional aid to deserving groups such as single-parent families in which the father had either died or deserted (90 per cent) and homeless families or those in very poor housing (85 per cent). Similarly, it was not surprising to find that respondents were unwilling to give aid to two particular types of family: (i) those in which parents drink, smoke or gamble (55 per cent); (ii) those in which the father is unwilling to work (53 per cent). More surprising, however, was the fact that may respondents were willing to give unconditional help to three groups commonly perceived as being undeserving – families in which the father was in prison (82 per cent); unmarried mothers and their children (74 per cent); and families with delinquent children (68 per cent).

Evidence from Clifford's survey in the Republic of Ireland lends support to Glastonbury et al.'s findings. Clifford found that a large proportion of his interviewees were willing to give unconditional help to deserving groups such as the elderly (97 per cent and above): families with a sick wage earner (93 per cent) and widows with children (92 per cent).[169] (See Table 2.18.) Similarly, respondents were unwilling to help 'undeserving' groups such as single men who were unwilling to work (83 per cent) and families which run up debts (51 per cent). Clifford also found that there was a good deal of public support for unmarried mothers with children and families in which the father was in prison. Widows, somewhat surprisingly, elicited a rather unfavourable response from those interviewed – only 34 per cent said that they would offer unconditional aid to this group.

In comparing the surveys of Clifford and Glastonbury et al. it is possible to detect certain regional differences in public attitudes towards potential recipients of welfare aid. For example, needy large families were viewed far more favourably in the Republic of Ireland than in south Wales (81 per cent of Clifford's respondents stated that they would offer unconditional help to this group whereas only 52 per cent of Glastonbury et al.'s sample said that they would act likewise (see Tables 2.17 and 2.18).

It is important to note that caution should be exercised when interpreting the results obtained in these two studies. For example, in both surveys favourable attitudes were displayed towards unmarried mothers. This may well indicate, as Clifford suggests, a change in public attitude towards this group.[170] However, the precise phrasing of the question used in this and other cases is likely to have affected the results obtained. In both surveys respondents were generally asked to consider whether

Table 2.18 Respondents' attitudes to giving help in specific family circumstances

Class of person	Proportions of interviewees		
	Help without conditions	Help with conditions	Should never help
Old who are poor	98.4	1.6	0.0
Old who are ill	97.3	2.7	0.0
Families whose husband is sick and out of work	93.0	7.0	0.0
Families whose husband has deserted without trace	87.9	11.4	0.7
Very big families whose fathers' wage is small	81.2	18.5	0.3
Families whose father is too lazy to seek work	29.2	50.7	20.1
Families whose fathers drink most of the wages	35.8	48.2	16.1
Single men who are unwilling to work	1.7	15.1	83.3
Wives of alcoholic husbands	68.5	27.9	3.7
Unmarried mothers who keep their child	86.6	12.4	1.0
Widows with children	9.2.3	7.0	0.7
Widows without children	33.6	55.7	10.7
Itinerant men not in work	33.7	45.8	20.5
Families of itinerants not at work	63.1	32.9	4.0
Families whose fathers are in jail	80.3	17.7	2.0
Families where both parents drink	38.6	41.9	19.5
Families where both parents gamble	27.9	40.7	31.3
Families where wife is an alcoholic	46.6	38.9	14.4
Families who run up debts and have large Hire Purchase arrears	14.1	34.2	51.3

Source: D. Clifford, Table 7, p. 43.
Note: Based on 300 interviewees.

they would offer help to certain groups within the context of family situations (i.e. they were not asked to consider providing aid solely for specific groups such as criminals, immigrants or unmarried mothers). The inclusion of dependants may therefore have neutralized underlying public hostility towards such groups. Indeed, in the case of widows, Clifford found that the inclusion of children was significant. Whilst 92 per cent of his respondents were willing to give unconditional help to a widow with children only 34 per cent were willing to provide similar aid for a widow living alone (see Table 2.18).

In the third of these surveys in the British Isles, Pinker[171] asked his respondents to consider which of a number of specified groups should be given priority in terms of additional welfare aid. As Table 2.19 shows, the deserving or undeserving characteristics of the specified groups did not appear to have been a major consideration in respondents' evaluations. For example, both the bronchitic and control groups indicated that they would give higher priority to ex-convicts than to either the disabled or old age pensioners. In addition, all groups believed that priority should be given to ex-convicts as opposed to sick men. It is a matter for speculation as to why respondents made these distinctions. For example, those interviewed may have ignored the deserving or undeserving characteristics of the various groups specified when making their assessments of welfare priorities (alternatively, they may have had highly distinctive views about what precisely constitutes a deserving or undeserving group). Instead, they may have decided to make their assessments of welfare priorities on the basis of existing levels of welfare provision for each of the groups concerned (i.e. given low priority to those groups deemed to be currently receiving an adequate level of aid).

Social policy research on stigma: an assessment

The collectivist and problem-solving roots of the discipline of social policy and administration can clearly be seen in the research studies that have been conducted into the notion of stigma within the welfare field. For example, most researchers have accepted the collectivist assumption that considerations of stigma can unnecessarily deter citizens from using selectivist public welfare services. Accordingly, a good deal of research has been devoted towards investigating the various ways in which

Table 2.19   Respondents' attitudes towards welfare priorities

Vignette	Rank order			
	Overall	*Bronchitics*	*Coronaries*	*Control*
Low earner	1	2	1	1
Sick old age pensioner	2	4	3	3
Fit old age pensioner	3	5	4	4
Ex-convict	4	3	8	2
Sick child	5	1	6	9
Disabled man	6	9	2	8
Child in trouble	7	8	7	5
Backward child	8	7	9	6
Sick man	9	6	10	7
Bright child	10	10	5	10

Source: R.A. Pinker, *Dependency*, pp. 50-2.
Note: Low numbers = high priority.

stigma can lead to the under-utilization of this type of social service provision. In particular, attention has been paid to the way in which the take-up rate for various means-tested benefits can be adversely affected by considerations of stigma (see pp. 42-5).

This type of research has certainly been of some use, particularly in the realm of policy-making. For example, a number of researchers have suggested various ways in which 'the problem of stigma' can be countered: e.g. the abolition of modification of selectivist services; better training schemes for officials; more widespread publicity of various entitlements; less complex procedures; improvements in the furnishings and facilities provided in welfare offices used by the public.

In general, however, social policy research on the effect of stigma upon the actions and feelings of welfare recipients (or potential welfare recipients) has been rather disappointing. Importantly, the problem-solving ethos of the discipline has tended to militate against the use of sound theoretical frameworks. As a result, insufficient attention has been given to the various aspects of the concept (i.e. distinctions have rarely been made between stigmas, stigmatization, felt stigma and so forth: see chapter 1). For instance, in much of this research the impression has often been conveyed that selectivist forms of welfare provision are the major source (as opposed to one particular source) of stigma in society. The promulgation of this viewpoint has tended to result in stigma becoming commonly regarded not as a pervasive and highly resilient social phenomenon but, rather, as a technical problem which can be solved by purposeful government intervention. Indeed, the failure to give due emphasis to the way in which stigma can (by functioning as a means of social control) bolster the existing social and economic structure of society has been a serious weakness of social policy research in this area. It should be noted here, however, that the public attitude surveys have served to highlight the way in which stigma can help to sustain a particular value system within society. (These issues will be discussed more fully in chapter 4 of this book.)

When examining social policy research on stigma it is important to recognize that there are certain problems in measuring this particular phenomenon. For example, researchers are liable to encounter a number of problems when constructing questions which are designed to accurately tap the extent of felt stigma amongst a particular survey group. This can clearly be seen if one considers the questions employed in surveys conducted by Handler and Hollingsworth[172] and Horan and Austin.[173] The former (in a study of AFDC recipients) attempted to obtain data about felt stigma by the use of the following two questions:

(1) How embarrassed do you feel in the company of non-AFDC recipients?
(2) What is the attitude of people in the community towards AFDC recipients?

Respondents who stated that they always felt embarrassed in the company of non-AFDC recipients and who, in addition, thought that the public were very hostile towards AFDC recipients were adjudged to feel stigma most strongly.[174] In contrast, Horan and Austin measured felt stigma in terms of respondents' replies to two different questions:

(1) How often do you feel ashamed about being on welfare?
(2) How often do you feel bothered by being on welfare?

Respondents who always felt both ashamed and bothered were awarded the highest stigma ratings.[175]

Clearly, the questions used in both these surveys were rather imprecise. For example, the second question posed by Handler and Hollingsworth does not appear to be a particularly reliable indicator of felt stigma. Although it is likely that some of the respondents in this survey (who expressed the view that people in the community were very hostile towards AFDC recipients) were likely to have experienced feelings of stigma, it is equally likely that others may have responded to this community hostility in a markedly different way (e.g. indifference, resentment). In addition, it can be argued that felt stigma cannot be accurately measured by the use of terms such as embarrassment or shame. For example, it was suggested earlier that distinctions could be made between feelings of embarrassment, shame and stigma (see pp. 16-18).

It was also pointed out earlier in the chapter that individuals may be somewhat reluctant to admit to personal feelings of stigma (see p. 48). Indeed, Davies contends that those who have failed to claim welfare benefits to which they are entitled may be especially reluctant to admit to the fact that feelings of stigma had influenced their behaviour (i.e. refusing a benefit on the grounds of stigma may be seen as an irrational form of conduct).[176]

Given this possibility, it seems likely that the extent of felt stigma amongst welfare recipients may have been significantly under-estimated in a number of the surveys referred to earlier. To counter this problem, it may well be necessary to directly confront respondents with the possibility that their actions or inactions were influenced by considerations of stigma. Although methodological objections can be raised about the use of 'suggestive' questioning (i.e. it can be argued that respondents will tend to over-emphasize the importance of stigma if it is suggested to them that their behaviour may have been affected by this factor), it would appear that the very nature of this phenomenon demands this type of approach.

If the impact of stigma upon welfare recipients has been under-estimated in the research studies conducted in this area then there would appear to be even stronger grounds for doubting the assertion, made by a number of commentators, that undue emphasis has been given to the notion of stigma in the field of social policy.[177] On the contrary, given the theoretical and practical limitations of much of the research in this area, there would appear to be every reason to examine this phenomenon in a more detailed and extensive way.

In this chapter, then, we have seen that within the field of social policy and administration the concept of stigma has (largely as a result of the efforts of Titmuss and other advocates of welfare collectivism) become associated predominantly with private and selectivist public forms of welfare provision. Although extremely useful, this approach to the concept of stigma has (by its rather narrow focus) tended to stifle discussion about other aspects of the relationship between stigma and social policy (e.g. the rationale for the stigmatization of certain 'welfare' groups: the functions of welfare stigmatization). It is to these wider dimensions of stigma that attention will be given in the following two chapters.

3 Stigma and the unmarried mother

The aim of this chapter is to demonstrate how the social administration approach to the concept of stigma can be enriched by more extensive examinations of the reasons why, and the ways in which, certain 'welfare' groups have been stigmatized over the centuries. For present purposes, attention will be given to one such group – namely unmarried mothers.

Throughout the years, stigma has tended to attach to the unmarried mother for two main reasons. Firstly, the sexual conduct of these women has elicited disapproval from the Christian church. Secondly, secular authorities have responded unfavourably to what they have perceived to be the 'blame-worthy' public dependency of this group. Let us look at each of these main sources of stigma in turn.

Challenge to Christian doctrine

There are two main ways in which the conduct of the unmarried mother runs contrary to Christian teaching:

(i) Sexual relationship outside marriage.
(ii) Threat to the institution of the family.

The early church fathers were highly critical of both marital and non-marital sexual relationships. They believed that such relationships prevented individuals from devoting themselves fully to the service of God. A passage from St Paul's first letter to the Corinthians neatly captures their attitude in this regard.

The unmarried man cares for the Lord's business; his aim is to please the Lord. But the married man cares for worldly things; his aim is to please his wife; and he has a divided mind. The unmarried or celibate woman cares for the Lord's business; her aim is to be dedicated to him in body as in spirit; but the married woman cares for worldly things; her aim is to please her husband.[1]

The church fathers' disapproval of sexual relationships can also be linked to the notion of 'the fall'. For example, St Augustine of Hippo contended that Adam and Eve lost control of their sexual impulses after they had succumbed to temptation. As Bailey points out, this belief

led Augustine to a virtual equation of original sin, concupiscence, and venereal emotion, from which he drew the inference that while coitus in theory is good, every concrete act of coitus performed by fallen man is intrinsically evil – so that every child can be said literally to have been conceived in the 'sin' of its parents.[2]

It is important to note that the condemnatory attitude displayed by the church fathers towards sexuality was based in large part upon their belief that the end of the world was imminent (i.e. a commitment towards celibacy was seen as essential if the city of God was to be filled speedily and the end of the world hastened).[3]

The early Christians, by way of contrast, found much to commend in marriage and family life. The fact that Christ performed his first miracle at a wedding service in Cana was taken to indicate divine approval of the institution of marriage. Indeed, marriage was eventually accorded sacramental status (the uniting of a man and a woman was deemed to symbolize the relationship between Christ and the church;[4] in addition, marriage came to be recognized as the appropriate institution for the procreation of children).[5] Support for the family unit also had a strong theological underpinning. As Troeltsch points out, Christ drew upon the institution of the family

for symbols of the highest attributes of God, for the name of

the final religious goal, for the original description of the
earliest group of His disciples, and for material for most of His
parables; indeed, the idea of the family may be regarded as
one of the most fundamental features of His feeling for human
life.[6]

Given their firm commitment towards marriage and family life,
the early Christians tended to look disparagingly upon those
individuals (such as unmarried mothers) whose sexual conduct
contravened their ideals (i.e. monogamy, chastity before
marriage, fidelity within marriage, Christian upbringing of
children). The censorious attitude displayed towards unmarried
mothers was compounded by the fact that the early Christians
believed that all women were inherently inferior to men. The
rationale for this viewpoint can also be traced back to the notion
of 'the fall'. As St Paul states in a letter to Timothy:

> A woman must be a learner, listening quietly and with due
> submission. I do not permit a woman to be a teacher, nor must
> woman domineer over man; she should be quiet. For Adam
> was created first and Eve afterwards; and it was not Adam who
> was deceived; it was woman who, yielding to deception, fell
> into sin.[7]

Women thus came to be seen as potentially dangerous individuals
who needed to be kept under close control, particularly in the
realm of sexuality. As Russell comments, the importance
Christians placed on sexual virtue

> did a great deal to degrade the position of women. Since the
> moralists were men, women appeared as the temptress; . . .
> Since woman was the temptress, it was desirable to curtail her
> opportunities for leading men into temptation; consequently
> respectable women were more hedged about with restrictions,
> while the women who were not respectable, being regarded as
> sinful, were treated with the utmost contumely.[8]

The spread of Christianity in Europe had serious repercussions
for the unmarried mother and other sexual 'transgressors'. For
instance, by the end of the thirteenth century in England, the

Christian church had managed to secure for itself the exclusive right to deal with sexual offenders in its own courts. As Wrighton points out, the essential concern of these church courts 'was to maintain the boundaries of permitted behaviour and to enforce, by the imposition of public penance, the public reaffirmation of the norms which had been breached.'[9]

Individuals could be summoned to appear before an ecclesiastical court for various sexual misdemeanours – bridal pregnancy, incontinence (fornication and adultery), prostitution, incest, rape and bastardy. One of two courses of action were open to those individuals who were charged with any of these offences. They could either plead guilty and accept the punishment of the court or, alternatively, deny the charge and undergo purgation. In some cases, purgation merely involved the making of a solemn declaration of innocence. More commonly, such an oath would have had to have been made in the presence of two or more compurgators (of 'good' reputation). Provided the precise conditions of purgation were complied with the accused was deemed to be innocent.[10]

Obviously, unmarried mothers could be summoned to appear before the ecclesiastical courts on a number of the charges mentioned above. Like other sexual offenders, they were liable, upon conviction, to be ordered to undergo penance. This usually involved some form of public humiliation (the severity of which tended to vary according to the seriousness of the offence).[11] For example, one unmarried mother, convicted of bastardy by a church court in Farnham (Kent) in 1562, was ordered to attend her parish church on the following Sunday (barefoot and barelegged)

> in her petticoat with a white sheet about her, her hair loose, and a kercher upon her head, and there at the chancel door to remain standing with her face towards the people at all the time of morning prayer until the end; that done to go about the Church before the procession be read, and to come to the chancel door where she shall remain kneeling the whole time of the Litany until such time as the priest goeth into the pulpit and there to read the wholy homily of adultery, whereat she shall come and stand before the pulpit and then to depart.[12]

It is difficult to estimate what effect this form of stigmatization had upon unmarried mothers and other sexual offenders. One commentator who has given some thought to this question (in relation to bridal pregnancy) came to the conclusion that local parishioners were not particularly fearful of church discipline.

> Public penance was, of course, supposed to be humiliating, but it may be doubted whether there were many . . . who found it so. Any offence of ante-nuptial fornication had, of course, been common knowledge for months: public confession by the offenders was no revelation, indeed, it must often have seemed like a triumphant announcement of successfully completed courtship, marriage and parenthood. Above all, . . . the offence was too common to be regarded as scandalous.[13]

Hair holds to this theory despite finding (in his study of bridal pregnancy in a number of parishes in earlier rural England) that there were relatively few baptisms recorded to families whose names had appeared on the marriage registers.

> It might be reasonably argued that the failure of some of the brides to record maternities in the register of the parish of marriage was due to their obviously pregnant condition at or soon after marriage, so that shame drove them to another parish where their recent date of marriage was unknown. . . . In view of the high proportion of brides who were pregnant, including many who were obviously so at marriage, it is difficult to believe that this assumed shame was widespread, or indeed markedly existent.[14]

Certainly the absence of any widespread public hostility towards those convicted of offences such as premarital fornication or bridal pregnancy[15] is likely to have lessened the possibility of felt stigma amongst these groups of sexual transgressors. However, it seems equally likely (given the propensity of the general public to respond less favourably towards unmarried mothers)[16] that pregnant, unmarried women with no immediate marriage plans would have found their predicament much more stigmatizing. Such women may have attempted to abort their children or dispose of them shortly after birth in order to avoid the possibility of public humiliation.[17] There must have been a tendency for unmarried women to conceal their pregnancies because the harbouring of such women was a separate ecclesiastical offence.[18] For example, in 1564 an East Horndon man who had sheltered a pregnant girl pleaded that 'he took her in for God's sake', but was sentenced to public penance in the market and had to pay 2s to the poor.[19] Even members of an unmarried mother's own family were liable to be sanctioned under this law.

A cleric, apparently the curate, offended in 1595. William Vixar of Fyfield, let his own daughter 'go away unpunished'. His plea was that she departed without his knowledge, but he was enjoined to confess in church that 'he had offended God and the congregation in harbouring his daughter'.[20]

It is important to note that the vast majority of those who were summoned to appear before the church courts came from the poorer sections of society. In the case of bastardy, this is not altogether surprising. Unmarried women in the wealthier social classes were expected to observe the strictest standards of sexual propriety as the loss of virginity before marriage could seriously damage their social and economic worth (chastity was seen as essential in order to dispel any doubts about the legitimacy of those children who would eventually inherit titles and property).[21] Given that these women were likely to be closely chaperoned until they were married there was little possibility of premarital pregnancy amongst this group. However, if such a woman did become pregnant it is likely that a marriage would have been hastily arranged (provided that the putative father came from the right social background). If this proved difficult for any reason, it is likely that the woman concerned would have been persuaded to abort or (in the event of the pregnancy running to term) dispose of the child in some way.

The only group of upper-class women who ignored these restrictions on their sexual freedom were the mistresses of the nobility.[22] Owing to the influence of their benefactors, these women were rarely required to submit to the jurisdiction of the ecclesiastical courts (a notable exception, however, was Jane Shore, the mistress of Richard III, who was ordered to undergo penance in St Paul's Cathedral before the bishop of London in 1483).[23]

Due to increased secular intervention, ecclesiastical influence in the sphere of sexual misconduct slowly declined from the sixteenth century onwards.[24] Although sexual offenders continued to be brought before the church courts until well into the eighteenth century, there were relatively few prosecutions.[25] Indeed, by the end of the eighteenth century the ecclesiastical courts had become largely obsolete as a result of the demise of shame punishments (1704s)[26] and the abolition of the offence of incontinence (1788).[27] As Chadwick points out:

> the courts of the State were . . . much more efficient and commanded so much more of the public confidence . . . that a system of church courts was no longer needed, and it slowly withered away except for the internal needs of church life and the moral discipline of the clergy.[28]

It is important to note, however, that the declining influence of the ecclesiastical courts did not herald the development of a more liberal ruling class attitude towards the unmarried mother and other sexual offenders. For example, Puritan censoriousness was clearly at the heart of two pieces of secular legislation which were introduced in the first half of the seventeenth century. The first of these acts (1624) attempted to stem the incidence of infanticide. This act declared that the concealment of the death of a newly born illegitimate child would be regarded as murder unless evidence to the contrary could be produced (the sworn oath of a witness that the child was stillborn).[29] Unmarried mothers were frequently prosecuted and convicted for this offence.[30] The second act (1650) introduced severe penalties for adulterers (execution) and fornicators (imprisonment).[31] This measure proved to be so unpopular with the public, though, that it was repealed shortly after the end of the interregnum.

This concern with morality was not, however (at least in the case of unmarried mothers), a significant feature of post-1500 secular legislation. In general, attention was directed towards the consequences of sexual misconduct (i.e. the financial cost of supporting unmarried mothers and their children).

We have seen, then, that the Christian church attempted to

impose its authority in the realm of sexuality by means of sanctioning those members of the community who were deemed to have behaved in an immoral way. By subjecting unmarried mothers and other sexual offenders to the ordeal of public penance, the church hoped to engender and sustain a high level of public commitment towards Christian ideals. As we will see below, this pattern of stigmatization contrasts markedly with the sanctions used by the secular authorities to deal with the 'problem' of bastardy amongst the poorer groups in society.

'Blameworthy' public dependency

Two distinctive patterns of secular stigmatization can be identified in relation to the treatment of publicly dependent unmarried mothers over the centuries. From 1500 to 1900, the secular authorities employed a variety of physical and economic sanctions in an effort to minimize the number of unmarried mothers (and their dependants) seeking public aid. This formal type of stigmatization was compounded by the informal economic and social sanctions which were imposed by other members of the community. Since 1900, these harsh and direct forms of secular stigmatization have gradually withered away. However, implicit forms of secular stigmatization have continued to operate (i.e. inappropriate or inadequate 'welfare' services for this group). In addition, informal economic and social sanctions have continued to be applied to unmarried mothers by certain members of the public at large. Let us look, then, at each of these distinctive stigmatization periods in turn.

Stigmatization period 1: 1500-1900

Before examining the ways in which unmarried mothers were treated by the secular authorities in the sixteenth century, it is useful to refer briefly to the situation of this group under feudalism. During this period, the ruling class did not regard illegitimacy amongst the poor as a particularly serious social problem. Such an attitude is not surprising given that the financial consequences stemming from such behaviour were minimal at this time. The lord of the manor merely stood to lose the small contribution (a merchet – which was to be provided by fathers when their daughters married) he would have received by way of compensation for the loss of a member of his workforce. In order to obtain some form of recompense for this loss, the lord imposed fines on those unmarried women who were convicted of either incontinence (legerwite) or bastardy (childwite).[32] It seems unlikely, however, that there would have been large numbers of unsupported, unmarried mothers bringing up children on their own in feudal society: given the close-knit nature of manorial communities it would have been relatively easy to trace (and obtain financial contributions from) the putative fathers concerned.

The decline of feudalism seriously threatened the social and economic security of unmarried mothers and their children. 'Cut off from the ever-sustaining resources of an uncomplicated rural parish',[33] unmarried mothers were forced, along with others in a similar position, to travel around the country in search of work or alms. As was noted earlier (see p. 25), the ruling class regarded this vagrant group as a serious threat to public order. Accordingly, unmarried mothers, in common with other members of the 'undeserving' poor, were subjected to harsh, deterrent punishments. For example, under the Poor Law Act of 1531 all vagrants were liable to be whipped in the nearest market town and then returned to their place of birth or to the area in which they had resided in the previous three years.[34]

Public concern about the economic implications of illegitimacy intensified during the latter part of the sixteenth century. With increased geographical mobiliity it became more and more difficult to trace the parents (especially the fathers) of illegitimate children. Parishes were thus often faced with the prospect of supporting relatively large numbers of unmarried mothers and their children. Given that poor rate contributions had been made compulsory during this period,[35] it seems likely that local parishioners would have been deeply opposed to this form of parish expenditure, particularly if the women and children concerned had migrated from other localities.[36]

The Poor Law Act of 1576 attempted to deal directly with the problem of illegitimacy amongst the poor. Under this act, penalties (fines, whippings) were imposed on those parents who failed to support their illegitimate offspring. Such parents were also expected (on pain of imprisonment) to indemnify the parish against any further expenditure in this regard.[37]

Gill contends that this statute had three main purposes:[38]

(i) To reduce parish expenditure on bastardy.
(ii) To demonstrate public disapproval of reproduction outside marriage.
(iii) To strengthen public support for marriage and family life.

However, this act cannot be said to have been primarily concerned with bolstering the social and moral fabric of society (ii and iii). If this had been the case one would have expected all parents of illegitimate children to have been made equally liable to prosecution. Instead, only those parents who were unable to provide financial support for their illegitimate offspring were liable to be sanctioned under this act.[39] This concern with minimizing parish expenditure on bastardy is also clearly reflected in the treatment accorded to publicly dependent illegitimate (and other vagrant) children during this period. Such children were liable to be forcibly apprenticed with local families, where they were unlikely to be treated as anything more than slave labour.[40]

Publicly dependent unmarried mothers continued to be treated harshly by secular authorities throughout the seventeenth century. Legislation introduced in 1609 ordered that unmarried mothers who had given birth to 'chargeable bastards' should be detained in a house of correction.[41] These detentions (to which mothers who had given birth to more than one illegitimate child – repeaters – were particularly prone)[42] were often recommended on moral grounds. For example, at Warwick quarter sessions in 1627 it was proclaimed:

that one Bridget Walker of Asley . . . is of very rude and evil behaviour and hath had three bastards and hath not received any condign punishment for the same, whereby she taketh encouragement to go on still in that lewd course, it is therefore ordered by the court that she shall be sent to the house of correction there to remain a year and a day. . . .[43]

However, the fact that unmarried mothers could obtain a premature release from such an institution if they could convince local magistrates that they would not become dependent upon parish relief in the future tends to suggest that financial considerations were again of paramount importance. For instance, in Warwick in 1649, Alice Ireland was granted an early discharge from the house of correction after the putative father had 'given good security to the . . . parishioners to free them from any charge that may happen by reason of the . . . bastard child. . . .'[44] Indeed, the justices tended to take a dim view of any mother who declined to accept an offer of maintenance. In 1642, the Warwick justices decided to reduce the allowance paid by the inhabitants of Spernall towards the keep of Anne Mawdick because of this woman's refusal to accept an offer of financial support from a local gentleman.[45]

The conditions prevailing within houses of correction can only be described as abject. Inmates were not only forcibly set to work but also subjected to physical punishments for even the most minor breach of the regulations. Not surprisingly, therefore, the health of many of the unmarried mothers who were sent to these institutions declined to such an extent that they were unable to undertake any work. For instance, in 1631 the master of the Warwick house of correction informed the inhabitants of Sowe that Goodith Checkley and her child (for whom they were responsible) were 'likely to perish unless some speedy course be taken for their relief. . . .'[46] In the same year, Mary Barber was given 12d a week from the Studley poor fund because she was 'very sick and weak and not able to get work or get any livelihood or maintenance for herself or her . . . child . . . whereby they are likely to perish for want of sustenance. . . .'[47] Even those unmarried mothers who were fortunate enough to secure their release from a house of correction were liable to be readmitted for an indefinite period if they gave birth to another chargeable bastard.[48]

The Warwick judiciary's unfavourable treatment of unmarried mothers and other members of the undeserving poor contrasts markedly with the approach they adopted towards other needy groups during this period. For instance, the justices had no compunction about ordering the wardens of Woolverton to provide a servant (who had become unemployable – and hence destitute – as a result of lameness) with 'a convenient habitation . . . fit for a Christian to dwell in . . .'.[49]

At local level, parishes used every available means to prevent unmarried mothers and their children from becoming dependent on poor relief. For example, parish officers were not averse to forcibly removing an expectant, unmarried woman from their locality in order to prevent her from becoming a charge on parish funds.[50] A statute of 1662, which had been introduced to clarify the issue of settlement, tended to encourage action of this kind.[51] Under this act, local overseers were authorized to remove (within forty days) any recent arrivals in their parish (who were renting a tenement worth £10 a year or less) whom they considered likely to become dependent on parish aid in the future. The fact that illegitimate children were to be granted settlement in the area in which they were born clearly provided an incentive for parish officers to remove poor, expectant, single women from their locality. Unmarried women who became pregnant whilst being employed as domestic servants were particularly likely to be forcibly removed by parish officials (such women were often working away from home in an area in which they were not legally settled).

Clause nineteen of this statute (which permitted local churchwardens and overseers of the poor to seize, by way of recompense, the property of those parents whose illegitimate children were being supported by the parish) also had serious repercussions for poor, single, expectant women. Such women were frequently pressurized into naming the putative father of their child so that the parish could serve maintenance orders, where appropriate. Midwives often played a key role in securing this information: they would frequently refuse to provide assistance to unmarried women in labour unless the name of the putative father had been disclosed.[52]

The large increase in illegitimacy in the eighteenth century[53] (the causes of which are difficult to unravel)[54] led to further steps being taken to limit parish liability for unmarried mothers and their children. Legislation introduced in 1744[55] attempted to deal specifically with the problem of obtaining maintenance payments from putative fathers. To this end, substantial credence was accorded to the declarations of single women (who were expecting children deemed likely to become a burden on the poor rate) concerning the identity of putative fathers. On the basis of these oaths, putative fathers were liable to be summoned to appear at the local quarter sessions, where they could be ordered to make a regular payment towards the upkeep of their children.

Although this measure improved the financial situation of a small number of unmarried mothers (i.e. in cases where the putative father was relatively wealthy) it did little to help the vast majority of such women (many putative fathers proved difficult to trace or were very poor). Mothers in this latter category continued to be admitted to houses of correction and, subsequently, to workhouses (which were frequently used as maternity wards for poor, homeless, pregnant, single women).[56] As Oxley points out, many parish authorities believed that indoor relief was particularly suitable for unmarried mothers and their children.

> Outdoor accommodation was likely to be costly and the woman's time used inefficiently because the need to care for the child would keep her from work. In the workhouse a few could look after the children while the remainder were set on useful tasks.[57]

Public provision for unmarried mothers and their children did not improve during the eighteenth and early nineteenth centuries despite the growth of charitable activity in this area (e.g. foundling[58] and magdalen[59] hospitals). It was still commonly believed that unmarried mothers and their children were nothing more than an unnecessary burden on public expenditure. This viewpoint was never more clearly expressed than in the Poor Law Report of 1834.

The authors of this report contended that the immoral conduct of unmarried women was the root cause of the problem of bastardy. Accordingly, they recommended that unmarried mothers should be held legally responsible for the maintenance of their illegitimate children.

> This is now the law with respect to a widow; and an unmarried mother has voluntarily become a mother, without procuring to herself and her child the assistance of a husband and a father. There can be no reason for giving to vice privileges which we deny to misfortune.[60]

The Commissioners suggested a number of ways in which the public cost of illegitimacy could be reduced. For example, they recommended that other family members (i.e. parents) should be required to contribute towards the upkeep of an unmarried mother and her child.

> In a natural state of things they must do so, whether the child be legitimate or not; and when we consider that, in the vast majority of cases, the neglect or ill example, and in many cases the actual furtherance of those parents has occasioned their daughter's misconduct, it appears not only just, but most useful, that they should be answerable for it.[61]

Even some of the Commissioners' more humane recommendations were based on financial considerations. For instance, their disapproval of the hounding of expectant unmarried women by parish officials certainly fits into this category.

> We feel confident that if the woman were allowed to remain unmolested until she asked for relief, she would, in many cases, by her own exertions, and the assistance of her friends, succeed in maintaining herself and her infant; . . .[62]

As a result of the Commissioners' deliberations, the Poor Law (as it related to illegitimacy) was modified in six important ways.

1 Unmarried mothers were no longer to be detained in houses of correction.
2 An illegitimate child was to acquire the same settlement as its mother.
3 Affiliation orders were only to be made out if the mother's evidence concerning paternity could be independently verified.
4 Maintenance payments were to be fixed at realistic levels (i.e. the actual cost of supporting a child); these payments were to continue until the child was seven.
5 Money recovered from putative fathers was not to be paid directly to the mothers concerned.
6 Men who failed to comply with the terms of a maintenance order by virtue of poverty were not to be imprisoned.

These modifications proved highly unpopular. As Henriques points out:

> A stream of petitions flowed into parliament, complaining that bastardy cases in Quarter Sessions were far too expensive; that affiliation orders were only enforceable against propertied men, so that only the rich could be made to pay for fathering bastards; that parishes were prevented from recovering the cost of supporting mother and child; that the law dealt severely with the weaker party and overlooked the stronger and generally more blameable one; and that, relieved of the fear of punishment, the men did what they pleased.[63]

Although the Poor Law Commissioners attempted to counter these criticisms by arguing that their measures were proving successful in reducing the incidence of illegitimacy[64] (a highly dubious claim),[65] they eventually succumbed to this pressure, and the rights of parishes to obtain maintenance payments from putative fathers were accordingly restored.[66]

As a result of the 1834 Poor Law Amendment Act, poor, unmarried mothers were forced, along with other members of the undeserving poor, to enter the workhouse if they required public aid. In many of these institutions unmarried mothers were treated more harshly than other inmates. As Longmate points out: 'To remind them that they were moral outcasts, many unions put their unmarried mothers into a distinctive yellow uniform, the colour of a ship's plague flag, the wearers being nicknamed "canary wards,". . . .'[67] Some workhouse guardians also recognized the deterrent value of 'badging' unmarried mothers. For example, in 1837, the Andover guardians reported to the Poor Law Commissioners that the introduction of a yellow stripe on the uniforms of unmarried mothers 'had proved a great success and that several women had left the workhouse as soon as the stripe had been forced upon them.'[68]

Advances in welfare provision for pauper children during the latter part of the nineteenth century (e.g. 'scattered homes', boarding out and educational opportunities)[69] brought little benefit to those unmarried mothers who did not wish to be parted from their children (or to remain with their children in the workhouse). Such mothers were often left with no alternative but to leave their children in the 'care' of woefully inadequate baby farmers, if they wished to retain their economic independence in the wider community.

The poor standard of much of this provision was brought to public attention in the late nineteenth century when a number of foster mothers were prosecuted for neglect.[70] The public outcry which greeted these revelations improved the position of some unmarried mothers in society. For example, the bastardy laws were amended in 1872 in an effort to alleviate some of the economic difficulties which had necessitated unmarried mothers to place their children with baby farmers (under this act unmarried mothers were: (i) given more time in which to submit maintenance claims; (ii) provided with higher weekly allowances).[71]

These measures were, however, completely irrelevant to those unmarried mothers who had been forced to accept institutional relief. Indeed, workhouse mothers were even faced with the prospect of losing their last few remaining parental rights. Legislation introduced in 1889 and 1899 permitted boards of guardians to assume parental control over those children who were deemed to have unfit parents. Extensive use was made of this legislation (some 12,000 children were, for example, 'adopted' in this way in 1908).[72]

This compulsory form of adoption provides yet another example of the repressive way in which unmarried mothers were treated by secular authorities in the period from 1500 to 1900. Throughout this period, attempts were made to limit the demands made by unmarried mothers (and their children) for public aid. Given that the public dependency of unmarried mothers was deemed to be both wilful and unnecessary, it is not surprising to find that the secular authorities showed little compunction about using harsh sanctions to contain this particular source of public expenditure.

In addition to this institutional form of stigmatization, unmarried mothers were also liable to experience hostile reactions and sanctions (e.g. loss of accommodation or employment) from their immediate family, their employer and other members of the community.

From the end of the nineteenth century onwards, however, one can detect a gradual softening of secular attitudes towards unmarried mothers. There are a number of possible explanations for this change. First, unmarried mothers benefited from the growing concern that was displayed by both governments and the general public towards the poor during this period. For example, it can be argued that late nineteenth-century politicians were compelled, as a result of the enfranchisement of large numbers of the working class (which had been brought about by a series of legislative measures from 1867 to 1885) and the spectre of socialism, to re-examine their attitudes towards the poor. The Webbs contend, for instance, that government reforms aimed at improving the care of elderly paupers, which were introduced immediately prior to the 1885 general election, were a deliberate attempt to secure the support of some two million first-time working-class voters.[73] In addition, the social surveys conducted by Booth (London) and Rowntree (York) in the 1880s served to discredit the prevailing individualistic notions of poverty. Both researchers concluded that poverty was far more likely to be experienced as a result of an inadequate income from work, sickness or disability than through idleness, drunkenness or some other 'character' defect.[74]

Second, the more enlightened approach that was adopted towards the needs of deprived children during the twentieth century (the social and economic benefits of providing for the basic needs of all children was clearly recognized in this period) inevitably led to consideration being given to some of the various ways in which unmarried mothers could be helped to bring up their children. For example, the 1948 Children's Act encouraged local authorities to reunite children (who were in care) with their natural parents or guardians wherever possible.[75]

Third, the effects of war served to underline the fact that the material needs of unmarried mothers were very similar to those of other, supposedly more deserving, categories of single parents such as widows. As a result, unmarried mothers have become more generally regarded as a group worthy of some form of public support.

Fourth, recent (post-1940) social science research in the areas of sociology, social administration and psychology has helped to dispel the notion that unmarried mothers are immoral, promiscuous women who are undeserving of public support. It is important to note, however, that many researchers in this area may have hindered (often unwittingly) the development of even more favourable public attitudes being displayed towards unmarried mothers by their assertions that such women have a tendency to be psychologically disturbed and/or socially deprived (in terms of their social background). This contemporary source of stigma will be discussed more fully later in the chapter.

Fifth, the establishment of pressure groups such as the National Council for the Unmarried Mother and her Child (1918)[76] helped to increase public awareness of the problems faced by unmarried mothers and their children. In particular, the NCUMC played a key role in persuading the general public and central and local government of the need to provide unmarried mothers with an opportunity to care for their own children.[77]

Finally, the realization that harsh, deterrent sanctions had little effect in terms of regulating sexual behaviour in society prompted secular authorities to consider other ways of dealing with publicly dependent unmarried mothers. Let us now look in more detail at this second distinctive stigmatization period.

Stigmatization period 2: 1900 to the present day

The majority Poor Law Report of 1909 provides a good example of how secular attitudes towards publicly dependent unmarried mothers were changing at the beginning of the twentieth century. Unlike their predecessors, the majority did not accept the idea that all unmarried mothers should be treated in a uniform way. Instead, they argued that there were three distinctive types of unmarried mother:

1 the feeble-minded,
2 the depraved,
3 the unfortunate.

According to the majority, women who fell into the first category needed to be strictly supervised and controlled as they were liable to continually give birth to 'chargeable' illegitimate children.[78] The depraved ('women who habitually make a convenience of the workhouse for the purpose of being confined with illegitimate children')[79] were considered to be more amenable to treatment.

The majority therefore recommended that this group of mothers should be detained in a suitable institution for a fixed period of time in order to regain their respectability. The majority were even more optimistic about the rehabilitative potential of the unfortunates (young mothers who had lapsed for the first time).[80] They suggested that this group should be cared for in voluntary homes rather than in the workhouse. Although there was a degree of benevolence in this particular proposal it should be remembered that the conditions in many of these homes were little different from those pertaining in workhouses. As Middleton points out, the regimes in such homes were often 'callously punitive and exploitative, based on long hours of drugery in the damp, hot, working conditions of a steam laundry or an institutional kitchen, the only respite from the round of toil and sleep being religious services and limited food.'[81]

.The majority also made recommendations relating to maternity and after-care facilities for mothers and the system of affiliation awards. In terms of the latter, the majority questioned the advisability of the existing direct payments scheme. They argued that this procedure (which necessitated a mother making a visit to the putative father at his place of work or at his lodgings in order to collect her weekly allowance) could prove most unsettling for mothers who were trying to regain their respectability. 'it soon becomes well known why she is there . . . with the result that her shame is blazoned abroad and she becomes . . . the centre of a degraded notoriety.'[82]

Although Poor Law Guardians were continually reminded of the need to discriminate between these different categories of unmarried mothers,[83] they showed little inclination to act on the recommendations contained in the majority's report. As a result, most publicly dependent unmarried mothers continued to be sent to workhouses rather than voluntary homes.[84]

The plight of single parents was given considerable attention after the outbreak of the First World War. The government of the day accepted that it had a responsibility to protect the widows and wives (both lawful and illicit) of servicemen from Poor Law dependency. It was decided, therefore, to set up a national relief fund to help those who had suffered financial hardship as a result of the war (1914).

The Women's Advisory Committee at the Ministry of Reconstruction expressed particular concern about the situation of unsupported mothers during this period.[85] For example, in a report submitted in 1918, the committee suggested that pensions should be provided for all unsupported mothers.[86]. However, when statutory provision was eventually introduced in this area (1925) it was decided (on financial[87] and 'social'[88] grounds) to exclude all but widows from the scheme.[89] As Finer and McGregor point out:

> the mothers' pension movement broke down on its inability to translate an aspiration into an administrative system that was viable in itself and acceptable to currrent notions of family responsibility, legal and moral. Thus, for divorced, deserted or separated wives, and the mothers of illegitimate children, the situation remained at the outbreak of the last world war as it always had been: either they could secure maintenance from their husbands or the fathers of their children by agreement, or a court order, or failing such means of support, they had to seek subsistence from the public.[90]

Unmarried mothers did, however, derive benefit from a number of inter-war social policy initiatives. For example, maternity and child welfare services were substantially improved during this period. The high mortality rate amongst young illegitimate children (particularly workhouse children)[91] prompted the introduction of the Maternity and Child Welfare Act in 1918. This statute empowered local authorities (in conjunction with voluntary agencies) to improve services for expectant and nursing mothers and for children below school age.[92]

A number of unmarried mothers also benefited from the introduction of the 1926 Adoption Act. For example, this statute provided unmarried women with an alternative means of parting with an unwanted child (previously such women were forced to resort to either abortion or infanticide).[93] In addition, this act permitted unmarried mothers to adopt their own children (many young mothers experienced difficulties, however, when they attempted to exercise their rights in this regard).[94]

It is important to note, though, that this act was not universally welcomed. For example, a young, financially impoverished unmarried mother who expressed a wish to keep her child was liable (because of this statute) to be pressurised (by her family and welfare workers) into placing her child for adoption.[95] In addition, this statute enabled a number of adoption associations to exploit unmarried mothers. These organizations would often require mothers to make an undertaking that they would engage in unpaid domestic work (for periods of up to two years) before an adoption would be arranged. Given the heavy demand for 'unwanted' children, it was possible for the more unscrupulous of these agencies to obtain 'a double rake-off, the first payment coming from the girl for being relieved of her child, the second for finding a suitable child from couples who were willing to pay sums ranging from £5 to £100.'[96]

Further attention was given to the plight of the unmarried mother during the Second World War – a period in which the number of illegitimate maternities rose sharply.[97] As Ferguson and Fitzgerald point out:

> The war affected not only the size but also the character of the social problem which was caused by illegitimacy: unmarried mothers met with greater obstacles in trying to help themselves or to obtain help. They were often away from their home communities, living in hostels, billets or service camps. The social services were curtailed and disorganised. There were fewer beds in hospitals and homes. There was less chance of finding foster-mothers or places in nurseries for the babies. There were fewer welfare workers to devote their time to the problems of unmarried mothers.[98]

As the war progressed the government gradually recognised that the needs of unmarried mothers could not be adequately met by voluntary and Poor Law services.[99] For example, in a Ministry of Health circular issued in 1943, local welfare authorities were encouraged to improve the services they offered to unmarried mothers. In particular, it was suggested that these authorities should:

(i) appoint their own social workers;
(ii) introduce subsidized foster-mother schemes;
(iii) provide hostels and other residential accommodation.[100]

It is clear that the situation of publicly dependent unmarried mothers improved markedly as a result of the collectivist nature of much Second World War welfare policy-making. Accordingly, post-war unmarried mothers were no longer forced to rely on charity or Poor Law relief. Instead, they were seen as having a clear entitlement to various welfare benefits and services. For example, unmarried mothers (or expectant unmarried women) were to be provided with:

1 Free maternity care either at home or in hospital.
2 Sickness benefits during any period of incapacity prior to the birth of their child (employed women only).
3 Maternity allowances of 26s/week (for a period of thirteen weeks) during their absence from work at the time of their confinement (this allowance could also be supplemented by discretionary National Assistance Board payments).
4 Free accommodation in a public or voluntary home in the event of homelessness.[101]

It is important to note, however, that post-war income maintenance schemes for unmarried mothers still bore the remnants of the ethos of less eligibility. For example, in his report on social insurance, Beveridge contended that single parenthood was not a suitable case for this form of income support.[102] Accordingly,

> the principles on which the State made provision for one-parent families remained after the Beveridge Report precisely what they had been before. Widows received pensions with the possibility of supplementation, from the poor law or public assistance or, after 1948, from national assistance. But divorced, deserted or separated wives and unmarried mothers remained throughout dependent on the poor law or its substitutes, in the event of their receiving no support from their husbands.[103]

Unmarried mothers have experienced considerable degrees of stigmatization as a result of this continued dependency on means-tested social security benefits. The administrative procedures of the National Assistance Board (1948-66) and, subsequently, the

Supplementary Benefits Commission (1966-80) have been identified as an important source of this stigmatization.[104] For example, in line with previous legislation, the Supplementary Benefits Act of 1976 was designed to restrict demand for public aid. To this end, all potential claimants were deemed to have certain obligations with regard to both the maintenance of their immediate dependents and to the seeking of employment.[105]

Unmarried mothers have expressed concern about two particular aspects of the liability to maintain regulations. In the first place a number of mothers, who have exercised their right to withhold information about the whereabouts of the father of their child, have complained that they have been treated unfavourably by social security officials. In certain cases mothers have even been informed (quite incorrectly) that their benefit will be withdrawn if they fail to provide information about their child's father.[106] Secondly, unmarried mothers have complained about cohabitation regulations. Mothers suspected of cohabiting have frequently reported being harassed by social security officials.[107]

In addition, mothers who are not required to register for work (on the grounds that they are caring for a dependent child) have reported that officials have exerted considerable pressure on them to return to full-time employment. A good example of such pressure is provided by one of Marsden's respondents.

> They've [National Assistance Board officers] been right nasty with me. They're always trying to get me to get a job. They made me sign on twice a week at the Labour Exchange. They keep telling me, 'You've got to find a job,' and that used to make me nervous and insecure, because I used to think they might cut off my assistance and leave me with nothing.[108]

It should be noted that the distressing nature of both liable relative and seeking work regulations may be compounded by the attitude adopted by some of the officials who administer these rules (i.e. unmarried mothers may be subjected to adverse comments about their sexual conduct).

The difficulties experienced by unmarried mothers during their contact with social security officials was one of the issues considered by the Finer Committee in its report on one-parent families, which was published in 1974.[109] The publication of this report can justifiably be regarded as a landmark in terms of public recognition of the needs of unmarried mothers and other single-parent families. In the view of the committee a thorough-going review of the provision made for single parents in society was essential given the change that had occurred in post-war public attitudes towards sexual relationships and family life.

In this climate of opinion, compassion for the disadvantages suffered by one-parent families has grown quickly. The old tariff of blame which pitied widows but attached varying degrees of moral delinquency to divorced or separated women or to unmarried mothers is becoming irrelevant in the face of the imperative recognition that what chiefly matters in such situations is to assist and protect dependent children, all of whom ought to be treated alike irrespective of their mothers' circumstances.[110]

The committee devoted considerable attention to the question of the financial situation of one-parent families. They recommended that improvements should be made in both the administration of court orders and supplementary benefit.[111] For example, in terms of the latter, the committee proposed that:

1 A special additional allowance should be paid to all lone parents.
2 The full adult non-householder scale rate should be paid to lone parents under eighteen (provided that they are receiving supplementary benefit in their own right).
3 The withdrawal of benefit on grounds of cohabitation should be delayed until the mother concerned has been given a written statement of the facts and an opportunity to appeal.[112]

The proposed introduction of a new, non-contributory, benefit for all one-parent families (Guaranteed Maintenance Allowance) was the most important financial recommendation made by the committee. This new benefit was intended to:

1 Replace the existing, inadequate, system of maintenance payments.

2 Offer single parents a real choice about whether or not to work.
3 Provide help for those with part-time or low full-time earnings.
4 Be available to all categories of single parents.
5 Be simple to claim (i.e. postal application).
6 Be equitable vis-à-vis low income two-parent families.[113]

The proposed introduction of this benefit, which was to be paid (at a rate dependent on individual circumstances) to all single parents with sole responsibility for a dependent child was warmly received by a number of commentators. For example, Murch argues that GMA represented a

serious attempt to offer single fathers the opportunity of staying at home and single mothers the opportunity of going to work. Quite apart from the material benefits the symbolic significance is that 90 per cent of single parents would be spared prolonged dependence on a system which is still stigmatically associated with the poor law and pauperism. In this way GMA would offer some single parents a chance to recover their lost dignity.[114]

Others, however, have been rather critical of certain aspects of this scheme. For example, both Kincaid[115] and Townsend[116] have expressed reservations about the inclusion of a means test in the administration of this benefit and the high marginal rate of tax or benefit reduction that single parents would experience upon resuming work.

The committee also recognized that provision for single parents needed to be improved in other areas – housing,[117] employ-ment,[118] day care,[119] personal social services,[120] education[121] and family planning.[122] For instance, in the case of the personal social services, the committee were concerned that single parents were not using this form of provision because of ignorance or fear of disapproval.[123] The committee recommended, therefore, that social work services should be more effectively publicized and that improvements should be made in reception and interviewing facilities, office opening times and the system of financial payments.[124] The committee did not think it advisable, however, to recommend the establishment of some form of separate provision for one-parent families within each local social service department. 'Such an arrangement would tend to isolate one-parent families from other families with social problems, and a certain amount of stigma might come to attach to the new service.'[125]

The main recommendations of the Finer Report have shown little sign, however, of being implemented.[126] Importantly, there has been a complete absence of official support for the introduction of a Guaranteed Maintenance Allowance for single parents.[127] As a result, large numbers of single parents have been forced to rely on supplementary benefit (392,000 – November/ December 1981)[128] and family income supplement (65,000 – April 1982)[129] as a means of financial support. The unsatisfactory nature of this type of provision is reflected in the fact that substantial numbers of needy, single parents fail to claim the benefits to which they are entitled (single-parent take-up has been estimated at 89 per cent for supplementary benefit (1977)[130] and 53 per cent for family income supplement (1981)[131]). Take-up has also been disappointing for the special single-parent supplement – one-parent benefit (formerly child benefit increase) – which was introduced in 1977 (estimated take-up 70 per cent in December 1981).[132]

Although certain improvements have been made in both the supplementary benefits system (e.g. an increase in the earnings disregard for claimants;[133] the payment of supplementary benefit to schoolgirl mothers between the ages of sixteen and eighteen)[134] and in housing provision (e.g. the housing needs of single parents and other groups were given priority under the 1977 Housing (Homeless Persons) Act)[135] since the publication of the Finer Report, it can generally be concluded that there has been no major attempt to improve the material and social circumstances of single parents in recent years.

Unmarried mothers have undoubtedly benefited from a number of twentieth-century social policy initiatives (i.e. the provision of certain welfare benefits and services has enabled this group to obtain a limited degree of economic and social security). Nevertheless, despite the emergence of this more enlightened approach, unmarried mothers have continued to be denied full social acceptance. Indeed, instead of being seen as an integral part *of* society, unmarried mothers have tended to be regarded as a social problem *for* society.

Dependency on public aid is the principal reason why unmarried mothers continue to be regarded as a social problem. The demand for public aid made by unmarried mothers is only to be expected, though, given the difficulties this group face if they wish to remain financially independent. For example, financial self-sufficiency necessitates unmarried mothers (and other single parents with dependent children) finding:

1 A local job which is relatively well paid.
2 An employer who appreciates that there will be a need to take time off work at short notice.
3 Suitable day-care facilities for their children.

Given these difficulties, which are compounded by the precarious position of women in the labour market, it is not surprising that unmarried mothers are prone to public dependency.

The recent growth in the number of unmarried mothers (and of one-parent families in general: see Table 3.1) has tended to intensify public concern about this source of public dependency. It should not be assumed, however, that this increase results from some rapid rise in the number of illegitimate births (though there has been a marked increase since 1977: see Table 3.2). This increase in the number of unmarried mothers owes far more to the reluctance shown by such women to either marry or place their children for adoption.[136]

Doubts about the ability of unmarried mothers to perform certain vital familial duties is another (related) reason why this group continue to be regarded as a social problem. For example, according to Perlman an infant 'presents a problem of social concern when he is kept by a socially, economically, and culturally impoverished mother. There is question and concern whether children reared under such complex disadvantaged conditions can grow into "good citizens".'[137] The fact that relatively large numbers of illegitimate children have been received into care over the years[138] has often been cited as an example of the general inability of unmarried mothers to provide a secure home environment for their children. Obviously, the social standing of unmarried mothers has not been enhanced by

Table 3.1 Estimated number of one-parent families in Great Britain in 1971, 1976 and 1979

Sex and marital status	1971 Number (000's)	%	1976 Number (000's)	%	1979 Number (000's)	%	Percentage change: 1971-1979
Mothers							
Single	90	16	130	17	140	16	56
Widowed	120	21	115	15	110	13	−8
Divorced	120	21	230	31	310	36	158
Separated	170	30	185	25	200	23	18
Total	500	88	660	88	760	88	52
Fathers							
Total	70	12	90	12	100	12	43
TOTAL (All Families)	570	100	750	100	860	100	52

Sources: Compiled from, R. Leete, Table 4, p. 7 and National Council for One Parent Families, 1981, p. 2.

Table 3.2 Illegitimate live births in England and Wales since 1945 (selected years)

Year	Illegitimate live births	Percentage of all live births (the illegitimacy ratio)
1945	63,420	9.3
1950	35,250	5.1
1955	31,145	4.7
1960	42,707	5.4
1965	66,249	7.7
1970	64,744	8.3
1975	54,891	9.1
1976	53,766	9.2
1977	55,379	9.7
1978	60,637	10.2
1979	69,467	10.9
1980	77,372	11.8

Source: National Council for One Parent Families, 1982, Table 6, p. 20.

the expression of these doubts about their parenting skills.

When considering some of the reasons as to why stigma has continued to attach to unmarried mothers in recent years, it is important to reflect on the part played by social researchers in this process. Since the 1940s the unmarried mother and her child have been the subject of a number of social science research studies (particularly in Britain and the United States). Clearly, the results that have emerged from such investigations are likely to have some effect on the way in which the unmarried mother is regarded by both official bodies and the general public. It is useful, therefore, to look in some detail at research in this area.

Studies of the unmarried mother have generally been undertaken from either a psychological or sociological perspective. Let us look at each of these approaches in turn.

Psychological Studies

Like Bowlby, most 'psychological' researchers in this field have tended to assume that 'in a western community, it is emotionally disturbed . . . women who produce illegitimate children of a socially unacceptable kind.'[139] Accordingly, attempts have been made to identify the particular personality factors which predispose unmarried women to engage in behaviour likely to lead to the birth of an illegitimate child.

Extraversion, neuroticism, ambivalent ego identity, impulsivity, poor tolerance and low IQ have been identified as the predisposing factors which are likely to precipitate behaviour which will lead to illegitimacy. For example, a neurotic girl might become pregnant in order to secure a relationship with her boyfriend (see Figure 3.1).

It should be noted at this point that a number of researchers have specifically studied the unmarried mother from a psychoanalytical perspective. Crucial to this form of investigation (which derives largely from the work of Freud)[140] is the ideal that all behaviour has an underlying meaning. According to Young, this method of investigation has helped to dispel the myth

that having an out-of-wedlock child is something that just happens. On the contrary, everything points to the purposeful nature of the act. Although a girl would obviously not plan consciously and deliberately to bear an out-of-wedlock child, she does act in such a way that this becomes the almost inevitable result.[141]

Although psychoanalytical studies will be referred to in the subsequent discussion, it should be remembered that a number of psychologists have expressed grave doubts about the scientific rigour of this particular form of investigation.[142]

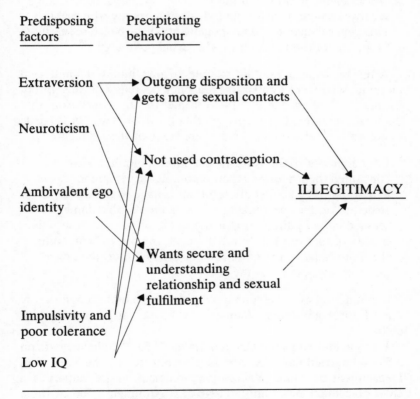

Source: J.A. Vincent, *Illegitimacy*, p. 128.

Figure 3.1 Psychological explanations of 'illegitimacy'

Evidence of psychological disturbance amongst unmarried mothers was found in a number of studies conducted in the 1940s. For example, in one such study Kasanin and Handschin[143] (United States: 1941) came to the conclusion that each of their sixteen respondents had displayed some form of unresolved oedipal conflict. In another survey (of ten unmarried mothers aged between thirteen and seventeen), Bernard[144] (United States: 1944) found that:

All the girls showed effects of early emotional malnutrition; they received too little parental love, protection, esteem, encouragement, and liberation to develop adequate emotional security or inner controls and ideals in harmony with reality. This general anxiety-ridden personality disturbance seems basic to the elaboration of their psychosexual pathology.[145]

After studying a random sample of one hundred unmarried mothers, who were known to an agency dealing with this group, Young[146] (United States: 1945) came to the conclusion that dominant parents (especially mothers) could have an adverse effect on the subsequent sexual behaviour of their daughters.

Fifty-eight out of the 100 girls had known mothers who controlled their lives and their emotional development to an extent that they could only result in damage to the whole structure of their personalities. The degree of that damage seemed to be in direct proportion to the power and destructive quality of that control. In other words, the more dominating, the more sadistic, the more rejecting the mother, the sicker and more hopeless was the girl.[147]

For Young, all of these 'unhappy' girls 'had blindly sought a way out of their emotional dilemma by having an out-of-wedlock child.'[148]

Pearson and Amacher (United States: 1956)[149]collected data on 3,594 unmarried mothers, who had been tested by the Minnesota Department of Public Welfare psychological service as part of a child placement programme (1946-51). Although 2,506 of these mothers were judged to be emotionally and behaviourally normal, some 657 were deemed to be neurotic (19 per cent); 123 – psychopathic (3.6 per cent); 116 – primary mental deficients

(3.4 per cent); 28 – psychotic (0.8 per cent) and 20 neurologically disordered in various other ways (0.6 per cent). As they were unable to draw any general conclusions from their study (a control group had not been used), Pearson and Amacher had to be content with merely expressing a hope 'that the incidence of rather serious personality or behavioural inadequacy (in the general population) would not approach the 27.4 per cent which we encountered in our sample of unwed mothers.'[150]

Psychological disturbance amongst unmarried mothers has also been found in a number of research studies which have been conducted since the 1940s. For example, Cattell[151] (United States: 1954) found that each of the 54 unmarried mothers he interviewed in a New York nursing home in the early 1950s were suffering from some form of personality problem (30 were deemed to have a character disorder; to be neurotic; and 17 to be schizophrenic).

In another survey (of 31, randomly selected, unmarried, pregnant women), Greenberg et al.[152] (United States: 1959) found that:

> the ego of most of the subjects appeared infantile and fragile. Generally speaking, their concerns and orientations appeared definitively preoedipal in quality and not primarily explainable by the dependency state of pregnancy. They were particularly sensitive to separations and often described themselves as both frequently and severely depressed.[153]

Further investigations indicated that these mothers (unlike a control group of 20 married mothers) 'had marked, overt psychopathology prior to pregnancy.'[154]

Eysenck[155] (Great Britain: 1961) compared the personalities of 100 primiparous women with a similar sample of married women. On the basis of her results, Eysenck provisionally concluded that 'girls who might be expected to become pregnant before marriage, would be those with high extraversion scores, or those with high neuroticism scores, or, most likely of all, those who score high on both.'[156]

In a study of 51 unmarried mothers (who had received casework services from the Children's Aid society of Pennsylvania during the years 1959 to 1962), Bonan[157] (United States: 1963) found that each of his subjects had a narcissistic character structure. According to Bonan, a woman with such a character structure is unlikely to become pregnant by accident.

> In her acting out she is trying to escape from a serious internal problem. Her level of ego development is infantile, or primitive, and she has not developed mature methods for resolving conflicts. Her reality-testing is defective; she is self-absorbed and she cannot love others.[158]

Kravitz et al.[159] (Canada: 1966) interviewed 83 unmarried mothers (aged between fourteen and thirty-nine) who had been referred to a special hospital clinic for unmarried mothers. They found that unmarried women became pregnant 'primarily as a result of a deficient ego control in the presence of sexual drive'.[160]

Two studies of the unmarried mother were undertaken by Naiman[161] (Canada: 1966 and 1971). In the first of these investigations, a group of 14 unmarried mothers (who had attended the Montreal Children's service between December 1963 and March 1965) were compared with 18 married mothers (who had attended the obstetrics clinic at a Montreal hospital between February 1964 and March 1965). Both of these groups were comprised of white, Protestant, Canadian born, women aged between eighteen and twenty-five. It was found that the unmarried mother group had 'a greater degree of impulsivity and a poorer ability to form stable relationships'[162] than the control group of married mothers. In the second of these surveys, the same group of unmarried mothers was compared with a group of 15, predominantly white, Canadian born, women (aged between eighteen and twenty-five) who had applied for a therapeutic abortion at a Jewish general hospital. After finding a similarity between the personalities of this 'abortion group' and the 'married group' in the previous survey, Naiman felt confident enough to suggest that:

> unmarried mothers constitute a distinct group, with particular if not unique psychodynamic characteristics and that other unmarried women either do not get pregnant or, if they do, handle the matter either by getting married or by getting an abortion. . . .[163]

Floyd and Viney[164] (Australia: 1974) attempted to test the applicability of a number of psychoanalytic hypotheses concerning the ego identity and the ego ideal of unmarried mothers. They compared 32, unmarried pregnant women (aged between fifteen and twenty-five, who were residing in charitable homes) with two control groups:

1 30, single, non-pregnant women who had been matched by age and socio-economic status.
2 15, married, pregnant women who had been matched by occupation, socio-economic status and education.

It was found that the unmarried pregnant women were more ambivalent about their ego identities (the ability to experience one's self as something that has continuity and sameness, and to act accordingly) and less inclined to view themselves as adequate feminine individuals than either of the control groups.[165]

Finally, evidence from a number of studies has suggested that unmarried mothers who keep their children are more likely to be psychologically disturbed than those who place their children for adoption. For example, Vincent[166] (United States: 1961) tested the personalities of 105 unmarried mothers who were living in two Californian maternity homes. Mothers who decided to keep their children were found to display a greater degree of neuroticism than those who opted to place their children for adoption.[167]

Jones et al.[168] (United States: 1962) studied 90 unmarried mothers who had been clients at a private New York city social welfare agency. When compared with the women who had surrendered their children for adoption, the 19 mothers who had kept their children were found in general to be: (a) lower in intelligence; (b) lower in ego strength or emotional stability; (c) more submissive.[169]

Yelloly[170] (Great Britain: 1965) compared 88 unmarried mothers who had kept their children with 72 mothers who had offered their children for adoption (all of these mothers had been referred to a voluntary social work agency in the west of England). She found that unstable or emotionally disturbed mothers were more likely to keep their children 'despite the presence of characteristics which would ordinarily tend towards adoption'[171] (e.g. a married putative father).

Two points should be borne in mind when considering the results obtained in these various psychological studies of the unmarried mother. Firstly, research in this area has tended to focus almost exclusively on those unmarried mothers who have been living in mother and baby homes or similar institutions. Clearly, respondents obtained from such sources are unlikely to provide a representative cross-section of the unmarried mother population. Secondly, results based on personality tests or professional evaluations of an individual's psychological make-up should be treated with the utmost caution given the highly subjective nature of these procedures. In particular, it should be remembered that unmarried mothers have often been encouraged (or, indeed, required) to adopt a psychological interpretation of their previous behaviour by the welfare professionals they have come into contact with.[172]

Public acceptance of the notion that unmarried mothers are likely to be psychologically disturbed owes much to the emergence of professional social work practice in both Britain and the United States. Psychological theories were widely adopted by social workers for two main reasons. Firstly, these theories were ideally suited to the dominant social work method – casework. For example, as Croxen points out, psychoanalytic theory provided social workers with 'a therapeutic procedure and a whole technique of enquiry'.[173] By the use of this theory, social work clients could thus be encouraged 'to analyse their situation, come to terms with their problem, adjust accordingly and re-enter the social system as "cured" individuals.'[174]

Secondly, the adoption of these theories enabled social workers to press their claims for professional status. By emphasizing the psychological basis of many of the problems that were being experienced by various members of society, social workers attempted to demonstrate that the care and therapy required by those in need necessitated the involvement of well-trained experts rather than unqualified voluntary workers.

Unmarried mothers were considered (amongst others) to be a particularly suitable client group for psychoanalytical casework. For instance, the fact that relatively large numbers of unmarried mothers tended to reside in maternity homes (of one sort or another) both before and after their confinements, provided social workers with a ready-made opportunity to establish the long-term casework relationships (which were deemed essential if this form of intervention was to prove beneficial) with this group. In addition, it was possible to gauge the effectiveness of this form of therapy with unmarried mothers in a relatively straightforward way (i.e. by examining the level of 'recidivism'[175] and the extent of dependency on welfare services).

It is now pertinent to consider the possible effect that this evidence of psychological disturbance has had upon the stigma attaching to the unmarried mother.

Cheetham, for example, argues that the development of psychological theories of unmarried motherhood

represents an attempt, most important and much needed, to challenge the sometimes sentimental or ill-informed stereo-types of unmarried mothers as either the innocent victims of predatory men or as over-sexed women whose uncontrollable urges make them careless and undiscriminating in their sexual relations.[176]

As she continues:

such explanations can be extremely useful in attempting to understand the pregnancies of women who seem very ambiva-lent about what course of action they should take; of those who are at a loss to explain how they became pregnant; of the older, educated or sophisticated woman whose pregnancies would seem, at first sight, to be a social and personal disaster which apparently they could have avoided; of some of those who repeatedly conceive outside marriage; and of the girls who seem caught in a web of unhappy family relationships. In some circumstances these explanations throw light on behaviour that is apparently meaningless, self-centred and self-damaging, and can alert workers to the importance of designing help which takes account of the complex needs and emotions contributing to such behaviour.[177]

Clearly, from this perspective psychological explanations of unmarried motherhood are seen as having a positive role to play in terms of countering the stigma that has attached to the unmarried mother. Indeed, Gill even suggests that a prior softening of public attitudes towards illegitimacy was necessary in order to facilitate the acceptance of these particular theories.[178]

In contrast, it can be argued that psychological explanations of unmarried motherhood have merely reinforced the stigma that has attached to such mothers. Individuals deemed to be psychologically disturbed in contemporary society are unlikely to be treated in a particularly favourable way by their fellow citizens.[179] On the contrary, they are liable instead to experience a considerable degree of social rejection (e.g. snubs, adverse comments, difficulties in obtaining and retaining a job). In addition, the psychologically disturbed are liable to be subjected to official forms of control and treatment on the grounds that they constitute some forms of threat to society. Indeed, unmarried mothers have been a target for a particularly repressive form of such control in the not-so-distant past (e.g. compulsory detention under the 1913 Mental Deficiency Act).[180]

This approach to the impact that psychological explanations of unmarried motherhood are likely to have upon the stigma attaching to this group appears to be far more plausible than the one previously outlined. Although psychological theories may be of some use in explaining the pregnancies of a small number of unmarried women, it seems highly questionable to suggest (or, at least imply), as many researchers appear to have done, that unmarried motherhood *per se* is evidence of some underlying psychological disturbance. Such a contention only serves to sustain the notion that unmarried motherhood is a social problem which requires containment and control. As a result, little or no attention is given to the possibility that women may deliberately choose to become (or, at least, are prepared to become) pregnant outside of marriage. Importantly, psychological explanations of unmarried motherhood can effectively serve to conceal the major, underlying reason why stigma continues to attach to unmarried mothers – namely, their dependency on public aid.

Sociological Studies

A number of sociological studies have tended to suggest that unmarried motherhood is more likely to be found amongst the poorer sections of society and in certain racial groups.

Unmarried motherhood: lower social class association

Evidence associating illegitimacy with the lower social classes has been found in a number of studies. For example, in a survey of 278 illegitimate births in a Midlands city ('Midboro') in the late 1940s, Hughes[181] (Great Britain: 1949) found that the majority of the mothers concerned came from the lower social classes. Similarly, after studying the records of all women who had given birth to an illegitimate child in Aberdeen during the years 1949 to 1952, Thompson[182] (Great Britain: 1956) came to the conclusion that 'illegitimacy tends to be associated with unskilled, unattractive, or menial occupations.'[183] This finding was confirmed in a subsequent survey of illegitimacy in Aberdeen in the early 1960s. (It should be noted, however, that the association between illegitimacy and lower social class membership was not found to be as strong as in the previous survey: see Gill[184] (Great Britain: 1977).)

Unmarried mothers have also been found to have a lower social class profile in a number of other surveys. For example, in a study of 39 cohabiting, and 27 non-cohabiting, unmarried mothers, who were living in south-east Essex, Yarrow[185] (Great Britain: 1964) found that 36 of the former and 22 of the latter could be classified as working class. Hopkinson[186] (Great Britain: 1976) also found that the vast majority (86 per cent) of the 116 unmarried mothers she interviewed in the early 1970s came from social classes III to V. In Addition, evidence from surveys conducted by Yelloly[187] (see pp. 105-6) and Weir[188] (Great Britain: 1970) suggests that lower social class unmarried mothers are more likely to keep their children than place them for adoption.

Before looking at the question of the potential impact of these sociological studies upon the stigma attaching to the unmarried mother, it is necessary to point out that neither Weir[189] (who collected data on 288 illegitimate maternities in an area of Scotland) or Crellin et al.[190] (Great Britain: 1971, who examined the social background of 679 illegitimate children as part of the

National Child Development Study) found any evidence to suggest that working-class women were over-represented in their surveys of illegitimacy.[191]

Despite the usual objections that can be made about the sampling procedures used in these research studies, there does not appear to be any valid reason why one should reject the notion that working-class women are more likely to become unmarried mothers than their middle class counterparts. However, greater caution needs to be exercised when one comes to examine some of the explanations that have been put forward to account for the fact that illegitimacy tends to be more prevalent amongst the lower social classes. For example, a number of commentators have argued that the higher rate of illegitimacy amongst this section of the population is directly attributable to the defective nature of working-class culture. As Thompson, an exponent of this viewpoint, states:

> Illegitimacy, like delinquency, thrives when social values,
> cultural as well as material, are low. Insecure family life, poor
> and overcrowded homes, lack of constructive recreational aims
> and outlets, lack of general planning ability, and permissive
> attitudes to extra-marital relations may all contribute to its
> occurrence.[192]

This 'working-class culture' explanation of illegitimacy has proved extremely popular despite the existence of alternative (and arguably more persuasive) explanations as to why working-class women are more likely to have illegitimate children. For example, it can be argued that working-class women run a far greater risk of involuntary unmarried motherhood because of the fact that they tend to (i) be more poorly informed about the availability and use of contraceptives; (ii) find it more difficult to obtain an abortion.[193]

The fact that most researchers working in this field have tended to accept the assumption that unmarried motherhood constitutes a serious social problem for society, is one of the reasons why this working-class culture explanation of illegitimacy has proved so popular (i.e. it is an explanation which suggests that the 'problem of unmarried motherhood' can be solved within the existing structure of society). Indeed, many researchers have presented and interpreted their survey findings in ways which have enabled this particular explanation of illegitimacy to flourish. For example, the interpretation that has frequently been placed on the fact that working-class unmarried mothers are more likely to keep their children than place them for adoption is that such women lack social responsibility because of the inadequacy of their cultural background. However, this type of explanation is clearly open to question. As Macintyre points out:

> it is equally plausible to attribute higher rates of keeping among working cass women to socially valued characteristics such as a greater love for children, a greater willingness to sacrifice reputation and personal advancement for the sake of a child, and on the part of kin and neighbours to provide support.[194]

The appeal of this working-class culture explanation of illegitimacy can be linked to other theoretical developments in the social sciences. In particular, it is necessary to refer (in this context) to the culture of poverty thesis which has been advanced by Lewis and others.[195] Lewis contends that the poor have, in response to their experiences of deprivation (e.g. ill-health, low incomes, unemployment, inadequate housing), developed their own distinctive culture. According to Lewis, this culture of poverty is characterized by: early sexual experience, promiscuity, high illegitimacy and desertion rates and non-participation in formal and informal social agencies such as trade unions or clubs. In addition, those imbued with the culture of poverty are deemed to be fatalistic, impulsive, helpless and prone to dependency.[196] Lewis lays great stress on the resilient nature of the culture of poverty, arguing that it can be transmitted from one generation to the next.

> By the time slum children are age six or seven they have usually absorbed the basic values and attitudes of their sub-culture and are not psychologically geared to take full advantage of changing conditions or increased opportunities which may occur in their lifetime.[197]

Despite the fact that Lewis's culture of poverty thesis has

attracted numerous theoretical and methodological criticisms,[198] it has nonetheless proved to be extremely popular in certain political quarters in both Great Britain and the United States.[199] For example, Sir Keith Joseph (paying scant regard to Lewis's assertion that a culture of poverty is unlikely to flourish in an advanced capitalist society with adequate welfare services)[200] has argued that a 'cycle of deprivation' exists in Britain. Joseph and others who subscribe to this hypothesis believe that:

> Certain inadequate parents do not provide the love, firmness, guidance and stimulus which most normal children receive. Being poorly socialized, their children do not acquire the motivation, skills and capacities necessary to avail themselves of educational and job opportunities. In turn, they will grow up only to transmit the same behaviour patterns to their offspring who, therefore, will also remain in poverty.'[201]

Importantly, unmarried mothers have been identified as one group of 'inadequate' poor parents who are likely to transmit such deprivation.[202]

By linking illegitimacy with the culture of poverty, it has been possible to reinforce the notion that unmarried motherhood is socially disreputable (i.e. it is a phenomenon peculiar to the poorer (and behaviourally deficient) sections of society).

Unmarried motherhood: the dimension of race

The racial dimension of unmarried motherhood has been given a good deal of attention in the United States.[203] In particular, illegitimacy has tended to be linked with negro culture. It has been argued, for example, that the 'acceptance' of illegitimacy by the negro population can be directly traced back to the forcible enslavement of their forebears (i.e. negro slaves were permitted, and often encouraged, to form illicit sexual relationships).[204] Following the 'emancipation' (latter half of the nineteenth century) and subsequent migration of negroes from the rural south to the industrial north (early twentieth century), the white community began to express considerable concern about what they perceived as deficiencies in the negro family structure. As

Gutman points out: 'The twin evils of familial "instability" and sexual "immorality" supported the advocacy of new forms of external control over blacks, including disenfranchisement and increasingly rigorous legal separation.'[205]

Sociological research studies on negro unmarried mothers have tended to reflect this 'white' concern about negro culture. For example, after studying 11 unmarried, pregnant negro women in North Carolina, Hertz and Little[206] (United States: 1944) came to the conclusion that 'illegitimacy can best be understood when examined in its cultural context, which may be responsible for the differential rate of illegitimacy between white and negro groups.'[207] Similarly, Knapp and Cambria[208] (United States: 1947) found (after interviewing 49 negro unmarried mothers who had been accepted for study and treatment by the Family Service Association of Washington during 1945) that the greater acceptance of illegitimacy amongst this group was primarily related to cultural factors.

The assertion that illegitimacy can be linked to deficiencies in negro culture has also received official support in the United States. For example, in a Department of Labor report[209] – *The Negro Family: The Case For National Action* (The Moynihan Report: 1965) – it was argued that high illegitimacy rates and welfare applications amongst the negro population could be explained by reference to cultural factors.

The assertion that the negro family structure is inherently unstable has, however, been challenged by a number of commentators.[210] For instance, Ryan has drawn attention to the way in which negro culture explanations can effectively serve to conceal the fact that the organization of American society provides disproportionate advantages for the white, middle-class section of the population.

Pointing to the supposedly deviant Negro family as the 'fundamental weakness of the Negro community' is another way to blame the victim. Like 'cultural deprivation,' 'Negro family' has become a shorthand phrase with stereotyped connotations of matriarchy, fatherlessness, and pervasive illegitimacy.[211]

Interestingly, there has also been a movement in the United

States (since the late 1950s) to distinguish between the culture of middle- and lower-class negroes (the former being seen as much more inclined to accept white, middle-class values). As the Billingsleys point out, middle-class negroes have come to be regarded as having 'tendencies towards monogamy, stable residence, the ideal of economic dominance by the father, rigid discipline and sex mores, heterogeneous occupations, thrift, caution, inhibition of aggression and sex, ambition, initiative and manners.'[212] In contrast, lower-class negroes have continued to be regarded as impulsive, aggressive and lacking in rigid sexual mores.[213]

Although illegitimacy has not been linked with race to anything like the same degree in Great Britain, it is important to note that a greater emphasis has been given to the factor of ethnicity in recent years. In particular, medical and other welfare personnel have been showing increased concern about the incidence of illegitimacy amongst young, 'West Indian' women.[214] It seems likely, therefore, that the racial dimension of unmarried motherhood will be subjected to more extensive scrutiny in forthcoming years. Indeed, there are already signs of a movement in this direction. For example, one notable commentator has recently argued that the civil disturbances in Brixton during the summer of 1981 can be attributed to the growth of West Indian single-parent families.[215]

What effect, then, is this association between illegitimacy and race likely to have upon the stigma attaching to the unmarried mother? It seems highly probable that this association will only serve to intensify the stigma which has come to be attached to the unmarried mother. By linking illegitimacy with racial groups, who are commonly regarded as socially inferior, it has been possible to highlight the unacceptable nature of unmarried motherhood. Similarly, persistent levels of illegitimacy amongst certain ethnic groups is likely to be regarded by many as yet further 'evidence' of the innate inferiority of this section of the population. Researchers working in this area who wish to avoid intensifying the stigma which has attached both to the unmarried mother and certain racial groups would be well advised, therefore, to exercise caution when presenting their 'findings'.

When considering the part social researchers may have played in reinforcing the stigma which has attached to the unmarried mother, it is also necessary to examine a number of social administration studies of the illegitimate child (the highlighting of the social and economic disadvantages suffered by illegitimate children who are not adopted can clearly help to sustain the belief that unmarried mothers are unlikely to make adequate parents).

Social administration studies of the illegitimate child

The National Child Development Study has provided some of the most detailed information about the circumstances of illegitimate children (see pp. 109-10). As part of this study, Crellin et al.[216] compared the development of a group of illegitimate children (679) with a sample of legitimate children (16,321). In this investigation, it was found that the mortality rate amongst illegitimate children (in the first seven years of life) was markedly higher than in the legitimate group[217] and that the former tended to be more clumsy and restless than the latter.[218]

Illegitimate children who remain with their natural mothers also showed poorer intellectual ability and attainment (i.e. in terms of arithmetic, reading, general knowledge, oral ability, creativity and perceptual development) than either illegitimate children who had been adopted or legitimate children.[219] In addition, illegitimate children who remained with their natural mothers were also found to experience greater difficulties in terms of their behaviour and adjustment in school.[220]

Non-adopted illegitimate children also fared less well in terms of their home environment than either of the other groups.

A high proportion among the illegitimate sample lived in a home which had no father figure; a majority of the mothers went out to work, both before and after the child went to school; mobility was high and so was the degree of over-crowding; a third of the children's homes lacked the use of one or more of such amenities as an indoor lavatory, hot water supply, a bathroom and their own cooking facilities; and a high proportion of the children experienced some form of substitute care, either on a day or residential basis.[221]

In the light of this evidence, it is not surprising to find that these authors came to the conclusion that illegitimate children:

> were beset by a multiplicity of unfavourable circumstances which not only gave them a relatively poorer start in life but which continued to build up into a complex web of cumulative and interacting disadvantages and deprivations. Thus at the present time, to be born illegitimate is still to be born disadvantaged.[222]

Subsequent surveys by Ferri[223] (Great Britain: 1976) and Lambert and Streather[224] (Great Britain: 1980) (which made use of the same population group) have merely served to confirm the fact that illegitimate children are prone to experiences of deprivation.

Unfavourable evidence relating to illegitimate children has also been found in other studies.[225] In one such study, the home backgrounds of 79 illegitimate children who were either living with their natural mothers (70) or with relatives (9) were assessed by caseworkers on behalf of Steel[226] (Great Britain: 1955). The care received by a third of these children was adjudged to be unsatisfactory.

> In some cases there were quarrels and rivalry over the upbringing of the child between the mother and the grand-mother, who often had the care of the child during the day when the mother was at work. In other cases the mother was backward or unbalanced, lazy or promiscuous. Some mothers frequently changed their work and their lodgings, their home background having little stability.[227]

In another study in which the circumstances of one- and two-parent families in five areas of Great Britain were compared, Hunt et al.[228] (Great Britain: 1973) found that children living in one-parent households were more likely to be deprived in some way (e.g. in terms of the level of household income, standard of housing and educational opportunity).

Evidence of maladjustment and emotional disturbance amongst illegitimate children (and amongst children from one-parent families in general) has also been found in a number of surveys in this field. For example, in a study of children in residential maladjusted schools, Pringle[229] (Great Britain: 1961) found that 15 per cent of the children concerned were illegitimate and that a further 53 per cent had suffered some form of family disruption. A Scottish Education Department working party[230] (Great Britain: 1964) also found evidence that illegitimate children brought up in female-headed households were quite frequently maladjusted.

Murchison[231] (Great Britain: 1974) has also drawn attention to the results obtained in two inner London educational reports. The first report was based on a study of an inner London maladjusted school. It was found that all of the 100 children who had been admitted to this school during the period from December 1964 to November 1970 (30 per cent of whom had come from single-parent families) 'had serious problems of behaviour or conduct, and all had severe learning disturbances, despite being of at least average intelligence.'[232] The second report was concerned with a study of 30,000, eight-year-old children who were attending inner London schools during 1968-9. It was found that children from one-parent families (of varying income levels) were more likely to experience emotional problems than other deprived children.[233]

Both Dell[234] (Great Britain: 1972) and Gill[235] (Great Britain: 1977) have found evidence that children living in single-parent families are poorer in terms of intellectual ability and attainment than children being brought up in two-parent households. Dell studied 1,562, fourteen-year-old Glasgow schoolchildren and found that pupils from one-parent families performed less well on reading tests than their two-parent counterparts. Gill, in a random survey of primary schoolchildren in Aberdeen, found that the educational attainment of those children who had spent the whole of their life in a single-parent family compared unfavourably with those children who had been brought up either in a two-parent family or in an 'anomalous' family situation (i.e. with step-parents or adoptive parents). However, Gill is quick to point out that the poorer educational achievements of children living in single-parent families 'may be attributed as much to the lower social class of these families as to the experience itself.'[236]

Surveys by Packman[237] (Great Britain: 1968) and Rowe and Lambert[238] (Great Britain: 1973) have also indicated that large numbers of illegitimate children are likely to be taken into (and remain in) some form of residential care. In a study of 4,500 applications for reception into care, Packman found that illegitimate children accounted for 28 per cent of the long-term admissions. Rowe and Lambert collected data on 2,812 children (aged 11 or under) who had been in the care of either a local authority or a voluntary agency for at least six months. They found that some 50 per cent of their total sample was illegitimate. Unlike legitimate children in care, this illegitimate group tended to: come into care when very young; have little contact with their natural parents; remain in care for relatively long periods of time; be in poorer health; be at greater risk of inherited illness; be lower in average intelligence and more prone to behavioural problems.

In other surveys, illegitimate children (and children living in single-parent families) have been found to be particularly prone to delinquency.[239] For example, in a study of 92 teenage illegitimate children (aged between fourteen and fifteen), who had been brought up by their natural mothers, The Unmarried Parenthood Committee of the Welfare Council of Toronto[240] (Canada: 1943) found that nearly a quarter of this group had engaged in some form of delinquent behaviour.

In another survey (based on a long-term investigation of 411 boys who had attended one of six junior primary schools in a working-class district of London), West[241] (Great Britain: 1969) found that illegitimate boys (25) were 'particularly delinquent-prone: 10 of the 25 became juvenile delinquents, of whom 7 had a record of at least two delinquencies, and when convictions of young adults were included 11 were delinquents, with 10 of them having more than one delinquent record.'[242]

More favourable evidence relating to illegitimate children has, however, been found in other surveys. For instance, in a study in Leicester (Macdonald[243]: Great Britain: 1956) health visitors were asked to assess the home circumstances and physical and emotional development of 238 five-year-old illegitimate children (the vast majority of whom (182) were living with their natural mothers). Macdonald reports that:

> In the great majority of cases the assessments in all respects
> were satisfactory, there being no financial or emotional
> problem in the home, the care, physical and mental develop-

ment of the child, and the child's emotional development being satisfactory.[244]

In a survey by Steel[245] (Great Britain: 1960), caseworkers also formed a favourable impression of the progress that a group of six-year-old illegitimate children, whom they had been asked to assess, had made (these children had all been brought up by their natural mothers).

Three studies in the United States lend support to the viewpoint that illegitimate children can be satisfactorily cared for by their natural mothers. In the first of these studies, Reed[246] (United States: 1962) found that the physical, mental and emotional development of illegitimate children being cared for by their natural mothers (118) was, in the majority of cases, highly satisfactory.

In a survey by Wright[247] (United States: 1965), caseworkers were asked to make an assesment of the progress that had been made by a group of three- and four-year-old illegitimate children who had been brought up by their natural mothers. Contrary to their expectations, the caseworkers found that the majority of these children had been well cared for and were progressing satisfactorily.

After comparing the care and development of a sample of black, illegitimate children, who had remained with their mothers, with a matched group of legitimate children, Oppel[248] (United States: 1969) could find no significant differences between the two groups. In addition, it should be noted that studies by Buchinal[249] (United States: 1964), Feldman and Feldman[250] (United States: 1975) and Raschke and Raschke[251] (United States: 1979) have all indicated that children are not adversely affected by living in single-parent households.

The fact that these favourable results can be used to counter the less favourable impressions of the circumstances of illegitimate children which have been presented in other social administration studies in this area, does not negate the need to give consideration to the possible impact that these latter findings may have had upon the stigma attaching to the unmarried mother in contemporary society.

At the onset, it must be stressed that researchers working in this field have not deliberately set out to stigmatize the unmarried mother. Indeed, many researchers have constantly drawn attention to the need for greater public support and improved levels of material aid for unmarried mothers and their children.[252] However, there has been a marked tendency to regard unmarried mothers, *per se*, as unsatisfactory parents. For example, when speculating about why unmarried mothers may find it difficult to satisfactorily carry out their parental obligations, many researchers have seen fit to focus exclusively on the individual characteristics of mothers themselves rather than on the impact that social and economic deprivation may have in this regard.[253] Crellin et al. provide a useful illustration:

> One would expect, for example, that a stable, well-educated woman of 25 with some professional training might well be able to provide a satisfactory environment for her child even though he lacks a constant father figure; at least, she is more likely to do so than say a 17-year-old, backward girl. . . .[254]

In addition, researchers often refer to the individual characteristics of unmarried mothers when making suggestions for reform in 'family policy'. Consider, for instance, the following suggestions that Pringle, a leading exponent in this field, has put forward.

> The myth of the blood tie should be replaced by the concept of responsibility and informed parenthood. The ability and willingness to undertake its responsibilities are neither dependent nor necessarily consequent upon, biological parenthood. Rather it is the unconditional desire to provide a caring home, together with the emotional maturity to do so, which are the hallmarks of good parenting. Responsible parenthood also includes having only as many children as the couple can emotionally tolerate and financially afford.[255]

> a social climate will have to be created in which it is considered irresponsible to have children before, say, the age of twenty-two or twenty-three.[256]

> Bringing up children is too important a task to be left entirely to those parents who are patently in need of support, guidance and, where necessary, sanctions on part of the community.[257]

Clearly, unmarried mothers, who are likely to: (a) experience financial difficulties in bringing up their children; (b) be under twenty-two years of age when their child was born (see Table 3.3); and (c) require various forms of community support are one group of parents whom Pringle would regard as potentially unsuitable parents. Indeed, she even seems to be suggesting that some unmarried mothers (perhaps the majority) should not be permitted to care for their own children.

Table 3.3 Illegitimate live births by mother's age at birth: 1980 (England and Wales)

Age of mother at birth	Illegitimate live births	%
Under 16	1,274	1.6
16-19	24,586	31.8
20-24	26,607	34.4
25-29	13,462	17.4
30-34	7,588	9.8
35-39	3,047	3.9
40-44	761	1.0
45-49	44	0.1
50 And Over	3	–
All Ages	77,372	100.0

Source: National Council for One Parent Families, 1981, Table 4, p. 19.

Such statements merely serve to sustain the belief that unmarried motherhood (being a reflection of some form of individual inadequacy) is a social problem requiring policies of containment and control. No credence is given to the possibility that unmarried motherhood might be better regarded as an alternative, but equally acceptable, family unit.

It is difficult to assess the impact that unfavourable social science research findings relating to unmarried motherhood may have upon the stigma attaching to this group. For example, it can plausibly be argued that the limited circulations of the journals in which social science research tends to be published will minimize the potential impact that unfavourable findings may have upon either the attitudes of policy-makers or the general public. Alternatively, though, research findings may (as a result of dissemination via the mass media) receive a good deal of attention and, as such, play a significant role both in the formation of public opinion and in terms of influencing policy-makers. From this latter perspective, the publication of unfavourable research findings could (in the absence of any reference to the various economic and social disadvantages which unmarried mothers are forced to endure) reinforce the stigma attaching to the single mother.

Before looking finally at the question of whether contemporary unmarried mothers are likely to feel stigmatized in their day-to-day lives, it is useful, at this stage, to briefly summarize the main arguments that have been presented in this chapter. It has been contended that there are two principal reasons why stigma has attached to the unmarried mother over the centuries – (1) the challenge presented to Christian beliefs; (2) 'blameworthy' public dependency. As was shown earlier, ecclesiastical authorities attempted to express their disapproval of illegitimacy by imposing some form of penance on those unmarried mothers who were brought before the church courts. Although it is difficult to assess the impact that this form of stigmatization had upon unmarried mothers, it seems likely that the public humiliation involved would have adversely affected a large percentage of those women who were sanctioned in this way.

Although 'Christian stigmatization' of the unmarried mother has markedly declined since the sixteenth century, it is important to note that unmarried motherhood is still regarded as a serious moral problem by certain sections of contemporary society. In addition, the Christian church has continued to take an active interest in the moral welfare of the unmarried mother and her child (e.g. by the employment of their own social workers).

'Blameworthy' public dependency has, however, been identified as the main reason why stigma has tended to attach to the unmarried mother over the centuries (particularly since 1500). During the period from 1500 to 1900, secular authorities attempted to limit the demand made by unmarried mothers upon public funds by means of the imposition of various physical and economic sanctions. Since 1900, however, there has been a detectable softening in secular attitudes towards the unmarried mother. Four possible explanations for this change were identified: (i) greater commitment towards the poor on the part of governments; (ii) more enlightened approach towards the needs of dependent children; (iii) the effects of war; (iv) the impact of social science research. It was pointed out, though, that implicit forms of secular stigmatization have still tended to persist in recent decades (e.g. unmarried mothers have tended to be given either inadequate or inappropriate forms of economic and social support).

In the latter part of this chapter attention was also given to one (rather neglected) way in which the stigma attaching to the unmarried mother may have been reinforced in recent years – namely the influence of social science research. It was argued that the tendency on the part of researchers working in this field to associate unmarried motherhood with other negative character-istics (e.g. psychological disturbance) could, in the absence of more detailed discussions about the social and economic disadvantages that these mothers are likely to experience, tend to create the impression that single motherhood is an unacceptable social phenomenon rather than an alternative (but equally acceptable) family formation.

Finally, in looking at the relationship between stigma and unmarried motherhood, it is useful to consider (albeit briefly) whether contemporary unmarried mothers actually feel stigma-tized in their day-to-day lives. A survey which I conducted in south-east England in the late 1970s is of some use in this regard.[258] Although the majority (86 per cent) of the 36 mothers who took part in this survey reported that they did not generally feel stigmatized in their day-to-day lives, they did admit to experiencing some form of felt stigma. For example, a number of mothers (13)[259] stated that they had felt stigmatized because of their dependency on supplementary benefit. These mothers outlined various reasons as to why they had felt stigmatized about receiving this form of welfare support:

1 Dependency per se ('I would much sooner earn it myself. I prefer to get it that way').
2 The possibility of being classified as a scrounger ('I don't like people pointing out that the state keeps me – you live off the state').
3 The attitude adopted by social security staff ('They're so sort of nosey when they come round. They just want to know

everything. How many sets of clothes you've got, how many pairs of pants, bras, etc. How many cigarettes do you smoke? What do you do with your money? They just want to know everything about your life and I'm not prepared to tell them').

4 The claiming procedure ('It's sitting in the social security office. Although there are people sitting around you in similar situations I hate having to go up to the desk within ear shot of other people').

In addition (when questioned directly about the attitude that had been displayed by supplementary benefits officers with whom they had come into contact) a number of mothers (13) stated that they had experienced feelings of stigma as a result of certain adverse comments which had been made by SB officials.

'You have to go for interviews, it's quite upsetting you know "How many times have you been to bed with anyone since." They upset me quite a bit.'

'It wasn't directly said that I don't like you going on the dole 'cause you're a single parent but it was indirectly said, the visiting officer said: "Our first priority is to the tax-payer and we've got to look after them before you." Those were his exact words. . . . I told the guy you don't have to come and insult me, it's not the sort of situation that I wanted to be in. They want to know all about your business, nosing in, sending spies round to see if you've got a man hidden in the cupboard.'

Respondents also referred to the social disgrace attached to unmarried motherhood when they were questioned about their experiences of felt stigma. For instance, 9 mothers admitted feeling stigmatized when they discovered that they were pregnant. As one mother commented:

'Things like that just don't happen in our family anyway. . . . It's the worst thing that could happen. It's worse than if you're dying, the sorrow and heartbreak. It's the biggest tragedy I'm telling you. It's the worst disgrace of all.'

In general, the respondents only tended to feel stigmatized on the grounds of social disgrace in particular circumstances. Three situations can be referred to for the purpose of illustration.

1 Disclosing information about their pregnancy to relatives ('I didn't exactly tell them (parents) myself. . . . I knew my mother was going to see the doctor so I asked him to tactfully tell her. I was really worried about telling them 'cause I just didn't know what their reaction would be').
2 Visiting time in hospital ('Why couldn't I have a husband to come and see me. . . . Why couldn't I be like everybody else? I thought the child's father might come into hospital just to see me. I was hoping but of course he didn't. It upset me a great deal').
3 Subsequent relationships with men ('They're going to think you're an easy lay. . . . You feel you don't want to meet other guys generally 'cause you think that's going to be their reaction').

A number of respondents also reported feeling stigmatized as a result of the reactions of certain people they had come into contact with during their 'unmarried mother career'. For example, 10 mothers stated that they had felt stigmatized during their period of confinement in hospital because of adverse comments which had been made by some members of the medical staff. As the following examples indicate this source of stigmatization could be quite savage:

'One morning she had me crying from half past eight to half past twelve. You're feeling depressed anyhow and I was reading a book and she said, "I think that ought to be the Bible you're reading." She told me I was very extravagant and a spoilt child and that I should have known better at my age . . . and did I realise I was bringing a child into the world without a father. It was pretty evil. She even brought another nurse over to my bed to help her make the bed and went on to her about me.'
(Hospital nurse)

'Matron said, "Mothers like you shouldn't be feeding your

children". I continued to breast feed my child so matron put me in a cubicle without curtains so all the porters and everybody coming past could see. She thought it would put me off . . . but it didn't stop me.'
(Hospital matron)

'She knew I was single, she turned round and said, "You mustn't have too many boyfriends because it will be upsetting for the child to have too many fathers," . . . I could just picture what she meant by that. I'd be going out every night with my boyfriends leaving the child and not looking after him properly.'
(Hospital paediatrician)

Five mothers also reported that they had experienced feelings of stigma as a result of the comments or actions of casual aquaintances. One mother's description of the response of a woman she had met at a playgroup provides a good illustration of this form of stigmatization.

'There was a girl I met up there – we used to sit and natter while the children were playing. One day she asked me what my husband did and I said, "Oh, I'm not married", and she just turned her back on me and started talking to the girl next to us. . . . She took her little boy away from my little girl and she wouldn't let him near her. She said, "You're not to play with that little girl again – you leave her alone." That annoyed me.'

It is important to stress, however, that experiences of stigma were (amongst this particular group of respondents) not only relatively rare but also highly situational in character (i.e. feelings of stigma only tended to be experienced in particular situations). Many mothers commented on the fact that they had received relatively favourable responses (often from quite unexpected sources – e.g. local authority housing officials) from many of the people whom they had come into contact with since becoming an unmarried mother. Clearly, this could be seen as indicative of a softening of public attitudes towards unmarried mothers. However, given the fact that all respondents in this study reported that they had been subjected to some form of stigmatization during their unmarried mother career, this conclusion would appear to be somewhat premature. What is interesting to note is the fact that such stigmatization did not tend to induce feelings of stigma amongst respondents. On the contrary, most mothers stated that the adverse reactions they had received from others had merely caused them to feel resentful. This may be a highly significant finding (i.e. it may indicate that stigmatized groups are much more willing than they were previously to contest the legitimacy of their disadvantageous economic and social position in society).[260] These mothers were, for example, highly resentful of the fact that they were:

1 Expected to live on meagre incomes

'I have to live on handouts from my family. Heating is the biggest problem. We have a meter which takes 50p per time and in the winter time you can put in £3 on just one fire with one bar and you go out into the hallway you might just as well go out to the North Pole, it's so cold. I feel resentful. I feel as though I should be able to buy decent food for myself which I can't do.'

'I could just buy the food for that week, pay the rent, gas, electricity and that was it, the money was gone. It used to annoy me because I couldn't add a little personal touch by doing something or buying a lamp or lampshade.'

2 Denied the opportunity to be independent

'I don't like living on social security. I don't like living off the state. I'd much rather be working.'

'Day care is so difficult to get. It's a case of me working, putting my child somewhere I'm not quite sure of or staying home. . . . I reckon there should be more day-care 'cause if I worked I'd be saving the state a lot of money.'

Given this more assertive tendency on the part of unmarried mothers, which owes much to the support and encouragement they have received from organizations such as The National Council for One Parent Families and Gingerbread, it is not surprising to find (as the following extract shows) that a number of mothers in this survey laid great stress on the fact that they had an entitlement to a decent standard of living.

'I'm doing a valuable job bringing up a member of the next generation. I've paid taxes in the past, I will pay taxes in the future. . . . It isn't a question of scrounging, it's a question of redistribution of resources.'
(Mother's opinion on why she was entitled to supplementary benefit)

Two important issues have been highlighted by this survey.

1 The need to distinguish between stigmatization and felt stigma.
2 The need for caution when one is confronted with evidence relating to felt stigma. (i.e. the absence of reports of felt stigma should not necessarily be taken to indicate that the general public and various institutional bodies have begun to adopt a more favourable attitude towards a particular stigmatized group. On the contrary, the absence of felt stigma reports may merely indicate that there has been a change in attitude on the part of the stigmatized rather than the stigmatizers.)

In conclusion, then, this chapter has attempted to demonstrate (through a case study of the unmarried mother) how the concept of stigma can be developed more fully by means of more detailed examinations of some of the various reasons why stigma has attached to certain welfare groups over the centuries. Appraisals of this kind inevitably lead one on to consider some of the wider functions of stigma in society. This theme will be taken up in the final chapter.

4 Stigma and social policy: wider dimensions

A number of commentators[1] have drawn attention to the atheoretical nature of much of the social administration literature. For example, Mishra contends that social administrators have, in general, tended to be far more concerned with intervention and reform than with theoretical issues.

> This reformist tradition is pragmatic and practical rather than theoretical and speculative. Its interest lies not so much in building a knowledge base about social welfare institutions as in understanding the nature and dimensions of a particular social problem – poverty, child abuse, homelessness – with a view to its solution. In short, the study of welfare is approached from an interventionist point of view: not academic knowledge *per se* but, rather, recommending a course of action or at least laying bare the choices facing a society with regard to a particular issue is the main objective. Given these practical concerns it is not surprising that social administration . . . deals far more in facts than in theories of welfare.[2]

Far greater attention has, however, been given to theoretical issues in recent years. This interest has been displayed in two inter-related ways. Firstly, a number of writers have attempted to clarify and refine some of the concepts most commonly referred to in discussions of social policy. By drawing attention to the complexities of concepts such as need[3] and equality,[4] these writers have significantly advanced the level of welfare theorizing. Secondly, emphasis has been given to the different ideological positions regarding the role and purpose of state welfare in contemporary society.[5] In particular, the emergence of Marxist analyses of the welfare state have done much to highlight the limitations of the institutional/residual approach to the study of social policy.[6]

The relationship between stigma and these theoretical developments will be the main subject matter of this final chapter. To this end, consideration will be given to two important issues:

1   The relationship between stigma and other 'welfare' concepts.
2   The social control function of stigma in contemporary society.

Finally, by way of conclusion, attention will be given to the question of whether stigma should be regarded as a key social policy concept.

The relationship between stigma and other 'welfare' concepts

As we saw in chapter 2, the fact that the concept of stigma has achieved such prominence in the field of social policy owes much to the efforts of those who can broadly be said to subscribe to the Fabian socialist or social democratic approach to welfare. From this perspective stigma has been commonly regarded as an unnecessary hindrance to the creation of a more just society.

Stigma and social justice

According to the Fabian socialists a more just society can be created by means of purposeful government intervention. It is argued, for example, that a government committed to social justice can, by pursuing policies of equality, gradually bring about a fundamental change in the very nature of society. As Tawney states, in discussing the achievements of Atlee's first post-war Labour government:

> the experience of 1945-50 established, I think, one important point. It showed that a capitalist economy is not the solid, monolithic block, to be endured as a whole, or overthrown as a

whole, that some simpletons suggested. It proved that a Socialist Government, with the public behind it, can change the power relations within the system, can ensure that a larger part of the resources yielded by it are devoted to raising the standard of life of the mass of the population, and can compel those directing it to work on lines which, left to themselves, they would not choose.[7]

Social policy is seen as having a key role to play in the creation of a more just society. According to Tawney,

It is possible, by means of a wisely planned system of communal provision, to ensure that the whole population enjoys, as far as environmental influences are concerned, equal opportunities of health and education, and is equally protected against the contingencies of life.[8]

In addition, as Titmuss points out, social policy can also serve to 'promote an individual's sense of identity, participation and community and allow him more freedom of choice for the expression of altruism . . .'[9]

For the Fabian socialists the pursuit of social justice is inextricably linked to the notion of need. This can clearly be seen if one considers their approach to the question of state welfare provision. They contend that the provision of state welfare services, on the basis of need, can help to counter the injustices and disadvantages which certain sections of the population are forced to endure as a result of the unfettered operation of the free market.

Given the importance that the Fabian socialists attach to 'institutional' forms of welfare, it is not surprising to find that they have been anxious to allay any fears that the public might have about using public welfare services. Accordingly, attempts have been made (e.g. the adoption of the principle of universalism; policies of positive discrimination – see pp. 31-4) to minimize the potentially negative impact that a factor such as stigma can have upon the public's willingness to use particular welfare services. Clearly, if public welfare services become tainted by stigma they are unlikely to advance the cause of social justice to any great extent.

It is important to note that the Fabian socialists' objection to stigma is not based solely upon the detrimental effect that this phenomenon can have upon both potential, and existing, welfare recipients. At the heart of their objection is the belief that no society can be regarded as socially just if it permits the stigmatization of certain of its minority groups.

Support for this contention can be found in Rawls's major work *A Theory of Justice*.[10] Rawls gives a good deal of attention to the principles of justice which individuals (under a 'veil of ignorance')[11] might formulate if they were given the opportunity to decide upon the way in which their society should be ordered. Rawls suggests that the following two principles might serve their purposes well:[12]

1   Each person is to have an equal right to the most extensive total system of equal basic liberties compatible with a similar system of liberty for all.

2   Social and economic inequalities are to be arranged so that they are both:
    (a) to the greatest benefit of the least advantaged, consistent with the just savings principle, and
    (b) attached to offices and positions open to all under conditions of fair equality of opportunity.

In constructing these principles, Rawls gives particular emphasis to the notion of primary goods. According to Rawls, all individuals require certain primary goods (e.g. rights, liberty, opportunities, power, income and wealth) if they are to enjoy a meaningful citizenship. As such, his principles of justice seek to maximise (as far as possible) every individual's access to such primary goods.

In terms of this particular discussion (i.e. the relationship between stigma and social justice) it is important to note that Rawls contends that self-respect is probably the most important primary good.[13]

> We may define self-respect (or self-esteem) as having two aspects. First of all . . . it includes a person's sense of his own value, his secure conviction that his conception of his good, his

plan of life, is worth carrying out. And second, self-respect implies a confidence in one's ability, so far as it is within one's power, to fulfil one's intentions. When we feel that our plans are of little value, we cannot pursue them with pleasure or take delight in their execution. Nor plagued by failure and self-doubt can we continue in our endeavours. It is clear then why self-respect is a primary good. Without it nothing may seem worth doing, or if some things have value for us, we lack the will to strive for them. All desire and activity becomes empty and vain, and we sink into apathy and cynicism. Therefore the parties in the orginal position would wish to avoid at almost any cost the social conditions that undermine self-respect.[14]

From this basis it is possible to infer that the stigmatization of certain individuals or minority groups would be incompatible with the pursuit of social justice.

However, this alleged incompatibility may be challenged by those who reject the possibility of formulating a contractual theory of justice. For example, Miller suggests that conceptions of social justice are likely to vary according to the primacy given to a particular underlying principle (e.g. rights, desert or need).[15] Thus, the stigmatization of certain individuals or groups might be deemed to be appropriate by those who adopt a desert-based theory of justice. For instance, from this perspective the stigmatization experienced by a relatively solvent family from both their neighbours (e.g. verbal abuse) and the local housing department (e.g. forcible eviction to a 'sink' estate) on the grounds of rent arrears could well be regarded as socially just.

Stigma, discretion and welfare rights

Over the centuries there has also been a strong link between the concepts of stigma and discretion, particularly in the realm of income-maintenance programmes. For example, it has only been in the comparatively recent past that the poor have been regarded as having some form of entitlement to financial support from public funds.[16] Previously, the acceptance or rejection of a request for public aid depended largely upon the discretionary benevolence, or otherwise, of local officials. This method of dispensing financial aid was clearly likely to have had a stigmatizing effect on some claimants. In particular, feelings of stigma were likely to have been engendered amongst those whose claims were refused on the grounds of some alleged character defect (e.g. the unemployed, unmarried mothers and other members of the 'undeserving' poor).

Attention has continued to be given to the stigmatizing potential of discretion in contemporary discussions of social policy. Before looking more closely at this debate, it is useful, firstly, to consider what is meant by the term discretion within the welfare field. For Davis: 'A public officer has discretion whenever the effective limits on his power leave him free to make a choice among possible courses of action or inaction.'[17] This definition is particularly appropriate for our present discussion given the fact that 'official discretion' has often been regarded as problematic not only by those who administer, but also by those who receive, various forms of welfare provision.

In looking at the notion of discretion within the welfare field, I think a distinction can be drawn between what can loosely be described as 'service' discretion and 'individual' discretion. Consider, for example, the provision of health care in this country. Although all health regions and districts are expected to have regard to the medical needs of all members of their target population, they will be able to exercise a good deal of discretion when deciding upon the precise facilities and services to be provided at any given time (service discretion). Discretion will also be exercised by medics during their consultations with patients. For instance, a GP has the authority to decide upon what initial treatment (if any) a patient requires (individual discretion). Both these forms of discretion can, either directly or indirectly, be potentially stigmatizing. In the case of the former (service discretion), a decision to give priority to patients with acute conditions may result in some patients with non-urgent complaints (e.g. hernias, varicose veins) coming to feel stigmatized. Similarly, in the case of the latter (individual discretion) a manual worker with a persistent backache may feel stigmatized when his GP implies (by suggesting that there is no good reason why he should not return to work immediately) that he may be malingering.

The negative dimensions of discretion have been highlighted by a number of commentators.[18] Not surprisingly (given the punitive forms of discretion which were employed in previous poor relief programmes) a good deal of this attention has been focussed on the supplementary benefits scheme.

The directives of the Supplementary Benefits Commission (which was abolished in 1980) (service discretion) and the apparently arbitrary nature of a number of the decisions made by individual officers (individual discretion) have been the subject of much criticism over the years. Concern has often been expressed, for example, about the guidelines which the SBC issued to its staff in relation to the payment of additional or exceptional allowances. For instance, the commission contended that exceptional needs payments for clothing should only be awarded (in general) when:[19]

   (a) the claimant has lived at or below supplementary benefits standards for some time before making a claim and may therefore be in difficulty over the replacement of major items;

   (b) there are dependent children (where ordinary clothing is concerned; school uniforms are the responsibility of local education authorities);

   (c) the claimant or one of his dependants is suffering from a chronic or serious disease where an adequate stock of warm clothing is essential, e.g. respiratory tuberculosis or other serious bronchial conditions;

   (d) hardship will result if a payment is not made to meet an urgent need.

These guidelines do not appear to offer much hope to certain 'short-term' claimants such as the single unemployed or childless couples under pensionable age. As such, it can justifiably be argued that this form of service discretion should be regarded as a form of stigmatization (i.e. some claimants are being seen as less worthy of additional support than others). However, claimants who have been refused additional allowances have tended to be far more critical of the official who actually dealt with their case than with the commission in general. Indeed, the discretion exercised by individual officers has been a major source of grievance for many claimants.[20]

SB officials are able to exercise a considerable degree of negative discretion in their work (i.e. they have the power to refuse, withhold or reduce benefit payments). For example, although such officials are not permitted (when processing a new claim) to arbitrarily decide on the amount of benefit that should be paid or the level of resources which should be taken into account for the purpose of determining entitlement, they are authorized to use their discretion in related matters (i.e. when deciding whether a claim for a rent allowance is 'excessive' or whether resources have been 'unnecessarily squandered' just prior to an application for benefit). In addition, SB officials can exercise negative discretion when:

(i) confronted with claimants who are suspected of defrauding the DHSS (e.g. claimants who neglect to inform the department that they are cohabiting with a wage earner or who fail to declare that they are in receipt of substantial part-time earnings).

(i) claims are submitted for exceptional circumstances additions (ECAs) or exceptional needs payments (ENAs).

Clearly, this type of negative individual discretion may cause some claimants to feel stigmatized. For example, a separated mother whose benefit is withheld because of a suspicion of cohabitation may well experience an intense feeling of stigma. Similarly, claimants who have had a request for an exceptional needs payment turned down may also feel stigmatized in certain circumstances. For instance, an unemployed man whose request for some new stair carpet is rejected may well feel stigmatized as a result of his experience, particularly if he discovers that other claimants in his locality have received awards for household items. Indeed, it has been suggested that some SB officers are likely to give vent to their own prejudices when making discretionary payments. As such, 'deserving' claimants (e.g. pensioners, the disabled) may find it relatively easy to obtain additional payments whilst the 'undeserving' (e.g. the unemployed, single parents) may experience considerable difficulties in this regard.

It is important to note, however, that highly stigmatizing negative forms of discretion also occur in other spheres of social policy. For example, a social worker may decide to curtail her much-appreciated visits to an elderly client on the grounds that her time can be spent more 'profitably' with other clients on her caseload. More significantly, social workers may employ negative forms of discretion when deciding which of their clients should receive financial aid (e.g. under section one of the 1963 Children and Young Persons Act) or material aid (e.g. under the 1970 Chronically Sick and Disabled Persons Act). Indeed, there has been growing concern expressed in recent years over the question as to whether social workers should be able to make the provision of financial assistance dependent upon improvements in the behaviour of their clients.[21]

One of the reasons why social workers and other welfare workers such as doctors and teachers may have been relatively immune from criticism relating to their discretionary powers may be linked to their professional status (i.e. they are generally seen to be using their 'professional judgment' as opposed to some form of arbitrary discretion). In contrast, relatively low-status employees such as SB officials have been continually portrayed as exercising their discretionary powers in an arbitrary, unprofessional manner.[22]

The stigmatizing nature of much welfare discretion, particularly in the field of income maintenance, has led a number of commentators to press for the introduction of a more extensive system of welfare rights.[23] As Jones points out, such advocates believe that once a 'right to welfare becomes a generally established conviction, then no stigma will attach to claimants or clients and that, conversely, without a basis of rights, welfare provision will inevitably be tainted with stigma.'[24] From this perspective, then, the establishment of welfare rights (by virtue of their capacity to enhance the self-esteem of those in need) is seen as being one of the most effective means for countering degrading forms of discretionary welfare provision (i.e. it is envisaged that individuals will eventually come to regard welfare services not as a form of charitable donation but as an entitlement of citizenship). As Jones states in a discussion of this issue:

> Charity precludes entitlement. The giving of charity is at the discretion of the charitable. The supplicant is, therefore,

dependent upon the will of the donor and has no right to complain if he does not receive; on the contrary, he should feel indebted when he does receive. The relationship between giver and receiver in charity is inherently unequal and it is understandable, therefore, that the receipt of charity should be thought to involve a loss of esteem both in one's own eyes and in those of others. By contrast, to receive what is one's right is to receive no more than one is entitled to expect, requires no debt of gratitude, and, in itself, involves no loss of status.[25]

It is open to question, though, whether a more extensive system of welfare rights will eradicate the stigma which has attached to discretionary forms of social service provision. For example, it is important to consider whether the establishment of welfare rights is intended to enhance the 'substantive' or merely the 'procedural' rights of individuals. As Adler and Asquith point out:

> Procedural rights refer to process – to a 'fair' trial, to having one's claims dealt with according to the rules or, in the absence of explicitly formulated rules, according to generally accepted conventions of natural justice. Substantive rights refer to outcomes – to the receipt of redundancy pay, or unemployment benefit at a given level for the unemployed, to the allocation of tenancies to homeless families or to medical (or social work) help of a certain kind to a sick person or someone with social or personal problems, etc. Most of those who have wished to limit discretion have wished to strengthen the procedural rights of those who are subject to it.[26]

Improvements in citizens' procedural welfare rights are unlikely to have any significant effect in terms of reducing the stigma which attaches to the receipt of public aid if the services or benefits being provided are of poor standard. For example, it would appear to be highly optimistic to expect an unemployed worker to retain his self-esteem if the level of his unemployment benefit compares unfavourably with the incomes of the lowest paid workers.

However, even if citizens' substantive welfare rights are dramatically improved there is no guarantee that this would have a positive effect on the self-esteem of social service recipients. For example, as was pointed out earlier (see p. 36), Pinker has suggested that the dependant are always likely to feel stigmatized in a society where market values predominate. If this assertion is correct, it is difficult to envisage how improvements in citizens' substantive rights can be expected to reduce the incidence of felt stigma amongst welfare recipients.

In addition, it should be noted that efforts to improve citizens' substantive welfare rights will only, at best, serve to remove one source of stigma in society (i.e. the stigma associated with the receipt of welfare benefits and services).[27] Such measures will do little to counter the stigma which has attached to individuals or groups with other negatively valued characteristics (see chapter 1).

It has also been suggested that a successful welfare rights campaign may have the unintended consequence of making the needy even more reluctant to apply for services to which they have no clear-cut entitlement. As Jones states:

the stronger the sense of entitlement, the stronger will be the sense of charity when that entitlement is exceeded. (There is, therefore, a danger that, while inducing people to think in terms of rights may make them more willing to claim that to which they believe they have a right, it will also make them more reluctant to receive anything to which they believe they have none.)[28]

Finally, it can be argued that some welfare rights advocates have, perhaps, tended to neglect the positive dimensions of welfare discretion. For example, in a discussion of the supplementary benefits scheme, Titmuss maintains that positive discretion (individualized justice) provides a necessary complement to the rights dimension of the service (proportional justice).

We need . . . individualised justice in order to allow a universal rights scheme, based on principles of equity, to be as precise and inflexible as possible. These characteristics of precision, inflexibility and universality depend for their sustenance and strength on the existence of some element of flexible, individualised justice. But they do not need stigma.[29]

Certainly, positive forms of welfare discretion have the potential to enhance the self-esteem of social service recipients. For example, the Supplementary Benefits Commission often used its discretionary powers in a humane and creative way (even to the extent, in one case, of providing funds for a new tyre for a man who had broken down on a motorway with a car-load of children).[30] Such positive forms of welfare discretion may also help in the identification of unmet need within the community, thereby aiding the development of a more comprehensive system of welfare rights. However, it is important to remember that the status-enhancing potential of positive welfare discretion may be seriously limited in a market economy. As Marshall notes:

> It would be nearer the truth to say that this notion of discretion as positive, personal and beneficient can only be fully realised in a 'welfare society', that is to say a society that recognises its collective responsibility to seek to achieve welfare, and not only to relieve destitution or eradicate penury.[31]

Stigma and rationing

The introduction of a comprehensive system of welfare rights is obviously likely to have serious resource implications. As Scrivens points out:

> For the past thirty years the British public have been able to receive free of charge or at a very reduced price, services such as health, education and personal social services. Expenditure on these services has increased over this period and has been accompanied by parallel increases in consumption and apparent demand which has mostly exceeded the resources available. The effect of demand increasing at a faster rate than available resources has led to concern about the ways in which the resources are allocated among the demands, and concern about how decisions are made to exclude some demands altogether. The methods by which these objectives are achieved have become known as rationing processes.[32]

A number of commentators have highlighted the various ways

in which rationing operates within the sphere of social policy.[33] From such discussions it is possible to identify seven principal devices which have been used to ration welfare services.

1 Charges[34]

The imposition of charges can stem the demand for a particular welfare service in two main ways. Firstly, charging can help to curb 'frivolous' forms of demand (i.e. the demands made by those who aren't 'really in need'). Secondly, and more importantly, charges can serve to limit the demands made by those in need who are unwilling or unable to contribute towards the cost of the provision they require.

2 Eligibility regulations

It is also possible to ration social services by means of highly restrictive eligibility criteria (e.g. qualifications, age, residence). For example, many local housing authorities have found residential qualifications to be extremely effective in terms of limiting the 'demand' for publicly rented housing.

3 Delay

Delay has also proved to be a highly effective way of rationing welfare services. Such delays may be organized and explicit (e.g. queues, waiting lists) or unplanned and implicit (e.g. a decision by a social worker to defer an elderly client's request for a residential home place).

4 Deflection

Potential social service recipients may also find that their requests for particular welfare services are 'deflected' (i.e. they are advised by one agency to apply elsewhere for the service they require). For instance, a woman with persistent backache may be advised by her GP to visit a local osteopath.

5 Dilution

Services can also be rationed by means of dilution. As Parker points out:

> There are many variations upon this theme. If more has to be
> done with the same resources standards have to be lowered

and the service spread more thinly. In the home help service, for instance, extra demand is not often deflected, turned away or kept waiting. Instead the amount of time allocated to each recipient is reduced.[35]

6 Inadequate information
Poor publicity can also be deemed to be a form of rationing. There is always likely to be a shortfall in the take-up rate for various benefits and services if potential recipients are inadequately informed about the availability of such provision.

7 Deterrence
The final rationing device that merits attention is that of deterrence. In this case, attempts are made to restrict the demand for a particular welfare benefit or service by making the receipt of such provision deliberately unattractive. Such deterrence can take a variety of forms (e.g. censorious staff attitudes, complex administrative procedures, forbidding offices). As Parker notes, the image acquired by a particular welfare service over the years may be of considerable importance in terms of its deterrent potential. 'How people *imagine* they will be treated, and what they *believe* they are entitled to may reflect the experience of a previous generation, and effectively stop them seeking assistance.'[36]

The notion of deterrence is the key element in the link between the concepts of stigma and rationing. Over the centuries, secular authorities have deliberately stigmatized certain sections of the poor in an effort to limit the demand for public aid. For example, under the 1834 Poor Law Amendment Act, relief was only provided for those who were willing to submit to a quite brutal form of personal and familial humiliation – namely the workhouse test (see p. 26). Although this particular form of welfare stigmatization has fallen into disrepute, other forms have persisted.

In examining the ways in which stigma has been used as a form of deterrence in contemporary social policy it is useful to distinguish between 'formal' and 'informal' procedures. An example of the former would be explicit references to the need for deterrence in official policy statements, directives or reports. In general, little reference has been made (except in the case of fraud or other kinds of abuse) to the need for deterrence in such documents. This absence should not, however, be taken to indicate that present-day governments are now unwilling to use stigma as a means of rationing welfare services. For instance, it is commonly acknowledged that substantial numbers of claimants are deterred from claiming the supplementary benefit to which they are entitled (the take-up rate for SB was only 70 per cent in 1979 according to official estimates[37]) because of considerations of stigma (see pp. 42-5). The failure of successive governments to deal effectively with this problem can be explained in part by their reluctance to dispense with stigma as a rationing device. Indeed, the new housing benefit scheme (under which claimants' rent allowances are 'paid direct') provides yet another example of central government's willingness to reinforce the stigmatizing propensities of the SB scheme (i.e. claimants are now deemed to lack even the necessary responsibility to pay their rent regularly).

At an 'informal' level, stigma is often used to restrict demand for welfare services. For example, patients who make frequent use of the services of their GP for minor complaints are likely to be reminded either implicitly ('I hope you're not becoming a hypochondriac') or explicitly ('You housewives are continually wasting my time') that their requests for consultations are 'unreasonable'. Similarly, a child who requests the opportunity to sit an 'O' level examination paper may be dissuaded from this course of action by the stigmatizing remark of a teacher ('You're only CSE standard').

Although there are difficulties in estimating the overall impact that stigma has on potential or existing welfare recipients, it can safely be concluded that its effect is far from minimal in terms of restricting demand for social service provision.

Stigma and participation

'Consumer participation' represents one possible way of combating the stigma associated with the receipt of public welfare. As was mentioned in chapter 2, stigma has tended to attach to three particular social services – namely, social security (especially the means-tested sector), local authority housing and the personal social services (see p. 40).

The introduction of some form of consumer participation would appear to be particularly apt in the case of these services given the fact that the vast majority of the recipients of such provision are unlikely to be in a position (owing to the nature or extent of their needs) to withdraw their 'custom' in the event of experiencing any of the stigma commonly associated with public dependency.

Consumer participation can help to reduce the possibility of welfare stigmatization in four main ways. Firstly, it can provide welfare recipients with an opportunity to express any grievances they might have about the quality of the services they are receiving. For example, consumers may want to draw attention to the stigmatizing nature of certain administrative procedures or highlight the patronizing treatment they have received from certain officials.

Secondly, consumer participation can help welfare administrators and professionals to minimize the stigma that might arise as a result of some form of misunderstanding on the part of those in need. For instance, an elderly person in receipt of a supplementary pension may have been experiencing feelings of stigma as a result of an erroneous belief that her allowance would be withdrawn if she permitted a relative to stay with her for a week.

Thirdly, the stigma that consumers are liable to experience as a result of being subjected to various forms of 'professional power' may also be reduced by more extensive forms of participation. For example, social workers may attempt to limit the negative aspects of their professional powers by taking their clients more fully into their confidence (e.g. by instigating joint consultations about the purpose and aims of the casework relationship).

Finally, the self-esteem of welfare consumers may be considerably enhanced if they are invited to become more fully involved in the decision-making processes of the various services which they use.

Consumer participation has certainly been a popular theme in social policy in recent decades. For example, the Seebohm Report on the personal social services stressed the need for effective forms of consumer participation.

Implicit in the idea of a community-oriented family service is a belief in the importance of the maximum participation of individuals and groups in the community in the planning, organisation and provision of the social services. This view rests not only upon the working out of democratic ideas at the local level, but relates to the identification of need, the exposure of defects in the services and the mobilisation of new resources. The consumer of the personal social services has limited choice among services and thus needs special opportunity to participate.[38]

Similarly, the 1973 NHS act provided for the establishment of Community Health Councils which were required to feed back local opinion and to act as 'visitors' to the health amenities in their locality.[39]

However, the effectiveness of such measures (in terms of reducing welfare stigma) is likely to depend to a large extent on the type of participation that is eventually established. For instance, Arnstein has argued that there are various types of 'participation' ranging from manipulation and therapy (non-participation) to informing, consultation and placation (tokenism) and finally to partnership, delegated power and citizen control (citizen power).[40] It can justifiably be argued that consumer participation within the social services has never extended far beyond the tokenism stage. Participation in the field of social policy has always been tightly controlled from 'above' (i.e. what constitutes a representative view or a justifiable grievance tends to be decided by those in authority). For example, although local housing authorities have actively encouraged tenant participation they have been extremely reluctant to concede to tenants' demands for a greater say over such matters as the level of rents, new building programmes or tenancy allocation procedures.[41]

The cosmetic nature of much social service participation has led a number of commentators to speculate about some of the underlying reasons for the introduction of such measures. For example, Plant et al. have suggested that:

Co-operative participation . . . does not challenge the structure of power and the existing distribution of benefits and burdens in society, but, on the contrary, it may well provide procedures for practical socialization in which the values of those who hold the power in society are learned and internalized by those who are involved in the participation. In this way people may learn to identify their needs or modify their identification of them as a result of internalizing the goals, norms and conventions of the existing social and political order through participatory schemes.[42]

From this perspective, it would seem highly optimistic to believe that welfare stigmatization can be dramatically reduced by the introduction of limited forms of consumer participation. On the contrary, the limited nature of existing forms of consumer participation in the social services only serves to highlight the need for consideration to be given to wider issues – such as the role and purpose of social policy in contemporary society.

The social control function of stigma in contemporary society

Ever since it was first coined by Ross[43] in the late nineteenth century the term social control has figured prominently in sociological[44] (and, much more recently, social policy[45]) literature. Despite its relative popularity, the theoretical development of this term has been somewhat stifled because of doubts about its value neutrality as a sociological concept. For example, some critics on the left have argued that because the concept was formulated and developed within a highly conservative sociological tradition it has become too closely associated with order or consensus models of society. In contrast, others have expressed disquiet about the more recent association of the term with social repression in western society. Limitations on the use of this concept should, however, be resisted as the term can usefully be employed in the study of any community or society. As Donajgrodzki states: 'The use of social control, like the concept of "socialisation" does not imply adherence to a sociology based on any particular ideology.'[46]

Stigma can justifiably be regarded as a major form of social control in contemporary society. Indeed, Pinker believes that:

The imposition of stigma is the commonest form of violence

used in democratic societies. Stigmatization is slow, unobtrusive and genteel in its effect, so much so, that when the stigmatized hit back physically in Londonderry or Chicago they can technically be accused of being the first to resort to force. Stigmatization is a highly sophisticated form of violence in so far as it is rarely associated with physical threats or attack. It can best be compared to those forms of psychological torture in which the victim is broken psychically and physically but left to all outward appearances unmarked.[47]

In general, stigmatization has tended to be regarded as an extreme form of psychological social control (i.e. persistent, negative, psychological sanctioning). It is useful, therefore, to look in a little more detail at the way in which psychological sanctions can be used as a form of social control.

At an informal level, it can be argued that virtually all members of society will resort, at some time or other, to the use of psychological sanctions in order to exert social control. This form of disapproval may be expressed in a variety of ways. Displeasure may, for instance, frequently be displayed in a non-verbal way. To be on the receiving end of a solemn facial expression, an outright glare or a 'forced' smile is likely to alert all of us to the possibility that our present or past conduct has caused offence. Confirmation of this possibility may lead many of us not only to offer an apology to the offended party but also to make an undertaking to improve our behaviour in the future (a variety of factors are, however, likely to determine the precise response adopted in any situation e.g. the relationship between the actors concerned). If this relatively minor form of psychological control fails to induce conformity, it is possible that a more direct type of sanction will be employed. In such circumstances, individuals may be directly informed about the unacceptable nature of some aspect of their conduct. For example, a woman may reprimand her former husband for failing to make regular maintenance payments. In this situation the woman concerned may attempt to induce feelings of shame in her ex-spouse (by drawing attention to the considerable hardship that their children are being forced to endure because of his neglect) in the hope that this will lead him to fulfil his obligations in a more satisfactory manner in the future. Such shaming can, of course, be intensified. In this particular case the woman concerned could decide to exert further pressure on her ex-husband by informing others of his reprehensible conduct.

Other types of psychological sanctions which are commonly used in informal social situations include snubbing, ridicule and ostracization. Snubbing can take various forms:

(i) A deliberate decision to engage only in the most superficial conversation with those individuals of whom one disapproves. (Former lovers who – having parted on less than favourable terms – find themselves obliged to engage in conversation with one another at a subsequent social gathering often employ this form of snubbing.)

(ii) The withdrawal of an invitation. (A university may decide to withdraw a lecture invitation because of the highly contentious political views of the prospective speaker.)

(iii) The return of a gift. (An elderly man may decide to return the birthday present he has received from his daughter in order to register some form of protest about her infrequent visits.)

Ridicule is another prominent form of psychological sanctioning. Most of us have been instigators of, as well as targets for, some form of ridicule. Individuals who stray a little too far from existing group norms may be subjected to relatively mild forms of ridicule. For example, a junior typist, who spends her lunch breaks reading literary criticism rather than engaging in other activities, is likely to find that her less academically inclined colleagues will make occasional jokes about her intellectual pursuits. In addition, individuals who conform too exactly to a particular norm may also experience mild forms of ridicule. As Roucek points out by way of illustration:

The college professor who is so typical as to meet every expectation which goes with the stereotype of his calling may be laughed at for his typicality. The 'Joe College' who looks and acts exactly as a college student is expected to act may thereby become the butt of many jokes. Such application of ridicule is aimed at making their subjects more 'human' and therefore less perfect in their roles.[48]

In other situations, individuals may be subjected to much harsher forms of ridicule. For example, in their interaction with one another, children will often use quite severe forms of ridicule as a means of social control. Accordingly, a child who attempts to curry favour with her teachers may well find herself subjected to intense ridicule from her classmates. Adults, on the other hand, tend to use severe forms of ridicule in a much more selective fashion. Indeed, they often reserve this form of disapproval exclusively for those individuals who have behaved in deceitful or hypocritical ways. For example, an ex-serviceman who has frequently let it be known that he was decorated for gallantry during his commission in the army may find himself subjected to considerable ridicule when it is revealed that he received no such award during what was, in reality, a rather undistinguished military career, notable only for the fact that it had been brought to a premature end as a result of a dishonourable discharge.

Another important psychological sanction which individuals are likely to experience is ostracization. For example, a man who refuses to support a union strike call in furtherance of a wage claim may well find that he is 'sent to Coventry' when his colleagues return to work after the dispute has been resolved. Similarly, a mother who is known to have neglected her children may find that her applications for membership of local women's organizations are continually turned down.

In many circumstances informal psychological sanctions can justifiably be regarded as 'positive' forms of social control – i.e. they are intended to induce conformity amongst those individuals who are deemed to have strayed too far from some particular behavioural norm. However, these sanctions can also be used in a negative way (stigmatization). For example, individuals with conduct stigmas are likely to be subjected to a whole range of psychological sanctions on the grounds that they constitute a threat to cherished norms and values. Accordingly, a homosexual may find that he is continually snubbed by his neighbours, ridiculed by local children and ostracized by work associates. In such cases, psychological sanctions can be said to serve two main purposes:

(i) They enable individuals to express their personal disapproval of certain types of conduct.

(ii) The attention of the public can be drawn to the fact that a particular individual has a serious character defect.

'Negative' forms of psychological sanctioning are even likely to be experienced by those with courtesy stigmas (see pp. 9, 16). For example, a woman may find that her neighbours and friends shun her after she has informed them that her husband is receiving psychiatric treatment at the local hospital.

Exposure to negative psychological sanctions may induce some individuals (who would, in general, tend to be acceptors rather than rejectors – see pp. 18-20) to seek ways of improving their public image (in such circumstances negative sanctions can be said to have had unintended 'positive' effects). For example, in the hope of regaining some form of social acceptance, an ex-convict may offer to organize fund-raising activities for various local charities. However, as was noted earlier, it may prove very difficult for such individuals to regain complete social acceptance (see p. 19).

In turning to the question of formal psychological sanctions it is useful, for the purpose of illustration, to examine certain aspects of the law enforcement process. Within this sphere, relatively mild psychological sanctions are often administered. For instance, a motorist who commits a minor traffic infringement is much more likely (at least in certain areas) to receive a stern lecture ('words of advice') from a police officer than to be formally charged with the particular offence. In situations of this kind the mere threat of a court appearance is often sufficient to prompt the offender concerned to make an undertaking to drive more carefully in future.

Criminal prosecutions, by way of contrast, frequently involve the use of more punitive psychological sanctions. Indeed, given their potential for tarnishing personal reputation,[49] court appearances can usefully be regarded as a highly effective form of social control in their own right. Accordingly, most of us will seek to minimize such appearances by behaving, whenever possible, in a law-abiding way.

A formal stigma is the most severe psychological sanction that can be imposed within the court setting. A conviction for an offence such as theft, soliciting or murder carries with it an inherent stigma. To be officially degraded[50] in this way can often have a detrimental effect on an individual's self-image. As Matza argues:

> To be signified a thief does not assure the continuation of such pursuits; but it *does* add to the meaning of a theft in the life of the perpetrator. . . . to be signified a thief is to lose the blissful identity of one who among other things happens to have committed a theft. It is a movement, however gradual, towards being a thief and representing theft.[51]

In addition, an individual's negative self-image can often be reinforced by the reactions of others. Those formally labelled as criminals may for example:

   (i) receive hostile reactions from their family, friends and other associates;
  (ii) experience difficulties in obtaining employment and/or accommodation;
 (iii) be continually subjected to official scrutiny (e.g. by the police).

There is likely to be considerable disagreement over the question of whether the imposition of formal psychological sanctions should be regarded as a positive or negative form of social control. For example, there are grounds for contending that criminal convictions are essentially a positive form of social control (i.e. this sanction enables social disapproval to be expressed in a way that maximizes the possibility of rehabilitation). Indeed, a number of measures have been introduced for the specific purpose of rehabilitation. For instance, the Rehabilitation of Offenders Act (1974) provides special forms of legal protection for 'rehabilitated' offenders. As Walker points out:

> A rehabilitated offender must be treated for all purposes in law as if he had not committed, been charged with, prosecuted for, convicted of, or sentenced for the offence in question, so that he can safely deny this, and sue for defamation if it is alleged in a defamatory way.[52]

In a similar vein, children are often given special forms of legal protection when they are brought before a juvenile court (e.g. the media are expressly prohibited from identifying any of the children who are required to attend these hearings).[53]

In contrast, though, the fact that many individuals have experienced severe forms of economic and social hardship as a result of a criminal conviction provides powerful support for the viewpoint that these sanctions should properly be regarded as a negative form of social control (i.e. certain types of offenders tend to be excluded from full social participation).

The impact of formal labelling has also been given serious consideration within the field of social policy. This is certainly not surprising given that most welfare service users are likely to be categorized in either a general (patient, client, claimant) or specific (homeless person, neurotic, educationally sub-normal) way. The question that concerns us here is whether some of these classifications can be used for the purpose of psychological social control. In certain cases there would appear to be valid reasons for supporting this supposition. For example, an individual who is informed that she requires compulsory psychiatric care is likely to experience a severe loss of self-esteem. As Schur remarks:

> Mental illness designations are highly stigmatizing and thus impose reductions in power and social standing . . . despite the undoubted benefits that voluntary psychotherapy may confer, and notwithstanding the good intentions of most therapists, compulsory impositions of psychiatric 'help' represent a significant mode of social control. Particularly when the state becomes implicated in its public uses, psychiatry may become a potent tool for controlling any or all individuals deemed to threaten or undermine the (political as well as social or cultural) status quo.[54]

In this passage, Schur also alludes to the principal argument that has been put forward to counter the suggestion made above. Proponents of this latter perspective contend that welfare categorizations are used solely for benevolent purposes. For instance, a classification such as 'educationally sub-normal' should not, it is argued, be viewed in a negative light. On the contrary, such a classification is seen as being extremely useful in terms of helping to ensure that children of limited intelligence are

placed in an educational environment that best serves their needs
(i.e. a school in which the other pupils have similar intellectual
capabilities). In short, from this perspective, welfare classifications are seen as being an entirely favourable form of social
control. However, the fact that many individuals have reported
feeling stigmatized as a result of welfare labelling[55] tends to
suggest that such categorizations should, at the very least, be
regarded as an unintentional form of negative, psychological
social control.

It is important to note that physical (e.g. bodily assaults and
other related forms of coercion such as imprisonment humiliation and
enforced exile) and economic (e.g. threat of unemployment,
fines) sanctions have also been, and continue to be, used for the
purpose of maintaining social control in society. Indeed, in some
instances, more than one type of sanction has been used for the
purpose of social control. For example, many of the punishments
meted out to the 'undeserving' poor in the sixteenth century (see
p. 25) were intended to be both physically and psychologically
painful (see Figure 4.1).

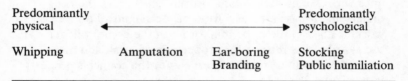

Figure 4.1 An example of combined physical and psychological
sanctions: the punishment of the 'undeserving' poor in the
sixteenth century

Psychological sanctions are also frequently used in conjunction
with physical and/or economic penalties in contemporary society.
For instance, in the field of international relations, a government
in one country may decide to use physical (armed aggression),
economic (trade embargo) and psychological (cutting of diplo-
matic ties) sanctions in order to exert control over another nation
state. Similarly, in the area of criminal justice psychological
sanctions (official labelling disseminated via the media) will often
be combined with either economic (fines) or physical (imprisonment) penalties.

Finally, although the term stigmatization has generally come to be associated with negative forms of psychological sanctioning, it should be remembered that the term can also be used in a much broader way. For example, any discussion of the stigmatization of ethnic minorities would necessitate consideration being given to the use of economic (e.g. the discriminatory recruitment policies of some employers) and physical (e.g. police harassment of black youths) as well as psychological (e.g. verbal insults, snubs) sanctions.

As was mentioned earlier (see the relevant sections in chapters 2 and 3) an appreciation of this wider perspective (i.e. the inclusion of physical and economic forms of discrimination) is useful when analysing welfare stigmatization. Consider, for instance, the case of local authority housing. Although the harsher aspects of the tenancy agreements imposed by the early 'philanthropists' have all but withered away, contemporary council tenants continue to be subjected to quite stringent forms of control. As Ginsburg argues:

> The local housing authority . . . manages tenants in accord-
> ance with the dictates of landlordism, and council housing
> management has acted as a form of social control of the
> working class in the hope that 'order in the home' will generate
> social order and respect for property in general, and the
> prompt payment of rent and respect for the council's property
> in particular.[56]

The furtherance of these aims has almost inevitably resulted in the adoption of stigmatizing administrative procedures. For example, in terms of allocation decisions, emphasis may be placed on the 'deserving' or 'undeserving' qualities of prospective tenants. Applicants who are assessed as being clean, quiet, respectable and improbable rent defaulters are likely to receive preferential treatment, at least in terms of the accommodation they are offered, than those with 'less eligible' characteristics. In addition, tenants who incur the displeasure of their local housing department by falling behind with their rent payments without 'good cause' or by behaving in an 'anti-social' way are likely to be stigmatized in a quite explicit way (e.g. forcible eviction).

The social control function of welfare stigmatization will be given further attention in the final section of this chapter which will, by way of conclusion, be concerned with the question of whether or not stigma should be regarded as a key social policy concept.

Stigma: a key concept in social policy?

One of the main aims of this book has been to challenge the assumption that stigma is some kind of 'natural' entity which can be examined in isolation from the economic and social structure of a given society. The fact that the concept of stigma has rarely been subjected to critical appraisal in its own right has tended to perpetuate the idea that the reasons for, and the effects of, stigma are self-evident.

Any attempt to link a society's prevailing pattern of stigmatiz-ation with its underlying economic and social structure necessi-tates some initial attention being given to the various aspects of stigma. Accordingly, in chapter 1 distinctions were made between stigmas, stigma recognition, stigmatization, felt stigma, responses to stigma acknowledgment, stigma disavowal and stigma management. A number of important issues were highlighted in this chapter. For example, it was argued that the process of stigmatization need not necessarily involve overt forms of hostility. In contrast to those with conduct stigmas (who are likely to be subjected to harassment and verbal abuse because of the 'blameworthy' nature of their 'failings'), the 'physically' stigmatized are unlikely (in general) to be treated in such an overtly hostile manner. However, they are likely to be stigma-tized in other ways (e.g. over-sympathetic or inhibited responses from normals; denial of adequate educational and employment opportunities). In addition, it was pointed out that it should not be assumed that all individuals who possess a stigma will automatically feel stigmatized. Many stigmatized individuals are likely, for example, to 'reject' (and resent) any suggestion that they should be denied full social acceptance. Indeed, in recent years collective forms of rejection have become commonplace. For instance (to cite just one case), people with physical impairments have formed pressure groups in an effort to publicize the various ways in which they are systematically 'disabled' by the very way in which economic and social activity is organized in society. The possibility of serious conflict between stigmatizers and the stigmatized serves to underlie the fact that any pattern of stigmatization is likely to further or sustain the interests of certain groups and classes at the expense of others.

The wider functions of stigma (i.e. its potential for bolstering the prevailing economic and social order) have tended to be somewhat neglected in the social administration literature (see chapter 2). This is not altogether surprising given the dominance of a problem-solving ethos within this field of study (i.e. attention has tended to be given to the notion of stigma for practical – e.g. the adverse effect that this phenomenon can have upon the take-up rate for various means-tested, state welfare benefits and services – as opposed to theoretical reasons). Indeed, the concern which has been expressed by some commentators about the theoretical relevance, and the practical applicability, of the concept of stigma for the study of social policy can be linked to the 'problem-orientated' nature of the social administration approach to this phenomenon (i.e. failure to appreciate the wider dimensions of stigma).

It is important, however, to give due credit to the strengths of the 'social administration' approach to stigma. By highlighting the stigmatizing propensities of social service provision, social administrators have played a major role in various campaigns for welfare reforms. At the heart of this approach has been a genuine commitment to the needs and aspirations of the various underprivileged members of society. By pressing for the intro-duction of more enlightened forms of social policy provision (e.g. improved levels of benefits, non-stigmatized administrative procedures), 'traditional' social administrators have shown a commendable desire to create a more humane type of society.

In order to emphasize the importance of linking welfare stigmatization with the economic and social structure of society, attention was given (in chapter 3) to some of the reasons why, and the various ways in which, one particular 'welfare' group – unmarried mothers – has been stigmatized over the centuries. It was argued that stigma has tended to attach to the unmarried mother for two main reasons:

(i) The challenge they present to Christian teaching on

marriage and family life.
(ii) The 'blameworthy' nature of their dependency on public aid (this was identified as the most important reason as to why stigma has attached to the unmarried mother, especially since 1500).

Although twentieth century unmarried mothers have not been subjected to the harsher forms of secular stigmatization which were all too familiar to their predecessors, it would be premature, it was contended, to claim that this group had achieved anything approaching full social acceptance. Indeed, the fact that unmarried motherhood continues to be regarded as a social problem (a view which has been reinforced, either intentionally or unintentionally, by a number of researchers working in the fields of sociology, psychology and social administration – see pp. 100-22) has tended to perpetuate the stigmatization of this group.

It is important to note that the continued stigmatization of unmarried mothers (and other welfare groups) is unlikely to elicit universal condemnation. On the contrary, there is likely to be considerable support amongst certain sections of the community for the introduction of more extensive forms of welfare stigmatization. With this in mind, it is useful to consider the question of welfare stigmatization from three divergent theoretical perspectives – namely – the anti-collectivist, the Fabian socialist (social democratic) and the Marxist.

The anti-collectivists (e.g. Hayek, Friedman and Seldon)[57] do not believe that there is any need for extensive institutional forms of state welfare provision. Instead, they contend that citizens' welfare needs can best be met by the free market and the family unit. It is acknowledged, however, that a minority of citizens will be unable to obtain support from these two sources. Accordingly, it is accepted that state welfare services, of a strictly residual kind, should be provided. (Such provision is advocated on the grounds of: (i) humanitarianism; (ii) neighbourhood effects – situations in which it is inappropriate or impossible for market forces to operate;[58] (iii) political stability – the prevention of civil disorder).

Not surprisingly (given their belief that state welfare services should only be provided for those in 'genuine' need), the anti-collectivists are firmly convinced that potential recipients of state support should be required to undergo stringent eligibility tests. For example, in the absence of a negative income tax scheme, the anti-collectivists believe that certain forms of means-testing are necessary in order to minimize the possibility of abuse in state social security programmes. However, the stigmatizing potential of such procedures tend to be ignored by free market advocates. Indeed, as was pointed out earlier (see p. 41), a number of anti-collectivists tend to favour the use of explicit forms of welfare stigmatization in certain cases (e.g. the voluntary unemployed).

The fact that the anti-collectivists tend (either explicitly or implicitly) to accept the need for potentially stigmatizing forms of state welfare provision reflects their generally favourable opinion of the existing economic and social order (though it should be remembered that they would like to see a substantial reduction in the level of public expenditure and an end to what they regard as completely unnecessary governmental regulation of commercial activity). In particular, the anti-collectivists believe that public commitment towards the dominant value system (with its stress on independence, self-help and competition) must be maintained if economic objectives such as high levels of growth (which, it is alleged, will benefit all members of society) are to be achieved. As such, the anti-collectivists tend to regard the existing pattern of welfare stigmatization (which is designed to limit the demand for public aid) as both necessary and just.

Unlike the anti-collectivists, the Fabian socialists (e.g. Tawney, Crosland and Titmuss)[59] do not believe that welfare stigmatization is either necessary or desirable. According to advocates of this latter perspective, the existence of welfare stigmatization can be directly linked to the primacy that has continually been given to economic as opposed to social values (e.g. equality, co-operation and fellowship). Importantly, though, the Fabian socialists contend that it is possible to redress the balance in favour of social imperatives. The state is seen as having a crucial role to play in this process. For example, Crosland contends that:

> the state and the political authority have removed a wide, and strategically decisive, segment of economic decisions out of the sphere of purely market influences, and made them subject to deliberate political control. Through fiscal policy, and a variety

of physical, legislative, and financial controls, the state now consciously regulates (or seeks to regulate) the level of employment, the distribution of income, the rate of accumulation, and the balance of payments; and its actions heavily influence the size of industries, the pattern of output, and the direction of investment-decisions. The passive state has given way to the active, or at least the ultimately responsible, state; the political authority has emerged as the final arbiter of economic life. . . .[60]

This belief in the benevolent potential of state intervention has led the Fabian socialists to press for the introduction of universal, socially integrative, need-based, public welfare services (complemented where necessary by positive forms of discrimination). It is contended that reformist measures of this kind can effectively counter the stigma that continues to attach to the recipients of state welfare provision.

The Marxists (e.g. Ginsburg, Gough and Navarro),[61] by way of contrast, reject the assertion that welfare stigmatization can be eradicated by the introduction of social reforms. Unlike the Fabian socialists, they do not believe that the 'state machine' can be used to challenge the long-term economic interests of the capitalist class.[62] As Gough points out:

The common element in all Marxist theories of the state, which distinguishes them from all other theories, is the subordination of the state to the particular mode of production and to the dominant class or classes within that mode. In other words, the *economically* dominant class is also the *politically* dominant or *ruling* class.[63]

Accordingly, the Marxists (although they would be the first to acknowledge the part played by the working class in terms of securing welfare reforms) contend that state welfare services have tended (in terms of their implementation and administration) to reflect the interests of the dominant economic class. Welfare stigmatization is thus seen as helping to sustain and reinforce the individualistic and competitive ethos of capitalist society. For example, the Marxists claim that stigmatizing, social security administrative procedures are designed not only to deter those in need from seeking public aid but also to reinforce the association between public dependency and inferiority. As Ginsburg states:

> Claimants are subject to expectations which stigmatize them as poor whatever they do, although the stigma is not as strong perhaps as in the days of the poor law. It is not an anachronism nor a vestige of the poor law which can be eradicated by administrative reform and repackaging. The stigma of being a claimant is an essential ingredient in a system designed to discipline claimants and to promote the values of insurance and individual and family self-help.[64]

The dispute between the Fabian socialists and the Marxists over the question of whether welfare stigmatization can be eradicated by means of social reform can be linked quite neatly to the earlier discussion on the unmarried mother. The Fabian socialists would argue that the stigma which has attached to this group (because of their 'blameworthy' public dependency) can be countered by well-formulated and skilfully executed social policies. A good deal of evidence can be cited in support of this assertion. For instance, a number of social policy initiatives during this century have done much to improve the life chances and, one would assume, the self-esteem of unmarried mothers (see pp. 89-98). However, the fact that the vast majority of unmarried mothers have continued to experience severe forms of economic and social deprivation tends to suggest that the stigma-reducing potential of welfare reforms may be seriously limited. If this is indeed the case then the Marxist approach to welfare stigmatization would appear to be particularly worthy of consideration. From this perspective, the stigmatization of any group would be expected to continue if it could be said to serve the interests of the dominant economic class. Certainly, it seems quite plausible to argue that the continued stigmatization of the unmarried mother would benefit the capitalist class to some degree (i.e. from the viewpoint of the capitalist class, unmarried mothers are likely to be regarded – because of their inability, in general, to remain economically independent – as an unnecessary burden on the productive sector of society). Accordingly, the continued stigmatization of unmarried mothers (an eventuality which would help to sustain the impression that such women are not only socially unacceptable but also undeserving of public support) is likely to be welcomed by members of the capitalist class on the grounds that such action is likely to ensure that only minimal forms of 'scarce' resources are devoted to the needs of this economically 'unproductive' group. Indeed, members of this class are likely to oppose any attempts to eradicate such stigmatization. For example, if it became widely accepted that unmarried mothers have a right to enjoy a standard of living which compares favourably with other, more affluent, sections of the community, it seems likely that attention would eventually have to be focused on the very way in which the organization of contemporary society militates against this group's interests (i.e. the mode of production, the position of women in society, the role of the family and so forth). It can be argued, therefore, that the stigmatization of unmarried mothers (and other negatively regarded groups) can help to forestall meaningful debate about the distribution of economic and social power in society.

The great strength of the Marxist approach is that it serves to highlight the importance of examining the link between welfare (and all other forms of) stigmatization and the mode of production. For instance, it seems likely, at least in theory, that there will be a significant difference in the pattern of stigmatization which prevails in a capitalist as opposed to a socialist society (i.e. groups which are prone to stigmatization in the former, such as the disabled and the unemployed, are likely to be treated far more favourably in the latter). Clearly, further research is needed in order to establish the strength, or otherwise, of this potential link between patterns of stigmatization and the mode of production. For example, such an association would appear to be far more easy to establish in the case of disability or race[65] than in the case of either homosexuality[66] or prostitution.

In conclusion, then, the concept of stigma (provided that it is not simply regarded as a 'technical' problem which can be resolved by a few administrative reforms) is likely to remain a key concept for both students and practitioners in the field of social policy. Indeed, an appreciation of the concept of stigma is essential if one wishes to examine, in a critical fashion, the frequently voiced claims about the establishment of a welfare state or a welfare society. For example, a society which permits the widespread stigmatization of groups such as ethnic minorities, the unemployed or single parents can hardly be said to be one in which the 'welfare ethic' predominates.

Notes

Chapter 1   The anatomy of stigma

1   My thanks to Bleddyn Davies for suggesting this title.
2   See C. Saunders, *Social Stigma of Occupations*.
3   R.M. Titmuss, *Social Policy: An Introduction*, p. 44.
4   J. Cumming and E. Cumming, 'On the stigma of mental illness', in S. Palmer and A.S. Linsky (eds), *Rebellion and Retreat*, pp. 449-50.
5   R.W. English, 'Correlates of stigma towards physically disabled persons', in R.P. Marinelli and A.E. Dell Orto (eds), *The Psychological and Social Impact of Physical Disability*, p. 162.
6   T. Kando, 'Passing and stigma management: the case of the transsexual', in C.D. Bryant (ed.), *Sexual Deviancy in Social Context*, p. 150.
7   L. Osborne, 'Beyond stigma theory: a literary approach', p. 72.
8   Though note the esteemed nature of this term in Christian teaching. See J. McCaffery, *The Friar of San Giovanni*, p. 142.
9   See, for example: N.J. Davies, 'Labeling theory in deviance research: a critique and reconsideration'; S. Dinitz et al., *Deviance: Studies in the Process of Stigmatization and Societal Reaction*; J.P. Gibbs, 'Issues in defining deviant behavior', in R.A. Scott and J.D. Douglas (eds), *Theoretical Perspectives on Deviance*.
10 R.K Merton and R. Nisbet (eds), *Contemporary Social Problems*. pp. 833-4.
11 K. Plummer, *Sexual Stigma*. p.26.
12 Ibid., p. 26.
13 S. Cohen (ed.), *Images of Deviance*, p.11.
14 See G. Christensen, 'A test of the labelling approach to deviance: the case of the disabled'; C. Haffter, 'The changeling: history and psychodynamics of attitudes to handicapped children in European folklore'.
15 See, for example, G.E. Markle and R.J. Troyer, 'Smoke gets in your eyes: cigarette smoking as deviant behaviour'.
16 E. Goffman, *Stigma*, p. 163; editorial in the *Daily Mirror*, 11.5.78.
17 E. Goffman, *Stigma*, p.14.
18 Ibid., pp. 14-15.

19   See T. Kando, op. cit., p. 151.
20   E. Goffman, *Stigma*, p. 14.
21   F. Davis, 'Deviance disavowal: the management of strained interaction by the visibly handicapped', in W.J. Filstead (ed.), *An Introduction to Deviance: Readings in the Process of Making Deviants*, p. 149.
22   W.J. Cahnman, 'The stigma of obesity', p. 294. See also, W. Dejong, 'The stigma of obesity: the consequences of naive assumptions concerning the causes of physical deviance'.
23   L.E. Pardo, 'Stigma and social justice. The effects of physical disability vis à vis moral turpitude'.
24   Ibid., p. 70.
25   Ibid., p. 71.
26   Ibid., p. 71.
27   Ibid., pp. 108-9.
28   E. Goffman, *Stigma*. p. 14.
29   Ibid., p. 13.
30   D.A. Reisman, *Richard Titmuss: Welfare and Society*, p. 128.
31   A. Raphael, 'Messiah of the militant left'.
32   J. Posner, 'The stigma of excellence: on being just right'. See also, J. Kwasniewski, 'Positive social deviancy'.
33   J. Posner, op. cit., p. 144.
34   Ibid., p. 143.
35   S. Dinitz et al., op. cit., p. 14.
36   E. Goffman, *Stigma*, p. 154.
37   K. Plummer, op. cit., p. 21. See also, M. Rotenberg, 'Self-labelling: a missing link in the "societal reaction" theory of deviance'.
38   E. Goffman, *Stigma*. pp. 45-6.
39   H. Beks, 'Learning to say "I am a homosexual" ', p. 58.
40   C.S. Suchar, *Social Deviance Perspectives and Prospects*, pp. 189-90. See also, H.S. Becker, *Outsiders: Studies in the Sociology of Deviance*, pp. 32-4; E.C. Hughes, 'Dilemmas and contradictions of status'.
41   See, for example, E. Goffman, *Asylums*; T.J. Scheff, *Being Mentally Ill: A Sociological Theory*; T.J. Scheff, 'The labelling theory of mental illness'; T.S. Szasz, *The Manufacture of Madness*, ch. 12.
42   See, for example, J.P. Gibbs, op. cit.; W.R. Grove (ed.), *The Labelling of Deviance*; E.M. Lemert, *Human Deviance, Social Problems, and Social Control*.
43   H.J. Parker, *View from the Boys*, p. 162.
44   See C.A.B. Warren and J.M. Johnson, 'A critique of labeling theory from the phenomenological perspective', in R.A. Scott and J.D. Douglas (eds), op. cit., ch. 3.
45   See, for example, A.N. Doob and B.P. Ecker, 'Stigma and compliance'; R. Kleck et al., 'The effects of physical deviance upon face-to-face interaction'; R. Kleck, 'Physical stigma and nonverbal clues emitted in face-to-face interaction'; L. Levitt and R.C. Kornhaber, 'Stigma and compliance: a re-examination'.

46 R. Kleck et al., 'The effects of physical deviance. . .'.
47 See, for example, R.A. Scott, *The Making of Blind Men*; R.B. Edgerton, *The Cloak of Competence: Stigma in the Lives of the Mentally Retarded*; R.B. Edgerton and S.M. Bercovici, 'The cloak of competence: years later'.
48 Quoted in E. Goffman, *Stigma*. p. 51.
49 See, E. Goffman, *Stigma*, p. 67.
50 F. Davis, op. cit., p. 149.
51 B. Berk, 'Face-saving at the singles dance', p. 538.
52 See, for example, S. Box, *Deviance, Reality and Society*, p. 243.
53 S. Sutherland, *Breakdown*, p. 35.
54 Quoted in E. Goffman, *Stigma*, p. 107.
55 F. Davis, op. cit., p. 145.
56 Quoted in E. Goffman, *Stigma*, p. 27.
57 See the *Evening News* (London), 11.9.78.
58 Quoted in E. Goffman, *Stigma*, p. 25.
59 M.S. Weinberg and C.J. Williams, *Male Homosexuals – Their Problems and Adaptions*, p. 154.
60 See, for example, R. Belson, 'Shame in Pregnancy'; S.E. Taylor and E.J. Langer, 'Pregnancy: a social stigma?'
61 J. Brundin, 'My special shame'.
62 Quoted in E. Goffman, *Stigma*, pp. 103-4.
63 See, on this subject, A. Birenbaum, 'On managing a courtesy stigma'; C.S. Suchar, 'The institutional reaction to child mental illness: co-deviant labelling'.
64 Quoted in E. Goffman, *Stigma*, p. 43.
65 Letters column, the *Evening News* (London), 18.12.79.
66 A. Modigliani, 'Embarrassment and embarrassability', p. 313. See also, E. Goffman, *Interaction Ritual*, pp. 97-112.
67 See, for example, K. Riezler, 'Comment on the social psychology of shame'.
68 F. Flynn, 'People like you should know better', p. 346.
69 See, for example, E. Goffman, *Interaction Ritual*, pp. 97-112; J. Miller, 'Exploring the inner man'.
70 D.W. Ball, 'The problem of respectability', in J.D. Douglas (ed.), *Deviance and Respectability: The Social Construction of Moral Meanings*, p. 334. See also on this issue, E. Goffman, *Stigma*, p. 18; L. Humphreys, *Out of the Closets*, pp. 136-7; J.W. Rogers and M.D. Buffalo, 'Fighting back: nine modes of adaption to a deviant label', p. 105.
71 See F. Flynn, op. cit., p. 346; J.W. Rogers and M.D. Buffalo, op. cit., p. 108.
72 See L. Humphreys, op. cit., p. 137.
73 R.H. Turner, 'Deviance avowal as neutralization of commitment', p. 316.
74 E. Goffman, *Stigma*, pp. 19-20.
75 See E. Sagarin and R.J. Kelly, 'Sexual deviance and labelling perspectives', in W.R. Gove (ed.), op. cit., p. 248 (Group 3).

76   See E. Goffman, *Stigma*, pp. 19-20.
77   See R.R. Anspach, 'From stigma to identity politics: political activism among the physically disabled and former mental patients'; L. Humphreys, op. cit., ch. 8; J. Weeks, *Coming Out*, ch. 16.
78   E. Goffman, *Stigma*, p. 139.
79   See M. Brake, *The Sociology of Youth Culture and Youth Subcultures*, ch. 3.
80   See D.W. Ball, op. cit.; E. Sagarin and R.J. Kelly, op. cit, p. 250; G.M. Sykes and D. Matza, 'Techniques of neutralization: a theory of delinquency'.
81   See, for example, S. Box, op. cit., pp. 189-97; T.J. Scheff, 'Negotiating reality: notes on power in the assessment of responsibility'; E.M. Schurr, *Labelling Deviant Behaviour: Its Sociological Implications*.
82   See E. Goffman, *Stigma*, ch. 2.
83   Quoted in E. Goffman, *Stigma*, p. 110.
84   See E. Goffman, *Stigma*, p. 98 and p. 117. See also, R.M. Harrison, 'Epilepsy and stigma'. Note also that a 'cycle' of passing may be adopted by certain individuals – see E. Goffman, *Stigma*, p. 100.
85   J. Miller, 'Jonathan Miller: the director's not for blocking', p. 175.
86   Quoted in E. Goffman, *Stigma*, p. 109.
87   Though we may all enjoy such experiences which have a habit of being associated with coach or railway journeys.
88   See E. Goffman, *Stigma*, p. 125.
89   Ibid., pp. 126-7.
90   See ibid., pp. 126-8.
91   See ibid., pp. 146-7.
92   See, for example, A. Birenbaum, op. cit.; J. Cumming and E. Cumming, op. cit.
93   See B. Berk, op. cit.; E. Goffman, *Interaction Ritual*, pp. 5-45.

Chapter 2   Stigma: the social administration approach

1   See K. de Schweinitz, *England's Road to Social Security*, chap. 3.
2   See A.L. Beier, 'Vagrants and the social order in Elizabethan England'; F. Fox-Piven and R.A. Cloward, *Regulating the Poor: The Functions of Public Welfare*, pp. 15-16; E.M. Leonard, *The Early History of English Poor Relief*, pp. 25-6; K. de Schweinitz, op. cit., ch. 3.
3   See D. Marshall, *The English Poor in the Eighteenth Century*, pp. 102-3; G.W. Oxley, *Poor Relief in England and Wales 1601-1834*, pp. 54-5.
4   See J.R. Poynter, *Society and Pauperism*, pp. 125-6; K. de Schweinitz, op. cit., ch. 13.
5   R.A Pinker, *Social Theory and Social Policy*, p. 58.
6   See M.E. Rose, *The English Poor Law 1780-1930*, pp. 145-6.
7   See S. and B. Webb, *English Local Government: English Poor*

Law History: Part II: The Last Hundred Years. Vol. I, pp. 378-81.
8   See R.A. Pinker, *Social Theory*, pp. 77-8; S. and B. Webb, Vol. I, pp. 316-47.
9   See M.E. Rose, op. cit., pp. 238, 252-4; S. and B. Webb, Vol. I, pp. 357-64.
10 See J.S. Heywood, *Children in Care*, ch. 5; I. Pinchbeck and M. Hewitt, *Children in English Society*, volume II, ch. 17.
11 See S. and B. Webb, vol. II, pp. 474-6.
12 See M. Bruce, *The Coming of the Welfare State*, pp. 203-4.
13 See B. Watkin, *Documents on Health and Social Services 1834 to the Present Day*, pp. 26-8.
14 See R.A. Pinker, *Social Theory*, pp. 82-3.
15 See D. Fraser, *The Evolution of the British Welfare State*, p. 149.
16 See, for example, W. Hannington, *Unemployed Struggles 1919-1936*, chs 2 and 3.
17 See A. Deacon, *In Search of the Scrounger*; A. Deacon, 'Concession and coercion: the politics of unemployment insurance in the twenties' in A. Briggs and J. Saville (eds), *Essays in Labour History, 1918-1939*, Vol. 3, ch. 3.
18 See A. Deacon, *In Search*; N. Ginsburg, *Class, Capital and Social Policy*, pp. 58-68.
19 See R.M. Titmuss, *Problems of Social Policy*, p. 515, note 1.
20 See B. Watkin, op. cit., pp. 94-6. See also, A. Deacon, 'Thankyou, God, for the means-test man'.
21 *Report on Social Insurance and Allied Services (Beveridge Report)*, para. 369, p. 141.
22 See V. George and P. Wilding, *Ideology and Social Welfare*, ch. 4.
23 See G. Room, *The Sociology of Welfare*, ch. 3, part IV.
24 See V. George and P. Wilding, op. cit., ch. 4.
25 See R.M. Titmuss, *The Gift Relationship*, ch. 1.
26 R.M. Titmuss, *Commitment to Welfare*, p. 191.
27 See R.M. Titmuss, *The Gift Relationship*.
28 Ibid., p. 269.
29 For useful discussions of the notion of social exchange see, P. Ekeh, *Social Exchange Theory: The Two Traditions*; A. Heath, *Rational Choice and Social Exchange*; G. MacCormack, 'Reciprocity'.
30 See A.W. Gouldner, *For Sociology*, ch. 9.
31 Ibid., p. 266.
32 For useful discussions of the anti-collectivist approach to welfare see, M. Friedman, *Capitalism and Freedom*; M. Friedman and R. Friedman, *Free to Choose*; F.A. Hayek, *The Road to Serfdom*; A. Seldon, *Charge*. See also, commentaries by V. George and P. Wilding, op. cit., ch. 2; G. Room, op. cit, ch. 3, part III; P.F. Taylor-Gooby and J. Dale, *Social Theory and Social Welfare*, pp. 58-69.
33 R.M. Titmuss, 'Introduction' in R.H. Tawney, *Equality*, p. 24.
34 R.M. Titmuss, *Social Policy: An Introduction*, pp. 42-3.

35 R.M. Titmuss, *Essays On The Welfare State*, pp. 216-17.
36 Ibid., p. 236.
37 R.M. Titmuss, *Commitment to Welfare*, p. 142.
38 Ibid., p. 134.
39 Ibid., p. 143.
40 Ibid., p. 134.
41 Ibid., p. 129.
42 See ibid., pp. 190-1.
43 See ibid., pp. 195-6.
44 R.M. Titmuss, *The Gift Relationship*, pp. 254-5.
45 R.M. Titmuss, *Commitment to Welfare*, pp. 196-7.
46 Ibid., p. 196.
47 See on this issue, P. Townsend, 'Introduction: does selectivity mean a nation divided' in Fabian Society, *Social Services For All?* ch. 1.
48 R.M. Titmuss, *Commitment to Welfare*, op. cit, p. 135.
49 See C. Clark, *Poverty Before Politics*; A. Seldon, op. cit.; A. Seldon and H. Gray, *Universal or Selective Benefits?*
50 R. Klein (ed.), *Inflation and Priorities*, p. 5.
51 See G. Rose, 'Stigma, illusion and means testing'.
52 G. Room, op. cit., p. 201.
53 M. Reddin, 'Local authority means-tested services' in Fabian Society, *Social Services for All?* p. 7.
54 R.A. Pinker, *Social Theory*, p. 141.
55 Ibid., p. 141.
56 See M.H. Cooper, *Rationing Health Care*, chs 7 and 8; L. Doyal with I. Pennell, *The Political Economy of Health*, pp. 195-7.
57 See, e.g. P. Morris, *Put Away; Report of the Committee of Enquiry into Allegations of Ill-Treatment at the Ely Hospital Cardiff.*
58 D.A. Reisman, *Richard Titmuss: Welfare and Society*, p. 54.
59 R.A. Pinker, *Social Theory*, p. 143.
60 Ibid., p. 170.
61 See ibid., p. 171. See also, A. Heath, op. cit., p. 154; R. Pruger, 'Social policy: unilateral transfer or reciprocal exchange'.
62 R.A. Pinker, *Social Theory*, p. 173.
63 See ibid., pp. 173-4.
64 See ibid., p. 174.
65 Ibid., p. 151.
66 See ibid., p. 143.
67 Ibid., p. 151.
68 Ibid., p. 160. See also, R. Pruger, op. cit., p. 295.
69 See R.M. Titmuss, *Social Policy*, p. 26.
70 R.A. Pinker, *Social Theory*, p. 139.
71 See DHSS, *Supplementary Benefits Handbook*, ch. 3; M. Hill, *Policies for the Unemployed: Help or Coercion?*
72 See for example, D. Marsden, *Mothers Alone*, ch. 12; J. Streather and S. Weir, *Social Insecurity: Single Mothers on Benefit.*
73 See, for example, R. Lister, *The Administration of the Wage Stop*;

D. Marsden, *Workless*, ch. 5.
74 B. Jordan, *Poor Parents*, p. 114.
75 R.A. Pinker, *Social Theory*, p. 201.
76 D. Donnison, 'Supplementary benefits: dilemmas and priorities', p. 358.
77 See ibid., p. 358.
78 See G. Rose, op cit. (Supplementary benefits) and B. Jordan, *Poor Parents*, p. 72. (Social work.)
79 R.A. Pinker, *Social Theory*, p. 206.
80 See P. Golding and S. Middleton, *Images of Welfare*.
81 See, for example, *Report of the Committee on Abuse of Social Security Benefits (Fisher Report)*; F. Field (ed.), *The Conscript Army*, ch. 4; F. Field, 'Scroungers: crushing the invisible'.
82 P. Golding and S. Middleton, 'Why is the press so obsessed with welfare scroungers?', p. 195.
83 *News Of The World*, editorial, 24.9.78.
84 See D.A. Reisman, op. cit., pp. 100-1.
85 R. Page, *The Benefits Racket*, p. 113.
86 R. Boyson, *Centre Forward*, p. 121.
87 P. Townsend, *The Family Life of Old People*, pp. 183-5.
88 See D. Cole with J.E.G. Utting, *The Economic Circumstances of Old People*, p. 10.
89 See ibid., ch. 8.
90 Ministry of Pensions and National Insurance, *Financial and Other Circumstances of Retirement Pensioners*.
91 V. George, *Social Security and Society*, pp. 115-16.
92 A.B. Atkinson, *Poverty in Britain and the Reform of Social Security*, p. 58.
93 See for example, *Report of the Committee of Inquiry into the Impact of Rates on Households (The Allen Report)*.
94 See V. George, *Social Security: Beveridge and After*, pp. 75-6.
95 J.C. Kincaid, *Poverty and Equality in Britain*, p. 64.
96 See P. Hall et al., *Change, Choice and Conflict in Social Policy*, pp. 457-60; J.C. Kincaid, op. cit., pp. 65-7.
97 See A.B. Atkinson, op. cit., pp. 75-6.
98 See for example, P. Moss, *Welfare Rights Project '68*; P. Moss, *Welfare Rights Project Two*; Coventry Social Services, *Looking for Trouble among the Elderly*; R. Cohen and M. Tarpey, *The Trouble with Take-up*.
99 P.J. Hennessey, *Families, Funerals and Finances. A Study of Funeral Expenses and How They are Paid*.
100 M. Meacher, *Rate Rebates: A Study of the Effectiveness of Means Tests*.
101 Ibid., p. 41.
102 Ibid., p. 41.
103 See Batley Community Development Project, *Welfare Rights Campaign Interim Report*; P.F. Taylor-Gooby, 'Rent benefits and tenants' attitudes. The Batley rent rebate and allowance study'.

104 P.F. Taylor-Gooby, 'Rent benefits', p. 44.
105 Ibid., pp. 44-5. See also, D. Page and B. Weinberger, *Birmingham Rent Rebate and Allowance Study*, pp. 38-9.
106 See M. Blaxter, 'Health "on the welfare" – a case study'.
107 Ibid., p. 48.
108 Ibid., pp. 48-9.
109 See ibid., p. 50.
110 See J. Nixon, *Fatherless Families on FIS*.
111 See, for example, N. Bond, *Knowledge of Rights and Extent of Unmet Need Amongst Recipients of Supplementary Benefit*; T. Lynes, 'The dinner money problem'; North Tyneside CDP, *In and Out of Work*.
112 See F. Field, *The Stigma of Free School Meals*. See also, F. Field, *Free School Meals: The Humiliation Continues*.
113 B. Davies in association with M. Reddin, *Universality, Selectivity and Effectiveness in Social Policy*.
114 See ibid., pp. 68-9.
115 See ibid., pp. 126-7.
116 Ibid., p. 127.
117 See D. Marsden, *Mothers Alone*, p. 238.
118 See P. Townsend, *Poverty in the United Kingdom*, pp. 842-7.
119 See R. Marshall, *Families Receiving Supplementary Benefit*, ch. 7. See also on the subject of felt sigma and the receipt of means-tested social security benefits: L. Burghes, *Living from Hand to Mouth*, ch. 2; H. Land, *Large Families in London*, ch. 7; P. Marris, *Widows and Their Families*, ch. 8; D. Marsden, *Workless*, pp. 93-5; J. Ritchie and P. Wilson, *Social Security Claimants*, ch. 3.
120 See, for example: F. Field and M. Grieve, *Abuse and the Abused*; Gingerbread, *As We See It*, ch. 1; H. Land, op. cit.; R. Marshall, op. cit.
121 See North Tyneside CDP, op. cit., pp. 149-57.
122 Ibid., p. 151.
123 See R. Lister, *Administration*.
124 Ibid., pp. 15-16.
125 See, for example, R. Lister, *As Man and Wife? A Study of the Cohabitation Rule*, pp. 18-19; D. Marsden, *Mothers Alone*, pp. 252-9; J. Streather and S. Weir, op. cit., pp. 13-14.
126 D. Marsden, *Mothers Alone*, p. 256.
127 See, for example, D. Marsden, *Mothers Alone*, pp. 247-51; J. Streather and S. Weir, op. cit., pp. 24-7.
128 See, for example, A. Hopkinson, *Single Mothers: The First Year*, p. 55.
129 See, for example, S. Jacobs, 'Rehousing in Glasgow: reform through community action' in D. Jones and M. Mayo (eds), *Community Work 2*; J. Lambert et al., *Housing Policy and the State*, ch. 3.
130 See, e.g., S. Rees, *Social Work Face to Face*, chs 2, 4, and 5.
131 See ibid, p. 21.

132 See E. Briggs and A.M. Rees, *Supplementary Benefits and the Consumer*.
133 Ibid, p. 73.
134 P.M. Horan and P.L. Austin, 'The social bases of welfare stigma'.
135 Ibid., p. 655.
136 See J.F. Handler and E.J. Hollingsworth, *The 'Deserving Poor'*.
137 Ibid., p. 169.
138 See H.R. Kerbo, 'The stigma of welfare and a passive poor'.
139 See ibid., p. 179.
140 See J.F. Handler and E.J. Hollingsworth, op. cit., p. 175.
141 H.R. Kerbo, op. cit., p. 182. See also on the question of possible causes of felt stigma, B. Davies in association with M. Reddin, op. cit., chs 4 and 5.
142 See R.A. Pinker, *Dependency and Social Welfare*.
143 See ibid., pp. 60-1.
144 See P. Golding and S. Middleton, *Images of Welfare*, chs 6 and 7.
145 See ibid., p. 172.
146 See ibid., p. 172.
147 See B. Glastonbury et al., 'Community perceptions and the personal social services'.
148 See D. Clifford, 'Stigma and the perception of social security services'.
149 See ibid., p. 49.
150 See ibid., pp. 49-50.
151 See J.B. Williamson, 'The stigma of public dependency: a comparison of alternative forms of public aid to the poor'.
152 See ibid., p. 222.
153 See ibid., p. 222.
154 See ibid., p. 220 (see p. 221 for 'General Relief' reasons).
155 See ibid., pp. 222-5.
156 See J.R. Feagin, 'America's welfare stereotypes'.
157 See J.P. Alston and K.I. Dean, 'Socioeconomic factors associated with attitudes toward welfare recipients and the causes of poverty' (see in particular Table 1, p. 15).
158 See ibid., pp. 14-16.
159 See P. Golding and S. Middleton, *Images of Welfare*, p. 195.
160 See ibid., p. 198.
161 See R.H. Lauer, 'The middle class looks at poverty'.
162 See L. Goodwin, 'How suburban families view the work orientations of the welfare poor: problems in social stratification and social policy'.
163 See J. B. Williamson, 'Beliefs about the motivation of the poor and attitudes toward poverty policy'. See also, J.B. Williamson, 'Beliefs about the welfare poor'.
164 See Commission Of The European Communities, *The Perception of Poverty in Europe*.
165 See ibid., p. 72.
166 See P. Golding and S. Middleton, *Images of Welfare*, p. 198.

167 See B. Glastonbury et al., op. cit., p. 196.
168 See ibid., p. 196.
169 See D. Clifford, op. cit., p. 43.
170 See ibid., p. 42.
171 See R.A. Pinker, *Dependency*.
172 See J.F. Handler and E.J. Hollingsworth, op. cit.
173 See P.M. Horan and P.L. Austin, op. cit.
174 See J.F. Handler and E.J. Hollingsworth, op. cit., p. 166.
175 See P.M. Horan and P.L. Austin, op. cit., p. 652.
176 See B. Davies in association with M. Reddin, op. cit., p. 81.
177 See E. Briggs and A.M. Rees, op. cit., pp. 41-2; B. Davies in association with M. Reddin, op. cit., p. 104, note 25; R. Klein, op. cit., p. 5.

Chapter 3   Stigma and the unmarried mother

1   1 Corinthians, 7, vv. 32-4. (This and all other biblical references are taken from *The New English Bible*, 1970, Oxford and Cambridge University Presses.)
2   D.S. Bailey, *The Man-Woman Relation in Christian Thought*, p. 55.
3   See ibid., p. 43.
4   See P. Sherard, *Christianity and Eros*, pp. 3-4. See also, Ephesians, 5, v. 32.
5   See P. Sherard, op. cit., p. 4. See also, Genesis, 1, v. 28.
6   E. Troeltsch, *The Social Teaching of the Christian Churches*, volume 1, p. 61.
7   1 Timothy, 2, vv. 11-14.
8   B. Russell, *Marriage and Morals*, pp. 45-6.
9   K. Wrightson, 'The nadir of English illegitimacy in the seventeenth century', in P. Laslett et al. (eds), *Bastardy and its Comparative History*, p. 178.
10 See on this subject, G. May, *Social Control of Sex Expression*, pp. 80-1.
11 See R.M. Helmholz, 'Infanticide in the province of Canterbury during the fifteenth century', pp. 383-4.
12 F.G. Emmison, *Elizabethan Life: Morals and the Church Courts*, pp. 283-4.
13 P.E.H. Hair, 'Bridal pregnancy in earlier rural England further examined', pp. 68-9.
14 P.E.H. Hair, 'Bridal pregnancy in rural England in earlier centuries', p. 239.
15 See K. Wrightson, 'The nadir of English illegitimacy', p. 178.
16 See ibid., pp. 178-9.
17 See A. Macfarlane, 'Illegitimacy and illegitimates in English history', in P. Laslett et al. (eds), op. cit., pp. 76-8
18 See F.G. Emmison, op. cit., pp. 25-30.

19 Ibid., p. 25.
20 Ibid., p. 27.
21 See L. Stone, *The Family, Sex and Marriage in England 1500-1800*, p. 502.
22 See Ibid., pp. 531-2; J. Teichman, *The Meaning of Illegitimacy*, pp. 20-2.
23 See M. Hopkirk, *Nobody Wanted Sam*, p. 11.
24 See G. May, op. cit., Ch. 8.
25 See J.W. Legg, *English Church Life from the Restoration to the Tractarial Movement*, ch. 8; L. Stone, op. cit., p. 633.
26 See L. Stone, op. cit., p. 633; A. Warne, *Church and Society in Eighteenth-Century Devon*, pp. 78-9.
27 See G. May, op. cit., p. 170.
28 O. Chadwick, *The Reformation*, p. 379.
29 See I. Pinchbeck and M. Hewitt, *Children in English Society*, vol. 1, p. 209.
30 See K. Wrightson, 'Infanticide in earlier seventeenth-century England'.
31 See G. May, op. cit., ch. 10; L. Stone, op. cit., p. 632.
32 See G. May, op. cit., pp. 128-30; B.A. Kellum, 'Infanticide in England in the later middle ages', p. 378.
33 W.K. Jordan, *Philanthropy in England 1480-1660*, p. 66.
34 See E.M. Leonard, *The Early History of English Poor Relief*, pp. 53-4.
35 See ibid., pp. 58-9.
36 See D. Gill, *Illegitimacy, Sexuality and the Status of Women*, p. 206.
37 See I. Pinchbeck and M. Hewitt, vol. 1, p. 207.
38 D. Gill, op. cit., p. 208.
39 See I. Pinchbeck and M. Hewitt, vol. 1, p. 207.
40 See ibid, p. 96.
41 See ibid., p. 208.
42 See K. Wrightson, 'The nadir of English illegitimacy', p. 181.
43 S.C. Ratcliff and H.C. Johnson (eds), *Warwick County Records* vol. 1, p. 46.
44 S.C. Ratcliff and H.C. Johnson (eds), *Warwick County Records* vol. 2, p. 247.
45 See ibid., pp. 114-15.
46 S.C. Ratcliff and H.C. Johnson (eds), vol. 1, p. 251.
47 Ibid., p. 243.
48 See I. Pinchbeck and M. Hewitt, vol. 1, p. 208.
49 S.C. Ratcliff and H.C. Johnson (eds), vol. 1, p. 117.
50 See E. Melling (ed.), *Kentish Sources: IV The Poor*, p. 35.
51 See K. de Schweinitz, *England's Road to Social Security*, ch. 5.
52 See K. Wrightson, 'Infanticide', p. 13; L. Stone, op. cit., p. 635.
53 See E. Shorter, *The Making of the Modern Family*, pp. 87-103.
54 See P. Laslett, 'Introduction: comparing illegitimacy over time and between cultures', in P. Laslett et al. (eds), op. cit., p. 27.

55   See I. Pinchbeck and M. Hewitt, vol. 1, pp. 208-9.
56   See G.W. Oxley, *Poor Relief in England and Wales 1601-1834*, p. 91.
57   Ibid., p. 90.
58   See M. Hopkirk, op. cit., pp. 31-3.
59   See ibid., p. 38; M.P. Hall and I.V. Howes, *The Church in Social Work*, p. 14.
60   *Royal Commission on the Administration and Practical Operation of the Poor Laws*, p. 347. See also, U.R.Q. Henriques, 'Bastardy and the new poor law'.
61   *Royal Commission on the Administration and Practical Operation of the Poor Laws*, p. 349.
62   Ibid., p. 347.
63   U.R.Q. Henriques, *Before The Welfare State*, p. 55.
64   See ibid., p. 55.
65   See P. Laslett, op. cit., p. 13.
66   See M. Finer and O.R. McGregor, 'The history of the obligation to maintain', in *Report of the Committee on One-Parent Families* Volume 2, *Appendices (Finer Report)*, Appendix, 5, Para. 62, p. 119.
67   N. Longmate, *The Workhouse*, p. 157. See also, A. Digby, *Pauper Palaces*, p. 152.
68   I. Anstruther, *The Scandal of the Andover Workhouse*, p. 113.
69   See J.S. Heywood, *Children in Care*, ch. 5; I. Pinchbeck and M. Hewitt, vol. 2, ch. 17.
70   See J.S. Heywood, op. cit., pp. 95-6; I. Pinchbeck and M. Hewitt, vol. 2, pp. 612-13.
71   See J.S. Heywood, op. cit., p. 99.
72   See ibid., p. 116.
73   See S. and B. Webb, vol. 1, p. 357.
74   See E.H. Hunt, *British Labour History 1815-1914*, pp. 120-5.
75   See J.S. Heywood, op. cit., pp. 157-8.
76   See S. Graham-Dixon, *Never Darken My Door*.
77   See H.A.L. Fisher. 'The unmarried mother and her child'.
78   See H. Bosanquet, *The Poor Law Report of 1909*, p. 246.
79   Ibid., p. 246.
80   See ibid., p. 246.
81   N. Middleton, *When Family Failed*, p. 279.
82   Quoted in H. Bosanquet, op. cit., p. 254.
83   See, for example, Local Government Board circular to Boards of Guardians (8.10.1914) in *Survey of Relief to Widows and Children*.
84   See Report of the *Royal Commission on the Poor Laws and Relief of Distress, Minority Report*, p. 788.
85   See M. Finer and O.R. McGregor, op. cit., paras 78-82, pp. 129-32.
86   See ibid., para. 80, p. 131.
87   See ibid., para. 83, p. 133.
88   See ibid., para. 84, p. 134.

89   See ibid., para. 85, p. 134.
90   Ibid., para. 86, p. 135.
91   See S.M. Ferguson and H. Fitzgerald, *Studies in the Social Services*, p. 85.
92   See M.P. Hall and I.V. Howes, op. cit., p. 33.
93   See on this subject, N. Middleton, op. cit., p. 285; R. Sauer 'Infanticide and abortion in nineteenth-century Britain'.
94   See N. Middleton, op. cit., p. 285; I. Pinchbeck and M. Hewitt, vol II, pp. 604-10.
95   See N. Middleton, op. cit., pp. 287-8.
96   Ibid, p. 279.
97   See S.M. Ferguson and H. Fitzgerald, op. cit., p. 103.
98   Ibid., p 103.
99   See ibid., ch. 4.
100 See ibid., pp. 127-9.
101 See ibid., p. 140.
102 See *Report on Social Insurance and Allied Services (Beveridge Report)*, para. 371, p. 142.
103 M. Finer and O.R. McGregor, op. cit., para. 111, p. 148.
104 See for example, R. Lister, *As Man and Wife? A Study of the Cohabitation Rule*; D. Marsden, *Mothers Alone*, ch. 12; O. Stevenson, *Claimant or Client?* ch. 6; J. Streather and S. Weir, *Social Insecurity: Single Mothers on Benefit*.
105 See DHSS, *Supplementary Benefits Handbook*, chs 13 and 14.
106 See A. Hopkinson, *Single Mothers: The First Year*, pp. 116-20; D. Marsden, *Mothers Alone*, pp. 253-4.
107 See, for example, R. Lister, *As Man and Wife? A Study of the Cohabitation Rule*; J. Streather and S. Weir, op. cit.
108 D. Marsden, *Mothers Alone*, p. 247.
109 See *Report of the Committee on One-Parent Families (Finer Report)*, volume 1.
110 Ibid., para. 2.6, p. 7.
111 See ibid., part 4.
112 See ibid., paras 5.251-5.276, pp. 335-43.
113 See ibid., para. 5.56, p. 269.
114 M.A. Murch, 'One-parent families', p. 175.
115 See J.C. Kincaid, *Poverty and Equality in Britain*, pp. 197-9.
116 See P. Townsend, 'Problems of introducing a Guaranteed Maintenance Allowance for one parent families'.
117 See *Report of the Committee on One-Parent Families (Finer Report)*, part 6.
118 See ibid., part 7.
119 See ibid., part 8, section 4.
120 See ibid., part 8, sections 1-3 and 6.
121 See ibid., part 8, section 5.
122 See ibid., part 8, section 8.
123 See ibid., paras 8.75-8.78, p. 448. Note that the Seebohm Committee also referred to the needs of unmarried mothers. See

*Report of the Committee on Local Authority and Allied Personal
Social Services (Seebohm Report)*, para. 211, pp. 62-3.

124　See *Report of the Committee on One-Parent Familes (Finer
Report)*, paras 8.78-8.92, pp. 448-53.

125　Ibid., para. 8.76, p. 448.

126　See, for example, M. Bramall, 'The Finer committee report';
National Council For One Parent Families, *Annual Reports*, 1974/5
to 1981/2.

127　See, for example, DHSS, *Social Assistance*, para. 2.16, p. 17.

128　See DHSS, *Social Security Statistics 1982*, Table 34.32, p. 187.

129　See ibid., Table 32.10, p. 174.

130　See DHSS, *Social Security Statistics 1980*, Table 34.28, p. 158.

131　See National Council For One Parent Families, *Annual Report
1980-81*, p. 2.

132　See DHSS, *Social Security Statistics, 1982*, p. 261.

133　See National Council For One Parent Families, *Annual Report,
1975-76*, p. 3.

134　See *One Parent Times*, 5.2.81, p. 3.

135　See Family Welfare Association, *Guide to the Social Services 1978*,
pp. 134-6. See also Department Of The Environment, 'Housing
For One-Parent Families'.

136　See R. Leete, 'One-parent families: numbers and characteristics',
p.7.

137　H.H. Perlman, 'Unmarried mothers', in N.E. Cohen (ed.), *Social
Work and Social Problems*, p. 279.

138　See, for example, DHSS, *Children in Care*.

139　J. Bowlby, *Child Care and the Growth of Love*, p. 115.

140　See, for example, S. Freud, *New Introductory Lectures in
Psychoanalysis*.

141　L. Young, *Out of Wedlock*, p. 22.

142　See, for example, H.J. Eysenck, *Sense and Nonsense in
Psychology*; B.A. Farrell, 'Psychoanalystic theory'; B.A. Farrell,
'Psychoanalysis – the method'.

143　See J. Kasanin and S. Handschin, 'Psychodynamic factors in
illegitimacy'.

144　See V.W. Bernard, 'Psychodynamics of unmarried motherhood in
early adolescence'.

145　Ibid., p. 44.

146　See L. Young, 'Personality patterns in unmarried mothers' in
R.W. Roberts (ed.), *The Unwed Mother*.

147　Ibid., p. 92.

148　Ibid., p. 93.

149　See J.S. Pearson and P.L. Amacher, 'Intelligence test results and
observations of personality disorder among 3594 unwed mothers in
Minnesota'.

150　Ibid., p.20.

151　See J.P. Cattell, 'Psychodynamic and clinical observations in a group
of unmarried mothers' in R.W. Roberts (ed.) *The Unwed Mother*.

152 See N.H. Greenberg et al., 'Life situations associated with the onset of pregnancy'.
153 Ibid., p. 298.
154 J.G. Loesch and N.H. Greenberg, 'Some specific areas of conflicts observed during pregnancy: a comparative study of married and unmarried pregnant women', p. 634.
155 See S.B.G. Eysenck, 'Personality, and pain assessment in childbirth of married and unmarried mothers'.
156 Ibid., p. 425.
157 See A.F. Bonan, 'Psychoanalytic implications in treating unmarried mothers with narcissistic character structures'.
158 Ibid., p. 324.
159 See H. Kravitz, 'Unwed mothers practical and theoretical considerations'.
160 Ibid., p. 462.
161 See J. Naiman, 'A comparative study of unmarried and married mothers'; J. Naiman, 'A comparison between unmarried women seeking therapeutic abortion and unmarried mothers'.
162 J. Naiman, 'A comparative study . . .', p. 468.
163 J. Naiman, 'A comparison between unmarried women seeking therapeutic abortion and unmarried mothers', p. 1088.
164 See J. Floyd and B.L Viney, 'Ego identity and ego ideal in the unwed mother.'
165 See ibid., p. 280.
166 See C.E. Vincent, *Unmarried Mothers*.
167 See ibid., pp. 179-97.
168 See W.C. Jones et al., 'Social and psychological factors in status decisions of unmarried mothers'.
169 See ibid., p. 277.
170 See M.A. Yelloly, 'Factors relating to an adoption decision by the mothers of illegitimate children'.
171 Ibid., p. 12.
172 See, for example, P.M. Rains, *Becoming an Unwed Mother*.
173 M. Croxen, 'Psychological theories of social problem causation', in Open University, *Social Work, Community Work and Society*, units 7-9, Part I, p. 26.
174 D. Gill, op. cit., p. 241.
175 See for example, V. Abernethy, 'Illegitimate conception among teenagers'; H.M. Adams and U.M. Gallagher, 'Some facts and observations about illegitimacy'; W.S. Kogan et al., 'Changes in the self-concept of unwed mothers'; W.S. Kogan et al., 'Personality changes in unwed mothers following parturition'; D. Levy, 'A follow-up study of unmarried mothers'; M. Schmideberg, 'Psychiatric-social factors in young unmarried mothers'.
176 J. Cheetham, *Unwanted Pregnancy and Counselling*, p. 62.
177 Ibid., pp. 63-4.
178 See D. Gill, op. cit., pp. 238-9 and 255-6.
179 See for example, E. Goffman, *Asylums*; E.M. Schurr, *The Politics*

of Deviance, pp. 29-45; T.S. Szasz, *The Manufacture of Madness*.

180 See, for example, National Council For Civil Liberties, *50,000 Outside the Law, Royal Commission on the Law Relating to Mental Illness and Mental Deficiency*, Minutes of evidence – 22nd day, 16.3.55, pp. 840-54.

181 The findings from this survey are presented in V. Wimperis, *The Unmarried Mother and her Child*, ch. 2.

182 See B. Thompson, 'Social study of illegitimate maternities'.

183 Ibid., p. 77.

184 See D. Gill, op. cit., ch. 1.

185 See A. Yarrow, 'Illegitimacy in south-east Essex'.

186 See A. Hopkinson, op. cit., pp. 23-5.

187 See M.A. Yelloly, op. cit., pp. 8-9.

188 See S. Weir, *A Study of Unmarried Mothers and their Children in Scotland*, pp. 65-6 and para. 9.9, p. 86.

189 See ibid., para. 9.3, p. 85.

190 See E. Crellin et al., *Born Illegitimate*, pp. 40-1.

191 Note, however, that the findings of E. Crellin et al., have been challenged by Gill. See D. Gill, op. cit., p. 137.

192 B. Thompson, op. cit., p. 86.

193 See on this issue, S. Macintyre, *Single and Pregnant*, ch. 8.

194 Ibid., p. 24.

195 See O. Lewis, *The Children of Sanchez*; O. Lewis, *La Vida*.

196 See O. Lewis, *The Children of Sanchez*, pp. xi-xxxi.

197 O. Lewis, *La Vida*, p. xiv.

198 See for example, N.J. Davies, *Sociological Constructions of Deviance*, pp. 116-18; P. Townsend, *Poverty in the United Kingdom*, pp. 65-70; C.A. Valentine, *Culture and Poverty*, ch. 3.

199 In the case of the United States see, L. Rainwater, 'The problem of lower-class culture and poverty – war strategy' in D.P. Moynihan (ed.), *On Understanding Poverty*, ch. 9; C.A. Valentine, op. cit., chs 3 and 4.

200 See O. Lewis, *La Vida*, p. xiv; B. Jordan, *Poor Parents*, p. 124.

201 R. Holman, 'Poverty: consensus and alternatives' in E. Butterworth and R. Holman (eds), *Social Welfare in Modern Britain*, p. 404. See also on this subject, K. Joseph, 'The cycle of deprivation', in ibid., pp. 387-93.

202 See K. Joseph, 'Speech in Birmingham', 19.10.74, op. cit.

203 In terms of general texts see, for example, P.A. Bruce, *The Plantation Negro as a Freeman*; E.F. Frazier, *The Negro Family in the United States*; G. Myrdal, *An American Dilemma*.

204 See, for example, H.G. Gutman, *The Black Family in Slavery and Freedom 1750-1925*.

205 Ibid., p. 532.

206 See H. Hertz and S.W. Little, 'Unmarried negro mothers in a southern urban community'.

207 Ibid., p. 79.

208 See P. Knapp and S.T. Cambria, 'The attitudes of negro

unmarried mothers toward illegitimacy'.

209 See Department of Labor, *The Negro Family: The Case for National Action*.

210 See, for example, F. Fox-Piven and R.A. Cloward, *Regulating the Poor*, pp. 192-6; L.H. Gutman, op. cit., pp. 461-8; C.A. Valentine, op. cit., ch. 2.

211 W. Ryan, 'Blaming the victim: ideology serves the establishment', in P. Wickman (ed.), *Readings in Social Problems: Contemporary Perspectives*, p. 65.

212 A. Billingsley and A.T. Billingsley, 'Illegitimacy and negro family life' in R.W. Roberts (ed.), op. cit., p. 145.

213 See ibid., p. 145.

214 For a general discussion of this subject see J. Cheetham, *Social Work with Immigrants*, pp. 119-35.

215 See P. Johnson, 'Family reunion', in *The Observer* (10.10.82).

216 See E. Crellin et al.; op. cit.

217 See ibid., chs 6 and 7.

218 See ibid., ch. 9.

219 See ibid., ch. 10.

220 See ibid., ch. 11.

221 Ibid., p. 67.

222 Ibid., p. 112.

223 See E. Ferri, *Growing up in a One-Parent Family*.

224 See L. Lambert and J. Streather, *Children in Changing Families*.

225 See for example, J. Spence et al., *A Thousand Families in Newcastle upon Tyne*, ch. 23.

226 See E.M. Steel, 'What happens afterwards: a survey of unmarried mothers and their children after three years'.

227 Ibid., p. 15.

228 See A. Hunt et al., *Families and their Needs with Particular Reference to One-Parent Families*.

229 See M.L.K. Pringle, 'The incidence of some supposedly adverse family conditions and of left-handedness in schools for maladjusted children'.

230 See *Report of a Working Party on the Ascertainment of Maladjusted Children*.

231 See N. Murchison, 'Illustrations of the difficulties of some children in one-parent families', in *Report of the Committee on One-Parent Families*, volume 2, *Appendices (Finer Report)*, Appendix 12.

232 Ibid., para. 29, p. 372.

233 See ibid., para. 23, p. 370

234 See ibid., para. 24, p. 370.

235 See D. Gill, op. cit., Ch. 5.

236 Ibid., p. 147

237 See J. Packman, *Child Care: Needs and Numbers*.

238 See J. Rowe and L. Lambert, *Children Who Wait*.

239 For the background to this association see, for example, J. Bowlby, op. cit., ch. 10; J. Packman, *The Child's Generation*, ch. 6.

See also, T. Morris, 'The crooked way to the top: crime and acquisitive mobility', p. 232.

240   See J. Bowlby, op. cit., pp. 118-19.
241   See D.J. West, *Present Conduct and Future Delinquency*.
242   N. Murchison, op. cit., para. 52, p. 379.
243   See E.K. Macdonald, 'Follow-up of illegitimate children'.
244   Ibid., p. 363.
245   See E.M. Steel, 'A final study of unmarried mothers and their children'.
246   See E.F. Reed, 'Unmarried mothers who kept their babies'.
247   See H.R. Wright, *80 Unmarried Mothers who kept their Babies*.
248   See W.C. Oppel 'Illegitimacy. A comparative follow-up study'.
249   See L.G. Burchinal, 'Characteristics of adolescents from un-broken, broken, and reconstituted families'.
250   See H. Feldman and M. Feldman, 'The effect of father absence on adolescents'.
251   See H.J. Raschke and V.J. Raschke, 'Family conflicts and children's self-concepts: a comparison of intact and single-parent families'.
252   See, for example, A. Hunt et al., op. cit., sections 12.1 - 12.3, pp. 62-4; L. Lambert and J. Streather, op. cit., ch. 16.
253   See, for example, E.K. Macdonald, op. cit., p. 364; E. M. Steel, 'What happens afterwards', p. 16.
254   See E. Crellin et al., op. cit., p. 110.
255   M.L.K. Pringle, *The Needs of Chldren*, p. 157.
256   Ibid., p. 157.
257   Ibid., p. 160.
258   A more detailed examination of the results which were obtained in this survey can be found in R.M. Page, 'The Concept of Stigma with Special Reference to the Unmarried Mother: A Social Policy and Administration Approach'.
259   Note that this subject was only applicable to 32 respondents.
260   See J.W. Rogers and M.D. Buffalo, 'Fighting back: nine modes of adaption to a deviant label'; E.M Schurr, *The Politics of Deviance*.

Chapter 4   Stigma and social policy: wider dimensions

1   See R.A. Pinker, *Social Theory and Social Policy*, ch. 2; P. Taylor-Gooby, 'The empiricist tradition in social administration'.
2   R. Mishra, *Society and Social Policy*, pp. 3-4.
3   See, for example, J. Bradshaw, 'The concept of social need' in M. Fitzgerald et al. (eds), *Welfare in Action*; A. Forder, *Concepts in Social Administration*, ch. 3; R. Plant, 'Needs and welfare' in N. Timms (ed.), *Social Welfare: Why and How?* ch. 6; P. Taylor-Gooby and J. Dale, *Social Theory and Social Welfare*, ch. 8.
4   See, for example, J. Le. Grand, *The Strategy of Equality*; A. Weale,

Equality and Social Policy.
5 See, for example, V. George and P. Wilding, *Ideology and Social Welfare*; R. Mishra, op. cit.; G. Room, *The Sociology of Welfare*; P. Taylor-Gooby and J. Dale, op. cit.
6 See, for example, N. Ginsburg, *Class, Capital and Social Policy*; I. Gough, *The Political Economy of the Welfare State*; L. Harris, 'The state and the economy: some theoretical problems' in R. Miliband and J. Saville (eds), *The Socialist Register 1980*; London Edinburgh Weekend Return Group, *In and Against the State.*
7 R.H. Tawney, *The Radical Tradition*, p. 180.
8 Ibid., p. 155.
9 R.M. Titmuss, *The Gift Relationship*, p. 253.
10 See J. Rawls, *A Theory of Justice.*
11 See ibid., pp. 136-42.
12 See ibid., p. 302.
13 See ibid., pp. 90-5.
14 Ibid., p. 440.
15 See D. Miller, *Social Justice.*
16 See K. Jones et al., *Issues in Social Policy*, p. 140.
17 K.C. Davis, *Discretionary Justice: A Preliminary Inquiry*, p. 4.
18 See, for example, M. Adler and S. Asquith (eds), *Discretion and Welfare*; H. Hodge, 'Discretion in reality', in M. Adler and A. Bradley (eds), *Justice, Discretion and Poverty*, ch. 5; O. Stevenson, *Claimant or Client?*, pp. 43-5; R. Wilding, 'Discretionary benefits' in M. Adler and A. Bradley (eds), op. cit., ch. 4.
19 See on this issue, Supplementary Benefits Commission, *Exceptional Needs Payments*, p. 12.
20 See pp. 65-8.
21 See J.F. Handler, *The Coercive Social Worker*, ch. 7; B. Jordan, *Poor Parents*, ch. 6.
22 See on this issue, D. Donnison, *The Politics of Poverty*, pp. 93-4.
23 See, for example, T. Lynes, *Welfare Rights*; H. Rose, 'Who can de-label the claimant?' in M. Adler and A. Bradley (eds), op. cit., ch. 11.
24 P. Jones, 'Rights, welfare and stigma', p. 140.
25 Ibid., p. 141.
26 M. Adler and S. Asquith, 'Discretion and Power', in M. Adler and S. Asquith (eds), op. cit., p. 17.
27 See P. Jones, op. cit., pp. 140-1.
28 Ibid., p. 142.
29 R.M. Titmuss, 'Welfare "rights", law and discretion', p. 131.
30 See D. Donnison, *The Politics of Poverty*, p. 94.
31 T.H. Marshall, *The Right to Welfare and other Essays*, p. 88.
32 E. Scrivens, 'Towards a theory of rationing', p. 53.
33 See, for example, K. Judge, *Rationing Social Services*; R. Parker 'Social administration and scarcity' in E. Butterworth and R. Holmes (eds), *Social Welfare in Modern Britain*; A. Rees, 'Access to the personal, health and welfare services'; E. Scrivens, op. cit.; A.G.

Stevens, 'Rationing in the social services'.

34   See in particular on this issue, K. Judge and J. Matthews, *Charging for Social Care*, ch. 6.

35   R. Parker. op. cit., p. 208.

36   Ibid., p. 206.

37   See DHSS, *Social Security Statistics 1982*, p. 261.

38   *Report of the Committee on Local Authority and Allied Personal Social Services (Seebohm Report)*, para. 491, p. 151.

39   M.H. Cooper, *Rationing Health Care*. See also on this subject, J. Hallas, *CHC's in Action*; R. Klein and J. Lewis, *The Politics of Consumer Representatives. A Study of Community Health Councils*; D. Phillips, 'The creation of consultative councils in the N.H.S.'.

40   See S.R. Arnstein, 'A ladder of citizen participation'.

41   See N. Boaden et al., *Public Participation in Local Services*, ch. 6.

42   R. Plant et al., *Political Philosophy and Social Welfare*, p. 112.

43   See E.A. Ross, *Social Control*. (This book was based on a series of articles which were published in the *American Journal of Sociology* in the late 1890s.)

44   See, for example, L.L. Bernard, *Social Control in its Sociological Aspects*; A.B. Hollingshead, 'The concept of social control'; P.H. Landis, *Social Control, Social Organisation and Disorganisation in Process*; R.T. LaPiere, *Theory of Social Control*; J.S. Roucek and associates, *Social Control*; C.K. Watkins, *Social Control*.

45   See, e.g., P.R. Day, *Social Work and Social Control*; J. Higgins, 'Social control theories of social policy'; B. Jordan, *Freedom and the Welfare State*, chs 5 and 11; D. Watson, *Caring for Strangers*, part III.

46   A.P. Donajgrodzki (ed.), *Social Control in Nineteenth Century Britain*, p. 10.

47   R.A. Pinker, *Social Theory*, p. 175.

48   R.T. Roucek and associates, op. cit., p. 321.

49   See R.D. Schwartz and J.H. Skolnick, 'Two studies of legal stigma'.

50   See H. Garfinkel, 'Conditions of successful degradation ceremonies'.

51   D. Matza, *Becoming Deviant*, p. 156.

52   N. Walker, *Punishment, Danger and Stigma*, p. 149.

53   See ibid., pp. 150-1.

54   E.M. Schurr, *The Politics of Deviance*, p. 30.

55   See for example, M. Rayman, 'My stigma – a care order'.

56   N. Ginsburg, op. cit., p. 156.

57   See, for example, F.A. Hayek, *The Road To Serfdom*; M. Friedman *Capitalism and Freedom*; A. Seldon, *Whither the Welfare State?*

58   See M. Friedman, *Capitalism and Freedom*, pp. 30-2.

59   See, for example, R.H. Tawney, *The Acquisitive Society*; C.A.R. Crosland, *The Future of Socialism*; R.M. Titmuss, *Commitment to Welfare*.

60   C.A.R. Crosland, *The Future of Socialism*, pp. 229-30.

61   See, for example, N. Ginsburg, op. cit.; I. Gough, *The Political Economy of the Welfare State*; V. Navarro, 'The crisis of the international capitalist order and its implications for the welfare state'.

62   Though there is considerable disagreement over the question of whether the state can be used in some way to undermine capitalism. See, for example, F. Block, 'Beyond relative autonomy: state managers as historical subjects' in R. Miliband and J. Saville (eds), op. cit.; L. Harris, op. cit.; R. Miliband, *Marxism and Politics*, chs. 3 and 4.

63   I. Gough, op. cit., p. 39.

64   N. Ginsburg, op. cit., p. 104.

65   See G.W. Allport, *The Nature of Prejudice*, ch. 13; O.C. Cox, *Caste, Class and Race*; J. Dollard, *Caste and Class in a Southern Town*.

66   Though see J. Weeks, 'Discourse, desire and sexual deviance: some problems in a history of homosexuality' in K. Plummer, *The Making of the Modern Homosexual*, ch. 4.

Bibliography

Abernethy, V., 'Illegitimate conception among teenagers', *American Journal of Public Health*, 64, 7, July 1974, pp. 662-5.

Adams, H.M. and Gallagher, U.M., 'Some facts and observations about illegitimacy', *Children*, 10, 2, March/April 1963, pp. 43-8.

Adler, M. and Asquith, S. (eds), *Discretion and Welfare*, London, Heinemann, 1981.

Adler, M. and Bradley, A. (eds), *Justice, Discretion and Poverty*, London, Professional Books, 1975.

Allport, G.W., *The Nature of Prejudice*, Massachusetts, Addison-Wesley, 1979.

Alston, J.P. and Dean, K.I., 'Socioeconomic factors associated with attitudes toward welfare recipients and the causes of poverty', *Social Service Review*, 46, 1, March 1972, pp. 13-23.

Anspach, R.R., 'From stigma to identity politics: political activism among the physically disabled and former mental patients', *Social Science and Medicine*, 13A, 1979, pp. 765-73.

Anstruther, I., *The Scandal of the Andover Workhouse*, London, Geoffrey Bles, 1973.

Arnstein, S. R., 'A ladder of citizen participation', *Journal of American Institute of Planners*, 35, July 1969, pp. 216-24.

Atkinson, A.B., *Poverty in Britain and the Reform of Social Security*, Cambridge, Cambridge University Press, 1969.

Bailey, D.S., *The Man-Woman Relation in Christian Thought*, London, Longmans, 1959.

Ball, D.W., 'The problem of respectability', in Douglas, J.D. (ed.), ch. 11.

Barber, D. (ed.), *One Parent Families*, London, Hodder & Stoughton, 1978.

Batley Community Development Project, *Welfare Rights Campaign Interim Report*, Batley, Batley CDP, 1974.

Becker, H.S., *Outsiders: Studies in the Sociology of Deviance*, New York, Free Press, 1963.

Beier, A.L., 'Vagrants and the social order in Elizabethan England', *Past and Present*, 64, August 1974, pp. 3-29.

Beks, H., 'Learning to say "I am a homosexual" ', *New Society*, 39, 745

(13.1.77), 1977, pp. 58-60.

Belson, R., 'Shame in Pregnancy', unpublished dissertation as part of DSW, Adelphi University, 1977.

Berk, B., 'Face-saving at the singles dance', *Social Problems*, 24, 5, 1977, pp. 530-44.

Bernard, L.L., *Social Control in its Sociological Aspects*, New York, Macmillan, 1939.

Bernard, V.W., 'Psychodynamics of unmarried motherhood in early adolescence' *Nervous Child*, 4, 1944, pp. 26-45.

Billingsley, A. and Billingsley, A.T., 'Illegitimacy and negro family life', in Roberts, R.W. (ed.), *The Unwed Mother*.

Birenbaum, A., 'On managing a courtesy stigma', *Journal of Health and Social Behavior*, 11, 3, September 1970, pp. 196-206.

Blaxter, M., 'Health "on the welfare" - a case study', *Journal of Social Policy*, 3, 1, January 1974, pp. 39-51.

Block, F., 'Beyond relative autonomy: state managers as historical subjects', in Miliband, R. and Saville, J. (eds).

Boaden, N. et al., *Public Participation in Local Services*, London, Longman, 1982.

Bonan, A.F., 'Psychoanalytic implications in treating unmarried mothers with narcissistic character structures', *Social Casework*, 44, 6, June 1963, pp. 323-9.

Bond, N., *Knowledge of Rights and Extent of Unmet Need amongst Recipients of Supplementary Benefit*, The Home Office And City Of Coventry Development Project Occasional Paper, no. 4, Coventry, Coventry CDP, 1972.

Bosanquet, H., *The Poor Law Report of 1909*, London, Macmillan, 1909.

Box, S., *Deviance, Reality and Society*, London, Holt, Rinehart & Winston, 1971.

Bowlby, J., *Child Care and the Growth of Love* (2nd edn), Harmondsworth, Penguin, 1965.

Boyson, R., *Centre Forward*, London, Temple Smith, 1978.

Bradshaw, J., 'The concept of social need', in Fitzgerald, M. et al. (eds), *Welfare in Action*.

Brake, M., *The Sociology of Youth Culture and Youth Subcultures*, London, Routledge & Kegan Paul, 1980.

Bramall, M., 'The Finer Committee report', in Barber, D. (ed.), *One Parent Families*, part. II.

Briggs, A. and Saville, J. (eds), *Essays in Labour History 1918-1939*, volume 3, London, Croom Helm, 1977.

Briggs, E. and Rees, A.M., *Supplementary Benefits and the Consumer*, Occasional Papers on Social Administration, no. 65, London, Bedford Square Press, 1980.

Bruce, M., *The Coming of the Welfare State*, London, Batsford, 1968.

Bruce, P.A., *The Plantation Negro as a Freeman*, New York, Putnam, 1899.

Brundin, J., 'My special shame', *The Guardian* (7.8.79), 1979.

Bryant, C.D. (ed.), *Sexual Deviancy in Social Context*, New York, New Viewpoints.

Burchinal, L.G., 'Characteristics of adolescents from unbroken, broken, and reconstituted families', *Journal of Marriage and the Family*, 26, 1, February 1964, pp. 44-51.

Burghes, L., *Living from Hand to Mouth*, Poverty pamphlet, No. 50, London, Family Service Units and Child Poverty Action Group, 1980.

Butterworth, E. and Holman, R. (eds), *Social Welfare in Modern Britain*, London, Fontana, 1975.

Cahnman, W.J., 'The stigma of obesity', *The Sociological Quarterly*, 9, 3, Summer 1968, pp. 283-99.

Cattell, J.P., 'Psychodynamic and clinical observations in a group of unmarried mothers', in Roberts, R.W. (ed.).

Chadwick, O., *The Reformation*, Harmondsworth, Penguin, 1964.

Cheetham, J., *Social Work with Immigrants*, London, Routledge & Kegan Paul, 1972.

Cheetham, J., *Unwanted Pregnancy and Counselling*, London, Routledge & Kegan Paul, 1977.

Christensen, G., 'A test of the labelling approach to deviance: the case of the disabled', unpublished Ph.D thesis, The American University, 1977.

Clark, C., *Poverty Before Politics*, Hobart Paper No. 73, London, Institute Of Economic Affairs, 1977.

Clifford, D., 'Stigma and the perception of social security services' *Policy and Politics*, 3, 3, March 1975, pp. 29-59.

Cohen, N.E. (ed.), *Social Work and Social Problems*, New York, National Association Of Social Workers Inc., 1964.

Cohen, R., and Tarpey, M., *The Trouble with Take-up*, London, Islington People's Rights, 1982.

Cohen, S. (ed.), *Images of Deviance*, Harmondsworth, Penguin, 1971.

Cole, D. with Utting, J.E.G., *The Economic Circumstances of Old People*, Occasional Papers on Social Administration, no. 4., Welwyn, Codicote Press, 1962.

Commission of The European Communities, *The Perception of Poverty in Europe*, Brussels, EEC, 1977.

Cooper, M.H. *Rationing Health Care*, London, Croom Helm, 1975.

Coventry Social Services, *Looking for Trouble among the Elderly*, Coventry, Coventry Social Services, 1973.

Cox, O.C., *Caste, Class and Race*, New York, Doubleday, 1948.

Crellin, E., et al., *Born Illegitimate*, Windsor, National Council For Educational Research in England and Wales, 1971.

Crosland, C.A.R., *The Future of Socialism*, London, Jonathan Cape, 1980.

Croxen, M., 'Psychological theories of social problem causation', in The Open University, *Social Work Community Work and Society*, units 7-9, part I.

Cumming, J and Cumming, E., 'On the stigma of mental illness', in Palmer, S and Linsky, A.S. (eds).

Davies, B. in association with Reddin, M., *Universality, Selectivity and Effectiveness in Social Policy*, London, Heinemann, 1978.

Davies, N.J., 'Labeling theory in deviance research: a critique and reconsideration', *The Sociological Quarterly*, 13, Fall 1972, pp. 447-74.

Davies, N.J., *Sociological Construction of Deviance*, Iowa, Wm. C. Brown, 1975.

Davis, F. 'Deviance disavowal: the management of strained interaction by the visibly handicapped', in Filstead, W.J. (ed.)

Davis, K.C., *Discretionary Justice: A Preliminary Inquiry*, Baton Rouge, Louisiana State University, 1969.

Day, P.R. *Social Work and Social Control*, London, Tavistock, 1981.

Deacon, A., *In Search of the Scrounger*, Occasional Papers on Social Administration, no. 60, London, Bell & Sons, 1976.

Deacon, A., 'Concession and coercion: the politics of unemployment insurance in the twenties', in Briggs, A. and Saville, J. (eds), ch. 1.

Deacon, A., 'Thankyou, God, for the means-test man', *New Society*, 56, 971 (25.6.81), 1981, pp. 519-20.

Dejong, W., 'The stigma of obesity: the consequences of naive assumptions concerning the causes of physical deviance', *Journal of Health and Social Behavior*, 21, 1, March 1980, pp. 75-87.

DHSS, *Children in Care*, London, HMSO, 1975.

DHSS, *Social Assistance*, London, HMSO, 1978.

DHSS, *Social Security Statistics 1980*, London, HMSO, 1980.

DHSS, *Supplementary Benefits Handbook* (7th edn), London, HMSO, 1981.

DHSS, *Social Security Statistics 1982*, London, HMSO, 1982.

Department of The Environment, 'Housing For One-Parent Families', Circular, 78/77 (26.8.77), London, HMSO, 1977.

Department of Labor (United States), *The Negro Family: The Case for National Action*, Washington, Department of Labor, 1965.

Digby, A., *Pauper Palaces*, London, Routledge & Kegan Paul, 1978.

Dinitz, S. et al., *Deviance: Studies in the Process of Stigmatization and Societal Reaction*, New York, Oxford University Press, 1969.

Dollard, J., *Caste and Class in a Southern Town*, New Haven, Yale University Press, 1937.

Donajgrodzki, A.P. (ed.), *Social Control in Nineteenth Century Britain*, London, Croom Helm, 1977.

Donnison, D., 'Supplementary benefits: dilemmas and priorities', *Journal of Social Policy*, 5, 4, October 1976, pp. 337-58.

Donnison, D., *The Politics of Poverty*, Oxford, Martin Robertson, 1982.

Doob, A.N. and Ecker, B.P., 'Stigma and compliance', *Journal of Personality and Social Psychology*, 14, 4, April 1970, pp. 302-4.

Douglas, J.D. (ed.), *Deviance and Respectability: The Social Construction of Moral Meanings*, New York, Basic Books, 1970.

Doyal, L. with Pennell, I., *The Political Economy of Health*, London, Pluto, 1979.

Edgerton, R.B., *The Cloak of Competence: Stigma in the Lives of the Mentally Retarded*, Berkeley, University of California Press, 1967.

Edgerton, R.B. and Bercovici, S.M., 'The cloak of competence: years later', *American Journal of Mental Deficiency*, 80, 5, 1976, pp. 485-97.

Ekeh, P., *Social Exchange Theory: The Two Traditions*, London, Heinemann, 1974.

Emmison, F.G., *Elizabethan Life: Morals and the Church Courts*, Chelmsford, Essex County Council, 1973.

English, R.W., 'Correlates of stigma towards physically disabled persons', in Marinelli, R.P. and Dell Orto, A.E. (eds).

Eysenck, H.J., *Sense And Nonsense in Psychology*, Harmondsworth, Penguin, 1958.

Eysenck, S.B.G., 'Personality, and pain assessment in childbirth of married and unmarried mothers', *British Journal of Mental Science* (now the *British Journal of Psychiatry*), 107, 1961, pp. 417-30.

Fabian Society, *Social Services For All?*, London, Fabian Society, 1968.

Family Welfare Association, *Guide to the Social Services 1978*, London, Macdonald and Evans, 1978.

Farrell, B.A., 'Psychoanalytic theory', *New Society*, 38 (20.6.63), 1963, pp. 11-13.

Farrell, B.A., 'Psychoanalysis – the method', *New Society*, 39 (27.6.63) 1963, pp. 12-13.

Feagin, J.R., 'America's welfare stereotypes', *Social Science Quarterly*, 52, March 1972, pp. 921-33.

Feldman, H. and Feldman, M., 'The effect of father absence on adolescents', *Family Perspective*, 10, Fall 1975, pp. 13-16.

Ferguson, S.M. and Fitzgerald, H., *Studies in the Social Services*, London HMSO and Longmans, Green & Co., 1954.

Ferri, E., *Growing up in a One-Parent Family*, Windsor, National Council for Educational Research in England and Wales, 1976.

Field, F., *The Stigma of Free School Meals*, Welfare In Action: A CPAG Report, London, Child Poverty Action Group, 1974.

Field, F. (ed.), *The Conscript Army*, London, Routledge & Kegan Paul, 1977.

Field, F, *Free School Meals: The Humiliation Continues*, Welfare In Action: A CPAG Report, London, Child Poverty Action Group, 1977.

Field, F., 'Scroungers: crushing the invisible', *New Statesman*, 98, 2539 (16.11.79), 1979, pp. 754-6.

Field, F. and Grieve, M., *Abuse and the Abused*, Poverty Pamphlet, no. 10, London, Child Poverty Action Group, 1972.

Filstead, W.J. (ed.), *An Introduction to Deviance: Readings in the Process of Making Deviants*, Chicago, Markham, 1972.

Finer, M. and McGregor, O.R., 'The history of the obligation to maintain', in *Report of the Committee on One-Parent Families*, volume 2, *Appendices (Finer Report)*, Appendix 5.

Fisher, H.A.L., 'The unmarried mother and her child', *The Contemporary Review*, 156, October 1939, pp. 485-9.

Fitzgerald, M., et al. (eds), *Welfare in Action*, London, Routledge & Kegan Paul in association with the Open University Press, 1977.

Floyd, J. and Viney, L.L. 'Ego identity and ego ideal in the unwed mother', *British Journal of Medical Psychology*, 47, 1974, p. 273-81.

Flynn, F., 'People like you should know better', *New Society*, 49, 680 (16.7.79), 1979, pp. 345-7.

Forder, A., *Concepts in Social Administration*, London, Routledge & Kegan Paul, 1974.

Fox-Piven, F. and Cloward, R., *Regulating the Poor: The Functions of Public Welfare*, London, Tavistock, 1972.

Fraser, D., *The Evolution of the British Welfare State*, London, Macmillan, 1973.

Frazier, E.F., *The Negro Family in the United States*, Chicago, University Of Chicago Press, 1939.

Freud, S., *New Introductory Lectures in Psychoanalysis*, Harmondsworth, Penguin, 1973.

Friedman, M., *Capitalism and Freedom*, Chicago, University of Chicago Press, 1962.

Friedman, M. and Friedman, R., *Free to Choose*, Harmondsworth, Penguin, 1980.

Garfinkel, H., 'Conditions of successful degradation ceremonies', *American Journal of Sociology*, 61, March 1956, pp. 420-4.

George, V., *Social Security: Beveridge and After*, London, Routledge & Kegan Paul, 1968.

George, V., *Social Security and Society*, London, Routledge & Kegan Paul, 1973.

George, V. and Wilding, P., *Ideology and Social Welfare*, London, Routledge & Kegan Paul, 1976.

Gibbs, J.P., 'Issues in defining deviant behavior', in Scott, R.A., and Douglas, J.D. (eds).

Gill, D., *Illegitimacy, Sexuality and the Status of Women*, Oxford, Basil Blackwell, 1977.

Gingerbread, *As We See It*, London, Gingerbread, 1975.

Ginsburg, N., *Class, Capital and Social Policy*, London, Macmillan, 1979.

Glastonbury, B. et al., 'Community perceptions and the personal social services', *Policy and Politics*, 1, 3, March 1973, pp. 191-211.

Goffman, E., *Stigma*, Harmondsworth, Penguin, 1968.

Goffman, E., *Asylums*, Harmondsworth, Penguin, 1968.

Goffman, E., *Interaction Ritual*, Harmondsworth, Penguin, 1972.

Golding, P. and Middleton, S., 'Why is the press so obsessed with welfare scroungers?', *New Society*, 46, 838 (26.10.78), 1978, pp. 195-7.

Golding, P. and Middleton, S., *Images of Welfare*, Oxford, Martin Robertson, 1982.

Goodwin, L., 'How suburban families view the work orientations of the welfare poor: problems in social stratification and social policy', *Social Problems*, 19, 3, Winter, pp. 337-48.

Gough, I., *The Political Economy of the Welfare State*, London, Macmillan, 1979.

Gouldner, A.W., *For Sociology*, London, Allen Lane, 1973.

Gove, W.R. (ed.), *The Labelling of Deviance*, New York, John Wiley, 1975.

Graham-Dixon, S., *Never Darken My Door*, London, National Council for One Parent Families, 1981.

Grand, J. Le., *The Strategy of Equality*, London, George Allen & Unwin, 1982.

Greenberg, N.H. et al., 'Life situations associated with the onset of pregnancy,' *Psychosomatic Medicine*, 31, 4, 1959, pp. 296-310.

Gutman, H.G., *The Black Family in Slavery and Freedom 1750-1925*, Oxford, Basil Blackwell, 1976.

Haffter, C., 'The changeling: history and psychodynamics of attitudes to handicapped children in European folklore', *Journal of the History of Behavioral Sciences*, 4, 1, January, 1968, pp. 55-61.

Hair, P.E.H., 'Bridal pregnancy in rural England in earlier centuries', *Population Studies*, 20, 2, November, 1966, pp. 233-43.

Hair, P.E.H., 'Bridal pregnancy in earlier rural England further examined', *Population Studies*, 24, 1, March, 1970, pp. 59-70.

Hall, M.P. and Howes, I.V., *The Church in Social Work*, London, Routledge & Kegan Paul, 1965.

Hall, P. et al., *Change, Choice and Conflict in Social Policy*, London, Heinemann, 1975.

Hallas, J., *CHC'S In Action*, London, Nuffield Provincial Hospital Trust, 1976.

Handler, J.F., *The Coercive Social Worker*, Chicago, Markham, 1973.

Handler, J.F. and Hollingsworth, E.J., *The 'Deserving Poor'*, Chicago, Markham, 1971.

Hannington, W., *Unemployed Struggles 1919-1936*, Wakefield, EP Publishing, 1973.

Harris, L., 'The state and the economy: some theoretical problems', in Miliband, R and Saville, J. (eds).

Harrison, R.M., 'Epilepsy and stigma', *New Society*, 37, 726 (2.9.76), 1976, pp. 497-8.

Hayek, F.A., *The Road to Serfdom*, London, Routledge & Kegan Paul, 1944.

Heath, A., *Rational Choice and Social Exchange*, Cambridge, Cambridge University Press, 1976.

Helmholz, R.H., 'Infanticide in the province of Canterbury during the fifteenth century', *History of Childhood Quarterly*, 2, 1975, pp. 379-90.

Hennessey, P.J., *Families, Funerals and Finances. A Study of Funeral Expenses and How They Are Paid*, DHSS Statistics And Research Division, Report, no. 6., London, HMSO, 1980.

Henriques, U.R.Q., 'Bastardy and the new poor law', *Past and Present*, 37, 1967, pp. 103-29.

Henriques, U.R.Q., *Before the Welfare State*, London, Longman, 1979.

Hertz, H. and Little, S.W., 'Unmarried negro mothers in a southern urban community', *Social Forces*, 23, 1, October, 1944, pp. 73-9.

Heywood, J.S., *Children in Care* (Rev. edn), London, Routledge &

Kegan Paul, 1978.

Higgins, J., 'Social control theories of social policy', *Journal of Social Policy*, 9, 1, January, 1980, pp. 1-23.

Hill, M., *Policies for the Unemployed: Help or Coercion?*, Poverty pamphlet, no. 15, London, Child Poverty Action Group, 1974.

Hodge, H., 'Discretion in reality', in Adler, M. and Bradley, A. (eds), ch. 5.

Hollingshead, A.B., 'The concept of social control', *American Sociological Review*, 6, April, 1941, pp. 217-24.

Holman, R., 'Poverty: consensus and alternatives', in Butterworth, E. and Holman, R. (eds).

Hopkinson, A., *Single Mothers: The First Year*, Edinburgh, Scottish Council for Single Parents, 1976.

Hopkirk, M., *Nobody Wanted Sam*, London, John Murray, 1949.

Horan, P.M., and Austin, P.L., 'The social bases of welfare stigma', *Social Problems*, 21, 5, June, 1974, pp. 648-57.

Hughes, E.C., 'Dilemmas and contradictions of status', *American Journal of Sociology*, 50, March, 1945, pp. 353-9.

Humphreys, L., *Out of the Closets*, New Jersey, Prentice-Hall, 1972.

Hunt, A. et al., *Familes and their Needs with Particular Reference to One-Parent Families*, Office Of Population Censuses And Surveys, Social Survey Division, vol. 1, London, HMSO, 1973.

Hunt, E.H., *British Labour History 1815-1914*, London, Weidenfeld & Nicolson, 1981.

Jacobs, S., 'Rehousing in Glasgow: reform through community action', in Jones, D. and Mayo, M. (eds).

Johnson, P., 'Family reunion', *The Observer* (10.10.82), 1982.

Jones, D. and Mayo, M. (eds), *Community Work 2*, London, Routledge & Kegan Paul 1975.

Jones, K. et al., *Issues in Social Policy*, London, Routledge & Kegan Paul, 1978.

Jones, P., 'Rights, welfare and stigma', in Timms, N. (ed.), ch. 7.

Jones, W.C. et al., 'Social and psychological factors in status decisions of unmarried mothers', *Journal of Marriage and the Family*, 24, 3, August, 1962, pp. 224-30.

Jordan, B., *Poor Parents*, London, Routledge & Kegan Paul, 1974.

Jordan, B., *Freedom and the Welfare State*, London, Routledge & Kegan Paul, 1976.

Jordan, W.K., *Philanthropy in England 1480-1660*, London, George Allen & Unwin, 1959.

Joseph, K., 'Speech in Birmingham' (19.10.74), reprinted in *The Times* (21.10.74), 1974, p.3.

Joseph, K., 'The cycle of deprivation', in Butterworth, E. and Holman, R. (eds).

Judge, K., *Rationing Social Services*, London, Heinemann, 1978.

Judge, K. and Matthews, J., *Charging for Social Care*, London, George Allen & Unwin, 1980.

Kando, T., 'Passing and stigma management: the case of the transsexual' in Bryant, C.D. (ed.).

Kasanin, J. and Handschin, S., 'Psychodynamic factors in illegitimacy', *American Journal of Orthopsychiatry*, 11, I, January, 1941, pp. 66-84.

Kellum, B.A., 'Infanticide in England in the later middle ages', in History of Childhood Quarterly, 1, 1974, pp. 367-88.

Kerbo, H.R., 'The stigma of welfare and a passive poor', *Sociology and Social Research*, 60, 2, Janaury, 1976, pp. 173-87.

Kincaid, J.C., *Poverty and Equality in Britain* (Rev. edn), Harmondsworth, Penguin, 1975.

Kleck, R., et al., 'The effects of physical deviance upon face-to-face interaction', *Human Relations*, 19, 4, November, 1966, pp. 425-36.

Kleck, R., 'Physical stigma and nonverbal clues emitted in face-to-face interaction, *Human Relations*, 21, 1, February, 1968, pp. 19-28.

Klein, R. (ed.) *Inflation and Priorities*, London, Centre For Studies in Social Policy, 1975.

Klein, R. and Lewis, J., *The Politics of Consumer Representatives. A Study of Community Health Councils*, London, Centre For Studies In Social Policy, 1976.

Knapp, P. and Cambria, S.T., 'The attitudes of negro unmarried mothers toward illegitimacy', *Smith College Studies in Social Work*, 17, 3, March, 1947, pp. 185-203.

Kogan, W.S., et al., 'Changes in the self-concept of unwed mothers', *Journal of Psychology*, 59, 1965, pp. 3-10.

Kogan, W.S., et al., 'Personality changes in unwed mothers following parturition', *Journal of Clinical Psychology*, 24, 1968, pp. 3-11.

Kravitz, H., et al., 'Unwed mothers practical and theoretical considerations', *Canadian Psychiatric Association Journal*, 11, 6, December, 1966, pp. 456-64.

Kwasniewski, J., 'Positive social deviancy', *Polish Sociological Bulletin*, 3, 1976, pp. 31-9.

Lambert, J., et al., *Housing Policy and the State*, London, Macmillan, 1978.

Lambert, L. and Streather, J., *Children in Changing Families*, London, Macmillan, 1980.

Land, H., *Large Families in London*, Occasional Paper on Social Administration, no. 32, London, Bell & Sons, 1969.

Landis, P.H., *Social Control, Social Organisation and Disorganisation in Process* (rev. edn), Chicago, J.B. Lippincott. 1956

LaPiere, R.T., *A Theory of Social Control*, London, McGraw-Hill, 1954.

Laslett, P., 'Introduction: comparing illegitimacy over time and between cultures', in Laslett, P., et al. (eds), ch. 1.

Laslett, P., et al. (eds), *Bastardy and its Comparative History*, London, Edward Arnold, 1980.

Lauer, R.H., 'The middle class looks at poverty', *Urban and Social Change Review*, 5, 1, Fall, 1971, pp. 8-10.

Leete, R., 'One-parent families: numbers and characteristics', *Population Trends*, 13, Autumn, 1978, pp. 4-9.

Legg, J.W., *English Church Life from the Restoration to the Tractarial Movement*, London, Longmans, Green & Co., 1914.
Lemert, E.M., *Human Deviance, Social Problems, and Social Control* (2nd edn), New Jersey, Prentice-Hall, 1972.
Leonard, E.M., *The Early History of English Poor Relief*, London, Frank Cass & Co., 1965.
Levitt, L. and Kornhaber, R.C., 'Stigma and compliance: a re-examination', *Journal of Social Psychology*, 103, October, 1977, pp. 13-18.
Levy, D., 'A follow-up study of unmarried mothers', *Social Casework*, 36, 1955, pp. 27-33.
Lewis, O., *The Children of Sanchez*, New York, Random House, 1961.
Lewis, O., *La Vida*, New York, Random House, 1966.
Lister, R., *The Administration of the Wage Stop*, Poverty Pamphlet, no. 11, London, Child Poverty Action Group, 1972.
Lister, R., *As Man and Wife? A Study of the Cohabitation Rule*, Poverty Research Series, no. 2., London, Child Poverty Action Group, 1973.
Loesch, J.G. and Greenberg, N.H., 'Some specific areas of conflicts observed during pregnancy: a comparative study of married and unmarried pregnant women', *American Journal of Orthopsychiatry*, 32, 4, July, 1962, pp. 624-36.
London Edinburgh Weekend Return Group, *In and Against the State* (rev. edn), London, Pluto, 1980.
Longmate, N., *The Workhouse*, London, Temple Smith, 1974.
Lynes, T., *Welfare Rights*, Fabian Tract No. 395, London, Fabian Society, 1969.
Lynes, T., 'The dinner money problem', *Poverty*, 10, Spring, 1969, pp. 13-15.
McCaffery, J., *The Friar of San Giovanni*, London, Darton, Longman & Todd, 1978.
MacCormack, G., 'Reciprocity', *Man*, II, 1, March, 1976, pp. 89-103.
Macdonald, E.K., 'Follow-up of illegitimate children', *Medical Officer* (14.12.56), 1956, pp. 361-5.
Macfarlane, A., 'Illegitimacy and illegitimates in English history', in Laslett, P. et al. (eds), ch. 2.
Macintyre, S., *Single and Pregnant*, London, Croom Helm, 1977.
Marinelli, R.P. and Dell Orto, A.E. (eds), *The Psychological and Social Impact of Physical Disability*, New York, Springer, 1977.
Markle, G.E. and Troyer, R.J., 'Smoke gets in your eyes: cigarette smoking as deviant behaviour', *Social Problems*, 26, 5, June, 1979, pp. 611-25.
Marris, P, *Widows and their Families*, London, Routledge & Kegan Paul, 1958.
Marsden, D., *Mothers Alone*, Harmondsworth, Penguin, 1973.
Marsden, D., *Workless*, London, Croom Helm, 1982.
Marshall, D., *The English Poor in the Eighteenth Century*, London, Routledge & Kegan Paul, 1969.
Marshall, R., *Families Receiving Supplementary Benefit*, DHSS Statisti-

cal Research Report Series, no. 1., London, HMSO, 1972.

Marshall, T.H., *The Right to Welfare and other Essays*, London, Heinemann, 1981.

Matza, D., *Becoming Deviant*, New York, Prentice-Hall, 1969.

May, G., *Social Control of Sex Expression*, London, Goerge Allen & Unwin, 1930.

Meacher, M., *Rate Rebates: A Study of the Effectiveness of Means Tests*, Poverty Research Series: 1, London, Child Poverty Action Group, 1973.

Melling, E. (ed.), *Kentish Sources: IV The Poor*, Maidstone, Kent County Council, 1964.

Merton, R.K. and Nisbet, R. (eds), *Contemporary Social Problems* (3rd edn), New York, Harcourt, Brace & Jovanovich, 1971.

Middleton, N., *When Family Failed*, London, Victor Gollancz, 1971.

Miliband, R., *Marxism and Politics*, Oxford, Oxford University Press, 1977.

Miliband, R. and Saville, J. (eds), *The Socialist Register 1980*, London, Merlin, 1980.

Miller, D., *Social Justice*, Oxford, Clarendon, 1976.

Miller, J., 'Jonathan Miller: the director's not for blocking', *The Listener*, 97, 2495 (10.2.77), 1977, p. 175.

Miller, J., 'Exploring the inner man', *The Listener*, 100, 2585 (9.11.78), 1978, pp. 594-7.

Ministry of Pensions and National Insurance, *Financial and Other Circumstances of Retirement Pensioners*, London, HMSO, 1966.

Mishra, R., *Society and Social Policy* (2nd edn), London, Macmillan, 1981.

Modigliani, A., 'Embarrassment and embarrassability', *Sociometry*, 31, pp. 313-26.

Morris, P., *Put Away*, London, Routledge & Kegan Paul, 1969.

Morris, T., 'The crooked way to the top: crime and acquisitive mobility', *New Society*, 49, 878 (2.8.79), 1979, p. 231-4.

Moss, P., *Welfare Rights Project '68*, Liverpool, Merseyside Child Poverty Action Group, 1969.

Moss, P., *Welfare Rights Project Two*, Liverpool, Merseyside Child Poverty Action Group, 1970.

Moynihan, D.P. (ed.), *On Understanding Poverty*, New York, Basic Books, 1968.

Murch, M.A., 'One-parent families', *Journal of Social Policy*, 4, 2, April, 1975, pp. 169-78.

Murhison, N., 'Illustrations of the difficulties of some children in one-parent families', in *Report of the Committee on One-Parent Families (The Finer Report)*, vol. 2., Appendix 12.

Myrdal, G., *An American Dilemma*, New York, Harper & Row, 1944.

Naiman, J., 'A comparative study of unmarried and married mothers', *Canadian Psychiatric Association Journal*, 11, 6, December, 1966, pp. 465-9.

Naiman, J., 'A comparison between unmarried women seeking therapeutic abortion and unmarried mothers', *Laval Medical*, 42, December, 1971, pp. 1086-8.

National Council for Civil Liberties, *50,000 Outside the Law*, London, National Council for Civil Liberties, 1951.

National Council for One Parent Families, *Annual Reports*, 1974/5 to 1981/2, London, National Council for One Parent Families.

Navarro, V., 'The crisis of the international capitalist order and its implications for the welfare state', *Critical Social Policy*, 2, 1, Summer, 1982, pp. 43-62.

Nixon, J., *Fatherless Families on Family Income Supplement (FIS)*, DHSS, Research Report, no. 4, London, HMSO, 1979.

North Tyneside CDP, *In and Out of Work*, North Tyneside, North Tyneside CDP, 1978.

Oppel, W.C., 'Illegitimacy. A comparative follow-up study', unpublished Ph.D thesis, National Catholic School of Social Services, Catholic University, Washington D.C., 1969.

Osborne, L, 'Beyond stigma theory: a literary approach', *Issues in Criminology*, 9, 1, Spring, 1974, pp. 71-90.

Oxley, G.W., *Poor Relief in England and Wales 1601-1834*, Newton Abbot, David & Charles, 1974.

Packman, J., *Child Care: Needs and Numbers*, London, Routledge & Kegan Paul, 1968.

Packman, J., *The Child's Generation*, Oxford and London, Basil Blackwell & Martin Robertson, 1975.

Page, D. and Weinberger, B., *Birmingham Rent Rebate and Allowance Study*, Centre For Urban And Regional Studies, University of Birmingham Research Memorandum, no. 44, Birmingham, University of Birmingham Press, 1975.

Page, R., *The Benefits Racket*, London, Tom Stacey, 1971,

Page, R.M., 'The concept of stigma with special reference to the unmarried mother: a social policy and administration approach', unpublished Ph.D thesis, University of Kent, Canterbury, 1984.

Palmer, S. and Linsky, A.S. (eds), *Rebellion and Retreat*, Columbus, Ohio, C.E. Merril, 1972.

Pardo, L.E., 'Stigma and social justice. The effects of physical disability vis à vis moral turpitude', unpublished Ph.D thesis, York University, Toronto, 1974.

Parker, H.J., *View from the Boys*, Newton Abbot, David & Charles, 1974.

Parker, R., 'Social administration and scarcity', in Butterworth, E. and Holman, R. (eds).

Pearson, J.S. and Amacher, P.L., 'Intelligence test results and observations of personality disorder among 3594 unwed mothers in Minnesota', *Journal of Clinical Psychology*, 12, 14, 1956, pp. 16-21.

Perlman, H.H., 'Unmarried mothers', in Cohen, N.E. (ed.).

Phillips, D., 'The creation of consultative councils in the N.H.S.', *Public Administration*, 58, Spring, 1980, pp. 47-66.

Pinchbeck, I. and Hewitt, M., *Children in English Society*, vol. I,

London, Routledge & Kegan Paul, 1969.

Pinchbeck, I. and Hewitt, M., *Children in English Society*, vol. II, London, Routledge & Kegan Paul, 1973.

Pinker, R.A., *Social Theory and Social Policy*, London, Heinemann, 1971.

Pinker, R.A., *Dependency and Social Welfare*, Social Science Research Council Report, HR 1129, London, SSRC, 1972.

Plant, R., 'Needs and welfare', in Timms, N. (ed.), ch. 6.

Plant, R., et al., *Political Philosophy and Social Welfare*, London, Routledge & Kegan Paul, 1980.

Plummer, K., *Sexual Stigma*, London, Routledge & Kegan Paul, 1975.

Plummer, K. (ed.), *The Making of the Modern Homosexual*, London, Hutchinson, 1981.

Posner, J., 'The stigma of excellence: on being just right', *Sociological Inquiry*, 46, 2, 1976, pp. 141-4.

Poynter, J.R., *Society and Pauperism*, London, Routledge & Kegan Paul, 1969.

Pringle, M.L.K., 'The incidence of some supposedly adverse family conditions and of left-handedness in schools for maladjusted children', *British Journal of Educational Psychology*, 31, 1961, pp. 183-93.

Pringle, M.L.K., *The Needs of Children*, London, Hutchinson, 1974.

Pruger, R., 'Social policy: unilateral transfer or reciprocal exchange', *Journal of Social Policy*, 2, 4, October, 1975, pp. 289-302.

Rains, P.M., *Becoming an Unwed Mother*, Chicago, Adline-Atherton, 1971.

Rainwater, L., 'The problem of lower-class culture and poverty – war strategy', in Moynihan, D.P. (ed.).

Raphael, A., 'Messiah of the militant left', *The Observer* (29.9.80), 1980.

Raschke, H.J. and Raschke, V.J., 'Family conflicts and children's self-concepts: a comparison of intact and single-parent families', *Journal of Marriage and the Family*, 41, 2, May, 1979, pp. 367-74.

Ratcliff, S.C., and Johnson, H.C. (eds), *Warwick County Records*, vol. I, Warwick, Warwick County Council, 1935.

Ratcliff, S.C. and Johnson, H.C. (eds), *Warwick County Records*, vol. II, Warwick, Warwick County Council, 1936.

Rawls, J., *A Theory of Justice*, Oxford, Oxford University Press, 1973.

Rayman, M., 'My stigma – a care order', *Community Care*, 288 (1.11.79), 1979, pp. 21-2.

Reddin, M., 'Local authority means-tested services', in Fabian Society.

Reed, E.F., 'Unmarried mothers who kept their babies', *Children*, 12, 3, May-June, 1965, pp. 118-19.

Rees, A., 'Access to the personal, health and welfare services', *Social and Economic Administration*, 6, 1, 1972, pp. 34-43.

Rees, S., *Social Work Face to Face*, London, Edward Arnold, 1975.

Reisman, D.A., *Richard Titmuss: Welfare and Society*, London, Heinemann, 1977.

Report on Social Insurance and Allied Services (Beveridge Report), Cmd

6404, London, HMSO, 1942.

Report of the Committee of Inquiry into the Impact of Rates on Households (Allen Report), Cmnd 2582, London, HMSO, 1965.

Report of the Committee on Local Authority and Allied Personal Social Services (Seebohm Report), Cmnd 3703, London, HMSO, 1968.

Report of the Committee of Enquiry into Allegations of Ill-Treatment at the Ely Hospital Cardiff, Cmnd 3975, London, HMSO, 1969.

Report of the Committee on Abuse of Social Security Benefits (Fisher Report), Cmnd 5228, London, HMSO, 1973.

Report of the Committee on One-Parent Families (Finer Report), vol. 1, Cmnd 5629, London, HMSO, 1974.

Report of the Committee on One-Parent Families (Finer Report), vol. 2, Cmnd 5629-I, London, HMSO, 1974.

Report of a Working Party on the Ascertainment of Maladjusted Children, Scottish Education Department, London, HMSO, 1964.

Richardson, S.A. et al., 'Cultural uniformity in reaction to physical disabilities', *American Sociological Review*, 26, 2, 1961, pp. 241-7.

Riezler, K., 'Comment on the social psychology of shame', *American Journal of Sociology*, 48, 1943, pp. 457-65.

Ritchie, J. and Wilson, P., *Social Security Claimants*, Office of Population Censuses And Surveys, Social Survey Division, London, HMSO, 1979.

Roberts, R.W. (ed.), *The Unwed Mother*, New York, Harper & Row, 1966.

Rogers, J.W. and Buffalo, M.D., 'Fighting back: nine modes of adaption to a deviant label', *Social Problems*, 22, 1, 1974, pp. 101-18.

Room, G., *The Sociology of Welfare*, Oxford, Basil Blackwell & Martin Robertson, 1979.

Rose, G., 'Stigma, illusion and means testing', unpublished paper.

Rose, H., 'Who can de-label the claimant?', in Adler, M. and Bradley, A. (eds), ch. 11.

Rose, M.E., *The English Poor Law 1780-1930*, Newton Abbot, David & Charles, 1971.

Ross, E.A., *Social Control*, New York, Macmillan, 1901.

Rotenberg, M., 'Self-labelling: a missing link in the "societal reaction" theory of deviance', *Sociological Review*, 22, 3, 1974, pp. 335-54.

Roucek, J.S. and associates, *Social Control* (2nd edn), Connecticut, Greenwood Press, 1970.

Rowe, J. and Lambert, L., *Children Who Wait*, London, Association of Adoption Agencies, 1973.

Royal Commission on the Administration and Practical Operation of the Poor Laws, London, HMSO, 1834.

Royal Commission on the Poor Laws and Relief of Distress, Minority Report, Cd 4499, London, HMSO, 1909.

Royal Commission on the Law Relating to Mental Illness and Mental Deficiency, Minutes of Evidence – 22nd Day (16.3.55), London, HMSO, 1955.

Russell, B., *Marriage and Morals*, London, George Allen & Unwin, 1976.

Ryan, W., 'Blaming the victim: ideology serves the establishment', in Wickman, P. (ed.), ch. 13.

Sagarin, E. and Kelly, R.J., 'Sexual deviance and labelling perspectives', in Gove, W.R. (ed.).

Sauer, R., 'Infanticide and abortion in nineteenth-century Britain', *Population Studies*, 32, 1, March, 1978, pp. 81-93.

Saunders, C., *Social Stigma of Occupations*, Farnborough, Gower, 1981.

Scheff, T.J., *Being Mentally Ill: A Sociological Theory*, Chicago, Aldine, 1966.

Scheff, T.J., 'Negotiating reality: notes on power in the assessment of responsibility', *Social Problems*, 16, Summer, 1968, pp. 1-17.

Scheff, T,J., 'The labelling theory of mental illness', *American Sociological Review*, 39, 3, June, 1974, pp. 444-52.

Schmideberg, M., 'Psychiatric-social factors in young unmarried mothers', *Social Casework*, 32, 5, 1951, pp. 3-7.

Schurr, E.M., *Labelling Deviant Behaviour: Its Sociological Implications*, New York, Harper & Row, 1971.

Schurr, E.M., *The Politics of Deviance*, New Jersey, Prentice Hall, 1980.

Schwartz, R.D. and Skolnick, J.H., 'Two studies of legal stigma', *Social Problems*, 10, Fall, 1962, pp. 133-42.

Schweinitz, K. de, *England's Road to Social Security*, New York, Perpetua, 1961.

Scott, R.A., *The Making of Blind Men*, New York, Russell Sage Foundation, 1969.

Scott, R.A. and Douglas, J.D. (eds), *Theoretical Perspectives on Deviance*, New York, Basic Books, 1972.

Scrivens, E., 'Towards a theory of rationing', *Social Policy and Administration*, 13, 1, Spring, 1979, pp. 53-64.

Seldon, A., *Charge*, London, Temple Smith, 1977.

Seldon, A., *Wither the Welfare State?* Occasional Paper, no. 60., London, Institute of Economic Affairs, 1981.

Seldon, A. and Gray, H., *Universal or Selective Benefits*, Research Monographs, no. 8., London, Institute of Economic Affairs, 1967.

Sherard, P., *Christianity and Eros*, London, SPCK, 1976.

Shorter, E., *The Making of the Modern Family*, Glasgow, Fontana, 1977.

Spence, J. et al., *A Thousand Families in Newcastle Upon Tyne*, London, Oxford University Press, 1954.

Steel, E.M. 'What happens afterwards: a survey of unmarried mothers and their children after three years', *Moral Welfare*, January, 1957, pp. 12-17.

Steel, E.M., 'A final study of unmarried mothers and their children', *Moral Welfare*, 1960, pp. 79-87.

Stevens, A.G., 'Rationing in the social services', *The Welfare Officer*, 1972, pp. 5-9, and 12.

Stevenson, O., *Claimant or Client?*, London, George Allen & Unwin, 1973.

Stone, L., *The Family, Sex and Marriage in England 1500-1800*, London,

Weidenfeld & Nicolson, 1977.
Streather, J. and Weir, S, *Social Insecurity: Single Mothers on Benefit*, Poverty Pamphlet, no. 16., London, Child Poverty Action Group, 1974.
Suchar, C.S., *Social Deviance Perspectives and Prospects*, New York, Holt, Rinehart & Winston, 1978.
Suchar, C.S., 'The institutional reaction to child mental illness: co-deviant labelling', *Journal of Social Issues*, 34, 4, 1978, pp. 76-92.
Supplementary Benefits Commission, *Exceptional Needs Payments*, SB Administration Paper, no. 4, London, HMSO, 1973.
Survey of Relief to Widows and Children, Cmd 744, London, HMSO.
Sutherland, S., *Breakdown*, St Albans, Paladin, 1977.
Sykes, G.M. and Matza, D., 'Techniques of neutralization: a theory of delinquency,' *American Sociological Review*, 22, 6, December, 1957, pp. 664-70.
Szasz, T.S., *The Manufacture of Madness*, St Albans, Paladin, 1973.
Tawney, R.H., *Equality*, London, George Allen & Unwin, 1964.
Tawney, R.H., *The Radical Tradition*, Harmondsworth, Penguin, 1966.
Tawney, R.H., *The Acquisitive Society*, Brighton, Wheatsheaf, 1982.
Taylor, S.E. and Langer, E.J., 'Pregnancy: a social stigma?', *Sex Roles*, 3, 1, February, 1977, pp. 27-35.
Taylor-Gooby, P.F., 'Rent benefits and tenants' attitudes. The Batley rent rebate and allowance study', *Journal of Social Policy*, 5, 1, January, 1976, pp. 33-48.
Taylor-Gooby, P.F. 'The empiricist tradition in social administration', *Critical Social Policy*, 1, 2, Autumn, 1981, pp. 6-21.
Taylor-Gooby, P.F. and Dale, J., *Social Theory and Social Welfare*, London, Edward Arnold, 1981.
Teichman, J., *The Meaning of Illegitimacy*, Cambridge, Englehardt, 1978.
Thompson, B., 'Social study of illegitimate maternities', *British Journal of Preventative and Social Medicine*, 10, 1956, pp. 75-87.
Timms, N. (ed.), *Social Welfare: Why and How?*, London, Routledge & Kegan Paul, 1980.
Titmuss, R.M., *Essays on the Welfare State*, London, George Allen & Unwin, 1963.
Titmuss, R.M., 'Introduction' in Tawney, R.H., *Equality*.
Titmuss, R.M. *Commitment to Welfare*, London, George Allen & Unwin, 1968.
Titmuss, R.M., *Problems of Social Policy*, Connecticut, Greenwood Press, 1971.
Titmuss, R.M., 'Welfare "rights", law and discretion', *Political Quarterly*, 42, 2, 1971, pp. 113-32.
Titmuss, R.M., *The Gift Relationship*, Harmondsworth, Penguin, 1973.
Titmuss, R.M., *Social Policy: An Introduction*, London, George Allen & Unwin, 1974.
Townsend, P., *The Family Life of Old People*, Harmondsworth, Penguin, 1963,

Townsend, P., 'Introduction: does selectivity mean a nation divided?', in Fabian Society.

Townsend, P., 'Problems of introducing a Guaranteed Maintenance Allowance for one parent families', *Poverty*, 31, Winter/Spring, 1975, pp. 29-39.

Townsend, P., *Poverty in the United Kingdom*, Harmondsworth, Penguin, 1979.

Troeltsch, E., *The Social Teaching of the Christian Churches*, vol. 1, London, George Allen & Unwin, 1931.

Turner, R.H., 'Deviance avowal as neutralization of commitment', *Social Problems*, 19, 3, Winter, 1972, pp. 308-21.

Valentine, C.A., *Culture and Poverty*, Chicago, University of Chicago press, 1968.

Vincent, C.E., *Unmarried Mothers*, Chicago, Free Press, 1961.

Vincent, J.A., 'Illegitimacy', unpublished Ph.D thesis, University of Surrey, Guildford, 1978.

Walker, N., *Punishment, Danger and Stigma*, Oxford, Basil Blackwell, 1980.

Warne, A., *Church and Society in Eighteenth-Century Devon*, Newton Abbot, David & Charles, 1969.

Warren, C.A.B. and Johnson, J.M., 'A critique of labeling theory from the phenomenological perspective', in Scott, R.A. and Douglas, J.D. (eds), ch. 3.

Watkin, B., *Documents on Health and Social Services 1834 to the Present Day*, London, Methuen, 1975.

Watkins, C.K., *Social Control*, London, Longman, 1975.

Watson, D., *Caring for Strangers*, London, Routledge & Kegan Paul, 1980.

Weale, A., *Equality and Social Policy*, London, Routledge & Kegan Paul, 1978.

Webb, S. & B., *English Local Government: English Poor Law History: Part II: The Last Hundred Years*, vol. I, London, Longmans, Green & Co, 1929.

Webb, S. & B., *English Local Government: English Poor Law History: Part II: The Last Hundred Years*, vol. II, London, Longmans, Green & Co, 1929.

Weeks, J., *Coming Out*, London, Quartet, 1977.

Weeks, J., 'Discourse, desire and sexual deviance: some problems in a history of homosexuality', in Plummer, K. (ed.), ch. 4.

Weinberg, M.S. and Williams, C.J., *Male Homosexuals – Their Problems and Adaptions*, New York, Oxford University Press, 1974.

Weir, S., *A Study of Unmarried Mothers and their Children in Scotland*, Scottish Home And Health Department, 1970.

West, D.J., *Present Conduct and Future Delinquency*, London, Heinemann, 1969.

Wickman, P. (ed.), *Readings in Social Problems: Contemporary Perspectives*, New York. Harper & Row, 1977.

Wilding, R., 'Discretionary benefits', in Adler, M. and Bradley, A.

(eds), ch. 4.

Williamson, J.B., 'Beliefs about the motivation of the poor and attitudes towards poverty policy', *Social Problems*, 21, 5, June, 1974, pp. 634-47.

Williamson, J.B., 'The stigma of public dependency: a comparison of alternative forms of public aid to the poor', *Social Problems*, 22, 2, December, 1974, pp. 213-28.

Williamson, J.B., 'Beliefs about the welfare poor'. *Sociology and Social Research*, 58, 2, January, 1974, pp. 163-75.

Wimperis, V., *The Unmarried Mother and her Child*, London, George Allen & Unwin, 1960.

Wright, H.R., *80 Unmarried Mothers who kept their Babies*, California, Children's Home Society of California and Los Angeles County Bureau Of Adoption, 1965.

Wrightson, K., 'Infanticide in earlier seventeenth-century England', *Local Population Studies*, 15, Autumn, 1975, pp. 10-22.

Wrightson, K., 'The nadir of English illegitimacy in the seventeenth century', in Laslett, P., et al. (eds) ch. 6.

Yarrow, A., 'Illegitimacy in south-east Essex', *Medical Officer* (24.1.64), 1964, pp. 47-8.

Yelloly, M.A., 'Factors relating to an adoption decision by the mothers of illegitimate infants', *Sociological Review*, 13, 1, March, 1965, pp. 5-14.

Young, L., *Out of Wedlock*, New York, McGraw-Hill, 1954.

Young, L., 'Personality patterns in unmarried mothers', in Roberts, R.W. (ed.).

Index of authors

202

Subject index